COLLECTIVE PROCESSES

COLLECTIVE PROCESSES

COUNTERPRACTICES IN EUROPEAN ARCHITECTURE

BIRKHÄUSER

Preface   6

QUESTIONING AUTHORIALITY: THE POSSIBILITY OF CHANGE   8

On the Collective and Other Kinds of Horizontal Organizations   13
Europe: a Socioideological Condition   15
The Gap Between Academia and Practice   18
New Ways of Working and Technological Possibilities   20
A New Type of Architectural Project: The Self-Initiated One   21

COLLECTIVE PROCESSES: COUNTERPRACTICES IN EUROPEAN ARCHITECTURE   24

How Do We Practice and Why Do We Practice? A Collective Discussion with the Actors   26

Proposing Alternative Ways of Practicing Architecture in the 2000s: Discussions with the Pioneers   50

baukuh   52
Architecture as a Collective Operation

raumlabor   60
Engaging the Public Eye

zuloark   76
A Liquid Professional Framework

Widening Up the Spectrum of Architecture in the 2010s: Seven Questions to Fourteen Contemporary Collectives   84

1. BEGINNINGS How To Get Together and Why   88
2. STATEMENTS Founding Acts   96
3. REFERENCES Question of Identity   106
4. WORKING SPACE Space of Interaction   122
5. ORGANIZATION Horizontality   138
6. DEVELOPMENT Fluidity and the Necessity to Morph   154
7. ARCHITECTURE Action for Reaction, Proposing an Alternative   168

Open Conclusion/s　　　　　　　　　　　　　　　　　　　　182
Rethinking Architecture

INDEX OF PRACTICES:　　　　　　　　　　　　　　　　　188
INTRODUCING THE ACTORS

(ab)Normal　　　　　　　　　　　　　　　　　　　　　　192
A-A Collective　　　　　　　　　　　　　　　　　　　　196
Assemble　　　　　　　　　　　　　　　　　　　　　　　200
CNCRT　　　　　　　　　　　　　　　　　　　　　　　204
Colectivo Warehouse　　　　　　　　　　　　　　　　　208
Collectif Etc　　　　　　　　　　　　　　　　　　　　 212
constructLab　　　　　　　　　　　　　　　　　　　　　216
false mirror office　　　　　　　　　　　　　　　　　　220
Fosbury Architecture　　　　　　　　　　　　　　　　224
la–clique　　　　　　　　　　　　　　　　　　　　　　　228
Lacol　　　　　　　　　　　　　　　　　　　　　　　　232
n'UNDO　　　　　　　　　　　　　　　　　　　　　　　236
orizzontale　　　　　　　　　　　　　　　　　　　　　240
X=(T=E=N)　　　　　　　　　　　　　　　　　　　　　244

Preface

This book developed from a series of discussions around the theme of the *collective*[1]—its beliefs, identity, organization, development and architectural output—during the end of 2019 and throughout 2020. After having contacted several collective practices acting in the European architectural context, a series of individual meetings was organized to discuss their working structure and to understand its impact on the architectural output. These meetings, conceived as physical encounters and visits of the space occupied by each collective, partially turned into virtual discussions after the explosion of Covid-19 pandemic.

1. The word *collective* is used within the publication to define all those architectural practices that are based on a horizontal organizational system, and whose founding members are greater than four. Some of the practices mentioned in this book do not actively call themselves collectives.

At some point, it became necessary to find a series of common thematics which would allow for an individual reading of each collective practice's entity, as well as for a general analysis of this large collective panorama, whose processes are as individual as varied. Therefore, after the first series of conversations, five common questions were sent to them:

- What are the key references behind your architecture?
- How is your working space?
- How is your collective structured?
- How has your collective changed since foundation?
- What is the key aim of your architecture?

These encounters, which continued throughout the year, and the written and visual responses to the above questions, inspired the creation of this publication, influencing not only its structure, but also its form and sub-thematics. On May 6, 2020, almost all the participants took part in a general conversation, by videoconference, on *How do we practice and why do we practice?*—a discussion centered around the possibilities and issues of working collectively as well as the role of architecture in the contemporary framework.

The aim of the book is to record the complex working dynamics of the different collectives through a series of fragments, which make apparent a contemporary evolving scenario and its future possible development. It was a real collaborative effort and therefore owes a debt of thanks to all the participants of this invisible collective that came into being while we cocreated this publication.

THE POSSIBILITY OF CHANGE

QUEST
AUTHO

On the Collective and Other Kinds of Horizontal Organizations 13
Europe: A Socioideological Condition 15
The Gap between Academia and Practice 18
New Ways of Working and Technological Possibilities 20
A New Type of Architectural Project: The Self-Initiated One 21

In recent years, the European architectural panorama has seen the emergence, increasingly marked, of a series of collective processes—initially isolated cases, which now, multiplying, seem to attract the general attention. Even if the well-established, conventional, hierarchical office remains the predominant organizational structure of today's architectural scape, these horizontal movements propose themselves as an alternative or as a form of resistance to the classical existing structure.

Some call themselves *collectives*, others *groups*, others *networks*, others *collaborative work-structures*, while others choose not to define themselves at all. However, what initially seems a rather overused term is the starting point of this research: the pretext to investigate this rather inclusive *fluid-something*, which might not necessarily be an encompassed form.

This publication aims to trigger a debate around the collective, its internal organization and architectural production, as well as its space of action—an expansive field of opportunities, where architects and other experts operate in agreement with the community. This emerging generation of architects, thanks to its public focus, social agenda, and ecological preoccupations, suggests other ways of approaching the project while making visible their network.

The emphasis is mainly on collectives that have emerged during the last decade, as these are far more sensitive to their surrounding evolving environment than longer-established ones. However, the choice of comparing two generations of collectives is key to understanding how these realities might have already evolved over a ten-year period. Therefore, the publication looks at a series of collective practices born in the 2000s in Europe—baukuh, raumlabor, and Zuloark can be considered some of the early examples—with a keen eye into a certain number of collectives formed since 2010: A-A Collective, (ab)Normal, Assemble, CNCRT, Collectif Etc, Colectivo Warehouse, constructLab, false mirror office, Fosbury Architecture, la−clique, Lacol, n'UNDO, orizzontale, and X=(T=E=N). This list does not pretend to be exhaustive, however it aspires to draw a general framework, as far as possible, of the contemporary European situation, thus sampling different realities according to their general activity, specific mission, and geographical distribution. The wish is to illustrate this rich panorama through a series of representative interventions, singular approaches, and different ways of working; and its relation to the fast-changing European situation, marked by the digital revolution, the change in economic structure and the gradual social transformation—from a centralized, hierarchical system to a decentralized, horizontal one.

The practices with which I formed a relationship during the writing of this book share a number of common factors: they work in groups of at least four people under a common name and for a shared ideology, while highlighting the possibility of making architecture collectively. Indeed, their architectural products—be they real or ideal, built or visionary—are the result of a collaboration, an ongoing discussion, a back-and-forth process authored as such. If these collectives do not reject their authorship on a work, since this is in any case held by a number of people grouped under a shared name or as individuals within a larger network, they all question the authoriality of the architect as a solo leading figure, which if exercised could not allow for equitable structures. The word *authoriality* refers to the "condition of being an author," and it is emphasized here due to its etymological derivation from the words *author* and *authority*, concepts that are examined within this publication. Furthermore, questioning the condition of being an architect today suggests rethinking the role and the potential of the architecture discipline itself. If these experiments might all rise from similar prerogatives, they are specific and diverse in their being. Nevertheless, they all equally understand that we might not need another architecture office; instead, we might need another kind of architecture, one that is more inclusive and less defined.

In the history of architecture, the concept of author has in many cases prevailed over the concept of collaboration: often, only the genius architect was credited for the work. For instance, the little-acknowledged influence of Lilly Reich in the architecture of Mies van der Rohe, or the many collaborators of Le Corbusier—to mention some, his cousin Pierre Jeanneret and the designer Charlotte Perriand—or the fact that Marion Mahony Griffin produced many of the drawings which established Frank Lloyd Wright's reputation, and so on. Indeed, to speak of collaboration is in a certain sense speaking of architecture itself: one might argue that the creative process would not exist without interaction and therefore the necessity to acknowledge the common making of architecture and the collective intents behind it. "Invisible labor and not valorizing collective labor enough are big problems in architecture right now. The pervasive, compelling myth still exists that someone called an architect designs a building; he might hire some people to draw it out for him or write up the details, but the idea belongs to this 'genius' figure."[1]

1. Charles Shafaieh, "The Death of the Genius: An Alternative History of Computation Lays Bare the Problem of Invisible Labor in Architecture," an interview with Matthew Allen, *Harvard Design Magazine online*, September 4, 2019.

One often also forgets that the architect is by far not the only actor in the creation of architecture, as this is made alongside many others—not only employees, but also clients, institutions, investors, municipalities, users, and so on.

Indeed, behind many large contemporary offices hides a huge workforce. In the early 2000s, when the hierarchical structure of the architectural firm reached its extreme and architects themselves began to be defined as "starchitects" and branded their practices through their name and surname, the concept of authoriality entered a crisis. In the same years a series of nonhierarchical countermovements emerged, which opposed themselves to architecture as a discipline governed by the economic system in place and subordinated to it, and which also rejected the scale that the architectural project had begun to take, with the aim of bringing architecture back to its social purpose. This does not mean that the traditional office based on a vertical hierarchy no longer exists—indeed this type of office is still the most common today. Instead, the collective proposed itself as an alternative to the traditional office, often contesting not only its structure but also its very architectural ambition. As Juan Chacón, from Zuloark, mentioned during our conversation on June 8, 2020: "We were a group of friends, having the same classes between 1998 and 2001 in the ETSAM, the school of architecture in Madrid. We started to ask each other questions about authorship—it was the time of Guggenheim, Zaha Hadid, all this star architecture. Zuloark is born against the concept of authorship, shaping a collective system and rejecting this egomania 'starchitecture.' The school was pushing us to become influential architects, so we thought about creating an entity, which had the power itself, and the people behind it."

The choice of a broader definition, which does not coincide with the architect's name itself, goes back to the great avant-garde movements of the early twentieth century, such as Futurism, Suprematism, or Constructivism, which were not limited to architecture, but rather included artists, architects, and thinkers driven by the same ideology. It also includes the Italian radical groups, such as Archizoom, Superstudio, and UFO and their collectivization with other architects and designers in the series of workshops called Global Tools, which took place between 1973 and 1975. These groups had already questioned the role of the architect as well as the possibility of architecture's being more than just a building. However this general critique detached architecture completely from reality and its problems, transforming it back to a visionary and elitist art, not accessible to everyone.

Today, the rediscovery of the social aspect of architecture and its opening towards the common user allows a different understanding of space and the opportunities it offers, highlighting its potential as a ground of exchange, confrontation, and experience. Even CIAM and Team 10 might be defined as some of the first examples of modern collectives, even though their agenda did not promote collectivism but rather created a platform for encounters between different renowned architects. However, one might say that the contemporary collective, which learns from all of these forms, does not coincide with any of them, remaining, in fact, extremely fluid in its nonform: "We hope that one day we will unite into the International Congress of Alternative Architecture in order to defend a social, democratic, sustainable production of spaces, places, cities! We guess it will be far away from previous CIAM's visions," says Collectif Etc.

ON THE COLLECTIVE AND OTHER KINDS OF HORIZONTAL ORGANIZATIONS

The word collective has its origins in the Latin adjective collēctīvus— *"gathered together," which derives from* collēctus, *past participle of* colligō *("I collect"), from* com *("together") plus* legō *("I gather").*

If the twentieth century *movement* was mainly based on a common direction—artistic, aesthetic and ideological—the twenty-first-century *collective* embraces a more varied production, less characterized by a particular style, but still linked to a specific vision. The term *collective*, before landing in the world of architecture, appears in the arts: architecture, as always, moves in the wake of art. In the architectural context, the term, mainly used as an adjective until a decade ago, is now commonly used in its noun form, and it is slowly becoming a fashionable banner. One might argue that the term has been assimilated by the culture it wanted to convert.

In 2012 the magazine *Arquitectura Viva* no. 145, titled "Colectivos españoles, Nuevas formas de trabajo: redes y plataformas," describes the proliferation of collectives in the Spanish architectural scenario as: "a set of practices that have been grouped under the name of 'collectives,' but whose definition of the term—a group of individuals—does not fully conform to the variety of experiences produced. A word that has been trivialized and does not respond to the plurality of a particular ecosystem, that of the Spanish architectural environment. Because what is meant by 'collectives' is a set of very different models of association, and they are not footnotes of previous conceptions, but realities that form a complex environment." Nine years later, this definition is still valid, even though the practices which in this book are generically defined as collectives might also define themselves, or prefer to be defined, with other terms: *group*, *network*, *not-for-profit association*, *distributed architecture*, *gathering*, *collaborative practice*, *family.* However, *collective*, more than these other words, manages to encapsulate the complexity and "plurality of a particular ecosystem."

Collective states, on the one hand, the possibility to aggregate—when for instance a series of individuals come together because they share the same vision—and on the other hand, a sense of multiplicity—when the same individuals, while still recognizing themselves as a joint entity, choose not to conform to it, relying on a system of collective trust and personal freedom. *Collective* also implies a strong relational bond between its members, often based on friendship and fairness, in an attempt to revive the motto "freedom, fraternity and equality," while underlining that everyone is able. The word suggests a certain openness and flexibility. For this reason some practices prefer the word *collective* to other definitions, such as the more standard *group*, which conveys a sense of unity. Said Jane Hall of Assemble (April 15, 2020, on Zoom), "It is easy to call ourselves a collective: over ten people it is automatically a collective. It is about communicating to other people what you are. It denotes a certain age or generation, as well as a political way of being, a political idea." Furthermore, today collectives are also formed for economic reasons: to maximize benefits and minimize risks, to share materials and equipment, work and exhibition spaces.

This way of collaborating is a direct consequence of the sociological and economic influences that impacted our generation. The postwar economic boom is over, and people today are skeptical to commit; the fluid environment a collective offers matches well this search for freedom.

When looking at the wider European scenario, it is necessary to take into account the historical and political connotation of the word *collective*, as it refers to a different common imagery according to location. In Northern Europe the term remains malleable. It indicates a way of practicing rooted in fair relations between the various members, a broad spectrum of collaboration, and a predominantly social orientation, with the goal of offering a renewed vision of space and architecture. In southern European countries such as Spain and Italy, the term still carries the weight of history. The 1970s collectives were spontaneous revolutionary movements of students fighting against the reform of the university, and against the corpus of professors. They then became extraparliamentary groups of the extreme left not represented in the Parliament. Despite the political weight of the term, the newest generations have a different connection to these terms than society had in the 1970s, following the thrust toward Englishization and globalization.

Indeed, does the word *collective* still hold potential politically today? Furio Montoli (A-A Collective, September 21, 2020, on Zoom) states: "For me the collective is an ideological fact. We needed a name that reflected a divided authorship and no desire for signatures. The word *collective* also gives the idea of something flexible, which might evolve, change over time, expand, involve more people. Perhaps this is the most beautiful feature of the collective: depending on the situation, one can choose its most pleasant and functional geometry."

EUROPE: A SOCIOIDEOLOGICAL CONDITION

"Europe is open-ended, vague, an unidentified political object with no final shape, no clear final borders, and no real definition of what it is as a political creature. In many ways this is still Europe's most attractive feature."[2]

2. Mark Leonard, *Why Europe Will Run the Twenty-first Century* (New York: Public Affairs, 2005).

The contemporary architectural collective is an all-European phenomenon. What could be defined as a new movement of collectives first appeared in the 1990s. Elise Macaire—in her doctoral thesis, titled *L'architecture à l'épreuve de nouvelles pratiques: Recompositions professionnelles et démocratisation culturelle* and presented on December 19, 2012, at the University of Paris-Est—highlights three collectives as pioneers of the movement: Action Group Gleisdreieck, a collective founded in Berlin in 1990; Ne Pas Plier, an association born in France in Ivry sur Seine in 1991; and Arpenteurs, an association created in Grenoble in 1993—a series of mixed entities where there was at least an architect within it, still very far away from what we describe as architectural collectives today.

In the same year, on November 1, 1993, the Maastricht Treaty, the act of creation of the European Union, entered into force shortly after the establishment of the Erasmus Programme (EuRopean Community Action Scheme for the Mobility of University Students), in 1987. Moreover, at the dawn of the 1990s, from January 1988 to January 1990, the Europan 1, titled *Evolution of Lifestyles and Housing Architecture* was launched, a biennial competition for young architects under forty, invited to present innovative urban and architectural projects on different European sites. If the newborn European ideal, oriented toward total openness and emancipation, morphed the geographical perception of the old continent forever, its consolidation into a single land free of borders—also achieved later on through the monetary union—transformed it into a captivating space of action: a fertile ground willing to host new architectural and urban planning experiences.

Today, the ability to move between countries has become an irrevocable right for European citizens, with the exception of the Covid-19 pandemic, which called into question all the achievements of the last thirty years. Although the European Union is under pressure, struggling to contain various populist and nationalist thrusts, a geographically interconnected Europe still is the status quo: a land of exchange whose common and individual movements seem to be motivated by the same prerogatives and therefore can be analyzed and compared precisely on a common scale.

The collectives analyzed in this publication were all conceived of in the European context: Belgium, France, Germany, Great Britain, Italy, Netherlands, Portugal, Spain, and Switzerland. And, according to the general analysis I carried out, these movements are more common in the southern regions of Europe as opposed to the north, where architectural offices headed by one, two, or three people are still the overwhelming majority. In the regions where there are lesser opportunities for stable work, joining together and creating a job for oneself becomes the only possibility. Conversely, in a flourishing job market, these movements become a reaction to the system in force, a way to destabilize and alter it. The large network of collectives in countries like France, Italy, Portugal, and Spain can be attributed partially to an economic situation, partially to an historical heritage, partially to a search for a political change through an action of some sort. In fact, some of these collectives had already developed in the same countries prior to the stalemate in the construction market resulting from the crisis, thanks to the support of public institutions open to these new practices.

In Germany the malleability of spaces after the fall of the Wall, especially in Berlin, played an important role in the creation of collective experiments, which have proposed themselves as an unofficial alternative to official urban planning, as mentioned by Markus Bader from raumlabor in the May 6, 2020, discussion hosted on Zoom, *How do we practice and why do we practice?* In countries like Great Britain and Switzerland, collectives are less common and isolated realities, very particular in their kind.

Also common are cases of entities created outside their country of origin by people of either the same nationality or mixed ones, meeting either in an academic or a professional environment. In most cases, the Erasmus scholarships and European funding have been important for the formation of these collectives; also important has been Europan, where they have often won mentions and awards; and the general borderless European situation, which allows people to study or work in countries other than their home country. Furio Montoli from A-A Collective, during our Zoom discussion on September 21, 2020, stresses the importance of the European dimension in their and other practices: "the European and international dimension is fundamental for us. I am Italian-Japanese, Srdjan is Serbian-Italian, Zygmunt is Polish-Italian, Martin is Danish, but we met in Switzerland, where we either studied or worked. This European dimension influences the very way in which collectives are formed and also their way of working."

As for the field of action of the collective, this might be local, European, or global, depending on its specific mission. In this alternative architectural environment, there has also been a growing interest in triggering discussions with other collectives on architectural and urbanistic practice, as well as on the possible political engagement of the two. In fact, a series of dense and extensive connections are being woven between different collectives through joint projects, dialogues, and festivals, as evidenced by various online and physical networks or by direct relationships. For instance, *Arquitecturas Colectivas* is a website which by mapping various collectives, especially in Spain, offers a possibility of connection between these different entities. In some cases, the collectives themselves are concerned with mapping their own network of action, for example the *cartographie des amis* created by Collectif Etc on their website. In other cases, they organize discussions and events, be they physical or online, such as *Superville*, initiated in 2013 also by Collectif Etc—a gathering of French collectives, organized every two or three years by one of them—and the first edition of the *Agora Live Talks* promoted by Colectivo Warehouse—a series of online discussions with other European collectives organized during the Covid-19 pandemic, in 2020. Others, like Zuloark, offer an *Inteligencias Colectivas* on their website as an open-source catalogue to share free information online about diverse urban agreements and strategies. Others see the project itself as a place of meeting, collaboration, and exchange. Casa do Vapôr, a small fishing settlement on the riverbank of the Tejo opposite Lisbon, marks not only the transition from EXYZT[3] to constructLab,[4] but also a ground of encounter between different people and collectives. In fact, some of the participants in the construction of Casa do Vapôr founded in the same year their own collective practice, Colectivo Warehouse.

3. EXYZT was a collective based in Paris with around 20 permanent members, active between 2003 and 2015. In 2012 they participated in the European Capital of Culture in Portugal, where they designed a scenography for the Curators' Lab with a 100% reusable timber construction. The timber was then transported by the team through the country in order to build Casa do Vapôr.
4. constructLab was initially an EXYZT initiative and then became itself a collective practice around the building site and construction. Some of the previous EXYZT members still work in constructLab.

THE GAP BETWEEN ACADEMIA AND PRACTICE

The activity of the collective challenges the traditional model of access into the professional world, mediated by a period of training in architectural firms, by proposing, after the completion of academic studies, the possibility of immediately starting to work independently, or partly independently: "the master and the student are now one and the same person."[5]

5. Thierry Paquot, "Tour, Detour, Retour," in *Détour de France, An Education off the Beaten Path...*, ed. Collectif Etc (Marseille: éditions Hyperville, 2015), 19.

Indeed, in many European countries, a certain amount of training is necessary in order to become a certified architect, which provides a more practical knowledge aimed at widening the academic one. However, depending on the experience, this period of training can vary enormously, and it is not always possible to see the complete building process, from concept phase to construction, which in some cases, compared to the size or complexity of the project, can last several years. Moreover, the disappointing reality of many work experiences, on the one hand due to the impossibility of taking direct decisions, and on the other hand due to distance to the construction industry, leads some individuals to reject the traditional practice of architecture. The nostalgia for the university environment, where each student can take direct decisions on a project, while profiting from a constant interaction with classmates, professors, and external outsiders, also plays its part.

The collective thus becomes a way to escape the rigid reality of the office; to have a direct experience on the construction site; to be able to express one's ideas directly, without having to constantly refer to a boss or a superior; to establish a continuity with the university system by triggering confrontation and dialogue, or to oppose an authoritarian message transmitted by the university; and finally to reject a prefixed and hierarchical method of work. These entities seek to create a gray area, a limbo, a void between academia and practice, where they can conceive space according to their own rules. The will is to maintain the best of both realities: the concreteness of the professional world and the openness of the academic one. "We never really went into the collective with the idea to build or having to build. This idea of creating a studio only started after the Swiss Art Awards. Before, we thought that our collective would eventually get a form without us controlling it. We did not know if we would do architecture. And it probably was not going to be architecture, otherwise we would probably all be working in architecture offices and building serious stuff. We are in Switzerland and we can do that, or we can go back to do that anytime. So why not suspend that possibility for a bit and do something else? That is probably why our work is so diverse, also thanks to the research we carry out in the Institute," says Scott Lloyd, from X=(T=E=N) when describing their initial intentions during our meeting in Zurich in their office on April 8, 2020. Indeed, their aim was to create a network inspired by the university methodology and based on a system of external critics for their various projects, as well as on internal competitions between the various collective's members of twenty-four hours, a kind of midterm submission within the university atelier.

The extreme fluidity of some collectives denotes an often temporary vision of this practice, as well as the search for something expanded and evolving. Many see this horizontal movement as an in-process without acknowledging if it will last forever and without feeling the need for it. It all comes down to the beauty and fleetingness of these moments of sharing, be it a design session or building together on the construction site. The collective is about sharing. It appears as anonymous from the outside, but inside each personality finds its own space within the work group. This does require an extreme amount of care from the collective, as well as attention for the psychological well-being of each member. The group has the risk of becoming a burden, which instead of coming from the top, as in a traditional office, comes from the inside. For this reason, some collectives have a more-defined structure in order to support its members; others have a less-defined structure in order to guarantee freedom and trust. In general, it becomes necessary to move away from the classic office model in order to maintain a certain degree of flexibility. Once something is established, it is necessary to defend it continuously. But if something is never established, morphing cannot hurt.

Many of these entities are research-based: political engagement occurs on a more theoretical level through consultations, competitions, publications, exhibition, lectures, and essays. n'UNDO aims to show how the act of building in many cases is a mere prerogative. To do so, their work is mainly organized through consultative actions, where, thanks to urbanistic analysis, the practice shows the need to minimize interventions and reuse, up to dismantling and not doing. For CNCRT, the collective itself is a research topic, investigated through a series of visual projects. In their case, the representation and drafting of charismatic texts thus become the main tools to communicate their intentions and self-analyze their own practice.

These experiences, though self-taught outside of conventional academic environments, possess a high level of erudition. While they may appear as spontaneous practices, they are in fact the result of continuous efforts and revised approaches. For these reasons, each of these entities is unique in its kind, offering a multifaceted general scenario, difficult to analyze in its totality. The strength of the collectives is in their will to return to an architecture stripped of all aesthetic charms, fulfilling the basic purpose of spatial problem-solving while implying the possibility of meeting, exchanging, and sheltering. Although the collectives are grounded in strong intentions, they are confronted by organizational difficulties and also by the risk of becoming a brand; thus, in the end they are not so different from the traditional architecture office.

NEW WAYS OF WORKING AND TECHNOLOGICAL POSSIBILITIES

"The rise of 'shared economies' in the culture and knowledge industries, triggered by the burst of technological innovation, has produced alternative 'corporate' entities such as Wikipedia, Kickstarter, Uber, and Airbnb, all of which are opening unprecedented possibilities to transform socioeconomic production as we know it."[6]

6. Alejandro Zaera-Polo, "Well into the Twenty-first Century, the Architecture of Post-Capitalism?," *El Croquis: Sergison Bates, 2004–2016*, no. 187 (December 2016): 257.

Today the enormous possibilities that technology offers us have completely revolutionized our way of living and working. Skype, Zoom, Jitsi, Teams, Google Meet, Google Drive, Dropbox, Slack, WhatsApp, Conceptboard, and Miro are just some of the many applications on the market that allow us to be hyperconnected and efficient, which allow us to host live meetings, share data, and exchange information in real time. Events, decisions, and actions in most cases take place in the digital space, generating what has been called the collective intelligence. Although this way of working is mostly used by collectives who do not share the same working space, the advent of digitalization is changing the approach of the entire architectural sector. This gradual but quick abstraction of the discipline detaches architecture more and more from the physical reality of space and buildings. It therefore also questions the need for a working space, which with the occurrence of the pandemic seems no longer a necessary condition. The atelier, where drawings were previously printed and regularly pinned up on the wall, is now reduced to shared boards, where different users can draw through a series of annotating tools.

If some do not have a physical workspace, others still consider it not only necessary but also their main project. One might think of Assemble's Sugarhouse Studios in London or Lacol's La Comunal in Barcelona. In terms of organization, all collectives largely base their practice on the use of these sharing applications and programs. Their horizontal and open work structures, be they web-like, constellations, or rhizomes, inevitably recall the invisible Internet network: "rather than forming a pyramid, as most movements do, with leaders at the top and followers below, it looks more like an elaborate web. In part, this web-like structure is inspired by the Internet-based organization."[7]

7. Flavien Menu, *Towards New Commons for Europe* (Leipzig: Spector Books, 2018), 8–9.

A NEW TYPE OF ARCHITECTURAL PROJECT: THE SELF-INITIATED ONE

The social and ecological situation of today challenges architecture and its role, inviting architects and other experts to rethink its scale, impact, and output. In order to respond to these general urgencies, these new collective structures stretch the boundaries of architecture, enlarging their spectrum of activity: the outcome is a fresh view on space and on its design possibilities—from the room to the city, from the temporary installation to the art piece, from the material object to immaterial research.

Perhaps driven by an initial impossibility, the collective is faced by the challenge of creating its own space of action. It is by finding different answers to commonly solved problems and by questioning the long-defined process of designing and building that it states itself as a forward-looking entity, open to collaborations with a wider network of people—sociologists, psychologists, artists, scenographers, choreographers, curators, etc. The collaboration with experts of different kinds allows the architecture practice to open up to new possibilities, informing it from different points of view, both in terms of technique and purpose. Broadening the spectrum of architecture means also pushing the discipline beyond simple architectural composition and construction. Indeed, the architecture envisioned or produced is often informed by theatre and performance and charged with social, ecological, and political activism. Architecture becomes the means to occupy space rather than a mere formalistic Subject: "the utopian spirit of bricolage that characterizes all of these projects demonstrates a new understanding of what architecture can be. Instead of being static, everlasting, inflexible and expensive, it can be removable, mobile, a stage for all kinds of scenarios."[8]

8. Niklas Maak, "A New Approach to Urbanity," in *Acting in Public*, ed. raumlaborberlin (Berlin: Jovis Verlag, 2008), 5.

In this context, the possibility of a new architectural project opens up. If historically it was always a client approaching the architect, now the reverse condition is equally feasible. The collective makes a possible client aware of a problem, while proposing to solve it in an unconventional, sometimes transitory way. This can be described as the new architectural project: the self-initiated one. "Do not wait for a client but provoke it. Do not respond to a program but create it. Consider no longer the architect as a producer of services or architecture as a product. These alternative attitudes reflect desire for immediacy."[9]

9. Flavien Menu, *Towards New Commons For Europe* (Leipzig: Spector Books, 2018), 10–18.

Collective discussion, Zoom, May 2020

COUNTERPRACTICES IN EUROPEAN ARCHITECTURE

COLLE
PROC

How Do We Practice and Why Do We Practice?: A Collective Discussion with the Actors	26
Proposing Alternative Ways of Practicing Architecture in the 2000s: Discussions with the Pioneers	50
Widening the Spectrum of Architecture in the 2010s: Seven Questions to Fourteen Contemporary Collectives	84

How Do We
Why Do W

A Collective Discus
(ab)Normal, Assem
Collectif Etc, construc
Lacol, raumlabo

Hosted via Zoom on
Berlin, Bern, Delft, Gh
Milan, Rotterdam

ractice and
 Practice?

on with the Actors:
e, **baukuh**, **CNCRT**,
ab, **false mirror office**,
and **X=(T=E=N)**

ay 6, 2020, between
t, Lausanne, London,
evey, and Zurich

MODERATOR

Natalie Donat-Cattin

PARTICIPANTS

(ab)Normal	Marcello Carpino
	Davide Masserini
Assemble	Jane Hall
baukuh	Andrea Zanderigo
CNCRT	Luciano Aletta
	Marson Korbi
Collectif Etc	Théo Mouzard
	Maxence Bohn
constructLab	Sébastien Tripod
	Bert De Backer
	Licia Soldavini
false mirror office	Boris Hamzeian
	Filippo Fanciotti
Lacol	Carles Baiges
raumlabor	Markus Bader
X=(T=E=N)	.Scott Lloyd

The collective discussion, which was supposed to be a physical encounter at the École Polytechnique Fédérale de Lausanne, instead took place on Zoom, following the outbreak of the Covid-19 pandemic. The conversation marked an opportunity for exchange between most of the practices which actively contributed to the creation of this publication, generating a ground of confrontation, as well as an informal environment of interchange and learning. These horizontal structures—here generically defined as *collectives*—given their recent birth are often particular in their organizational system. The dialogue therefore concentrated on common and noncommon aspects of their way of working and designing, as well as on larger questions regarding the possibility of changing the architectural process and the approach to the discipline itself. If, on the one hand, it shed light on issues related to the complex human environment of these structures, on the other, it underlined why it is necessary for architecture to find new outlets today, in order to respond to the social, ecological, and political problems.

    Much of the exchange focused on the word *collective* itself, its role as an entity and its architectural typology of interest, for instance the public or temporary project. The architect, throughout the discussion, is no longer seen and mentioned as a solo figure, but as a number of people cooperating. The very project of these structures is to develop an open and accessible model able to act on a public and political level, which offers an expertise, while proposing a counterarchitecture, faithful to its founding values.

General Greetings and Pretalk

Lacol, Carles Baiges: Did you only invite men to this conversation, Natalie?

raumlabor, Markus Bader: We have been discussing that a couple of times, the fact that *collective* has something to do with gender, and in the raumlabor story it is so in a way. raumlabor emerged from a shared shop front studio space—it was very "soft" and we did not know what we were doing. The boys were more willing to stick with this uncertainty than the girls—to gender it this way—and I would be very curious to hear from everybody if that is also your case. The women that were part of this "soft" phase created smaller, more reliable groups, and followed a less unpredictable path.

Lacol, Carles Baiges: Our case is very balanced. However, we realized that it was mainly men presenting our works in talks and conferences, so we had to encourage the women to put themselves forward.

Assemble, Jane Hall: In Assemble we gather ourselves around the building site itself. The active building is more important than trying to realize a set project. Part of that is about feeling empowered through building. We were very young when we started, fresh out of uni. In a traditional architecture office you perceive the hierarchy, as well as the fact that there are a lot of men around. Assemble is fifty-fifty, but for the women, at the start, part of the interest was wanting to have a more hands-on approach, to gain that construction knowledge, which takes a long time to build through practice, and women traditionally tend to drop out of the industry. However, now we have other concerns, and are sticking around for different reasons.

baukuh, Andrea Zanderigo: I agree with what Markus is saying. At the beginning we were six men and two women. It probably would not have happened because of the women pushing it along. Initially, the two who were involved were not convinced, and only one stayed at the end. I am sure it is different now, but at the time women were willing to follow a more reliable career, generally speaking. The boys were willing to take the risk, embracing the wait, whilst trying to do something.

Start of the Conversation

Natalie Donat-Cattin: The topic of today's conversation is: how do we practice? And why do we practice? I will open up the discussion with a quote from *Brussels: A Manifesto towards the Capital of Europe* "to realize built architecture, architects have to explicitly or implicitly, consciously or unconsciously, comply with the priorities of the power system in force. Architects whose principles oppose these priorities find themselves unable to realize their architecture and can only postulate, by means of projects, conjectures anticipating an alternative regime. Often they are the harbingers of the future."[1]

1. Pier Vittorio Aureli, Véronique Patteeuw, Joachim Deklerck and Martino Tattara, *Brussels: A Manifesto towards the Capital of Europe* (Rotterdam, NAi Publishers, 2007), 7.

I would like to open up the debate with these first questions, in response to the quote previously mentioned: can it exist, another architectural path or an alternative to the system in force? And if it does exist, until when does it remain true to its ideals without compromising itself? And if it does remain true to itself, what impact does it have on its outcome, on the architecture?

I leave the word to you.

X=(T=E=N), Scott Lloyd: I will talk about remaining true. We are all scared of selling out and for this reason we start off by creating something special, empowering us, which we are all seduced by at the start. However, then it fades, and it happens everywhere, even in relationships. If you cannot maintain the spark, then you might fall into what is expected and normalized. X=(T=E=N) has a constitution and a set of values, and it is structured in such a way that any member or any group of members can be voted out. It is a consensus-based system where the founders, if they do not stay true to the values, eventually will be out.

    We do not know how that is going to work, and we are not that old, so we are looking forward to testing it. The constitution of values is updated every six months. We have gone through a couple of fights already, because we realized we were not staying so true, so we made a break and restarted. We expect that it is always going to happen. Putting staying true into a protocol shows a hope that new and exciting energy will come from new people in order to put the agenda forward. For this reason I think remaining true is a really important point.

CNCRT, Luciano Aletta: Architecture is a collective process, a common practice. This dimension is never recognized by contemporary institutions of work, whether it is an office, university, or collective. As concrete (CNCRT) we decided to actively embrace this common dimension in our form of association and declare the social role of architecture within the construction of social life. What we try to do with our collective is to question the practice of architecture. Being limited to just ourselves, we can only question the way in which we work. Therefore, we try to create an open community, a space open to encounters, organized around the project of architecture.

    Our attempt is to focus on the role of architecture and the architecture project within the construction of the contemporary city. For us, the project acquires a salvific dimension. For this reason, we do not have a fixed structure or procedure of work, nor do we aim to achieve a general consensus. This collective participation has to be freely happening around the availability and interest of people and the possibility of having an open structure, allowing us to be more inclusive. For people who are not familiar with us, our collective since 2014 has expanded every year, we are currently twelve. In a way, our collective became the central point of our research, a project on common practices within architecture.

CNCRT, Marson Korbi: Concrete (CNCRT) started in 2014, but became a real project very recently, two years ago, following this idea of being more inclusive, when a core group of twelve people was regularly joining. Our starting point was a specific city in a specific environment, Brussels. I would like to return back to your question of why do we practice in this new innovative collective form. This question for me, even if it is difficult to answer, is very important because it indicates a moment of thinking: Why are we doing this? And this puts into question the profession as a whole. Some of you were discussing before the question of gender, which is, in my opinion, key, however it does belong to a more complex and general system, the profession as a whole, which is currently changing as the architecture labor is. We are all conscious that there are many collectives today. However, what is interesting is the way in which we produce things and their heterogeneity, which makes apparent the amount of labor. Texts, collages, competitions. In our case, we assume the project as a means to make more explicit the effort behind it, putting emphasis on how to communicate that architectural labor is changing and on how to give an architectural form to this new way of working together. If you take an ordinary architectural office, you know its name, where it is based, but you never have a clear idea of who is behind it. What I am trying to argue is that this is an important occasion for us, even if we are doing it via Zoom from a webcam, to see each other and make visible a category, a multitude of people working, which is something usually not so visible as it is today.

raumlabor, Markus Bader: The being against—this is what I read in your question—the possibility of a counterarchitecture or an architecture outside the system or as an alternative to the system, was very much part of raumlabor's beginnings. Berlin at the time was very accessible and "soft," you could experience the making of the city done by the people who were taking things in their own hands—it was very strong—while at the same time, master planning processes tried to superimpose an idea, an image, and a functional system of the city, which completely conflicted with this self-made city. And so from an architecture perspective, then, as a student or as a young professional, it seemed like two ways of city-making competing with each other, the official one and then the unofficial one. And we decided for the unofficial one. Now twenty years later, the question is still valid: to what extent can we, inside the capitalist reproductive system, offer any kind of countersystem? Of course it is about gradients. Our position at the moment is to allow for this counterarchitecture, to create situations of making otherwise and invite people in. This is probably why many of the situations in which we work are temporary, because we never found a way to make them last more or to accumulate more momentum. Indeed, we understand them as a window of opportunity into another potential reality.

Natalie Donat-Cattin: Markus, did you see temporariness as something you needed to give up in the process? To pursue your values, you had to give up on permanence.

raumlabor, Markus Bader: No. It was a psychological process of letting go as somebody who was trained in architecture and connected to the image or the imaginary, that I, architect, create things that last longer than I do. It was about learning that things that are fluid and temporary can be extremely valuable in themselves. So I am actively ignoring the question as the idea of giving up has a value attached to it that I do not agree with.

Assemble, Jane Hall: The question of value is important because, if we are thinking about how to do architecture differently or challenge the norms within the industry, why would organizing collectively be valuable or inherently part of that? Because it is hard work and sets itself up against being financially viable. As individuals, you take on burdens and risks. And it becomes difficult to explain your values to clients which would enable more permanent projects to happen. It is just not affordable. And that is something that we have been dealing with for the last ten years. We started off as a group of friends who were holding this idea of working collectively in balance with learning within the industry that we were in. So I would not say that working collectively was about being in opposition or finding alternatives. It was about creating agency for ourselves as individuals, which we thought we could do as a group to kind of question some of those norms. But over the years, it has cemented itself more as a practice. So that "why" is a big question for us: why are we doing this like this? And I think the reason why we continue to do it is that it is an enjoyable way of practicing. It is not just about a group of individuals working and celebrating together, implementing the collaborative nature of how architecture is produced, but about the spaces in which we do it. Our studio is really important to us. We have big workshops. We have ceramicists, graphic designers, and all sorts of people with whom we work in close proximity. The idea is not just about us being a differently structured architecture practice, but about creating a whole community that produces and makes work. This is where the value of working comes from as a way to change how architecture is made. It would be interesting to hear how everyone else is organized; working collectively can be very individual. Each collective has very different ways of working together and organizing groups into business models. We are twenty people in a limited partnership now, and we have a sort of top level of directors. But we still work very much in the initial way that we began working together, which is trying to do as much communally as possible, even though we are getting bigger and more permanent projects. Would be really interesting to hear more about how each group understands value in relationship to how we choose to work.

X=(T=E=N), Scott Lloyd: On that note, is there a typology of project which you think only works as a collective, because it is not necessarily about formulating an alternative to the practice, and you might inevitably start working on different typologies of projects if you are a collective. For us, we can work on small housing projects as a collective, we can do pavilions, installations, and experiments. But as soon as you have to split the labor and do more complicated work, we would not do it as a collective. It just would not happen.

So is there a typology of work which is still accessible by the collective to produce? We do not have experience with large-scale projects, with a collective of twelve people we are getting valuable inputs and still keeping that interest in the collective work. I guess you guys in Assemble have got more experience and it is interesting to see if it is still a collective practice when you start having project leaders and a fair system of wages. I am interested in the typology of work as a collective and the correlations it has with the structure of the collective.

Assemble, Jane Hall: What maybe all of us share in this conversation is the origins of the collective in any temporary or self-initiated environment. Assemble does different projects now, working across everything from the research scale to buildings and business planning, which can get siloed amongst a few individuals. A few people run each project because it gets confusing for clients to see a different face every week. We have a stable core group, but we safeguard time—a morning every week—where all together we work on each project and we schedule a couple of meetings each week to work in groups. One of the key elements, for us, is less about how to work collectively across projects of different types, but how to maintain the kind of coworking process which is about material experimentation mainly. For our biggest project, Goldsmith's Art Gallery in South London, we made the facade in our studio by collaboratively working with different skills and bringing them in. As it could all happen in our studio, it was much easier to make it happen in a spontaneous way. However, the projects that we were able to self-initiate, where everybody was part of it, are still the best ones. It can feel like there is an inability to share and learn new knowledge from each other's projects when you do have more stringent constraints on delivering and running projects of a different scale or with a different type of client. Having agency in projects has always enabled us to work more collaboratively and collectively because we can organize how we want to. It is very idiosyncratic.

Natalie Donat-Cattin: Andrea, I was thinking of something you guys wrote when you participated in Europan 7. You were saying about your project in Amsterdam, *Cassius*, that the project would remain social housing, but by dealing with the project in a certain way, an amount of quality could be produced in it, which was not necessarily valid in other circumstances. So to respond to what Scott was talking about, maybe it is not about typology, but about the way the project is taken on by the collective.

baukuh, Andrea Zanderigo: In a way both positions are valid. It is important to be trusted by clients in architecture, which is a big obstacle now. As a young collective it is difficult to be taken seriously by clients, whilst it might be easier to gain the support of cultural entities or clients driven by a certain political ideology or in a competition. Nobody knows if you are a collective or not when you participate in Europan. Indeed, my perception is that if you are understood by the architectural market as a collective, initially what you do is research, installations, and leftist progressive cultural projects. Eventually you might try to reposition yourself slightly more to the center, in the hope of having an impact on the architecture market and maybe on its process too, by adding an extra value.

It is difficult for everybody, collectives and not, especially in Italy in our times, where in order to build a hospital you need to have done hospitals for all of your life.

In our case we simply wanted to create a collective studio, because in the end architecture is produced collectively, even though during the twentieth century that idea got corroborated by critics, clients, and media. We always design collectively, and when we look at other people's work, we think that it is a collective production. It is always a collective process, and it always happens in a sort of political space: a space for debate, negotiation, and compromises. What is happening today is that this collective image, which was already part of the reality, is now emerging and proliferating.

false mirror office, Filippo Fanciotti: Andrea, do you normally introduce yourself as a collective to a new client or a new person?

baukuh, Andrea Zanderigo: Depends what you mean. We introduce ourselves as an office with many partners from the very beginning. However the people who reach for us in general sort of know us and know what they are going to get. Nobody looks for us from the real estate market.

false mirror office, Filippo Fanciotti: I am under the impression that the perception of the word *collective* changes from country to country. Indeed, it does carry along with it political baggage. So to talk about collectives in Italy is something productive in some sense and not productive in others. Probably in some other countries, the same word does not have the same effect and impact. The more you go north, the less you have this bad political tag on it. For us it is a topic of discussion: can we use the word *collective* or not? For a while we called ourselves a group because it is somehow more neutral. We've now reached a point in which we cannot even use the word *group* among us.

false mirror office, Boris Hamzeian: Compared to what Jane said before, regarding the genesis of Assemble, where there was a desire to stress its collective dimension, for us the process of coming together was more natural. Our case is not so different from baukuh, also because we started by looking at them as an example and also participated in Europan. We also decided to add the noun *office* in our name, false mirror office, because of this relationship of trust between us and the client.

Natalie Donat-Cattin: I already discussed the use of the noun *collective* with some of you. Jane mentioned how the word collective automatically referred to a certain generation, between their twenties and forties, and defined a larger group of people. Between all of you, there are various descriptions of yourself, collective or not. However in the end, the ambitions are not so different. On the one hand, how you define yourself is very individual to each one of you, because the way you got together is personal and unique; on the other hand, this chosen definition defines what you want to offer to a potential client or how you introduce yourself to the world.

Assemble, Jane Hall: Coming back to the notion of *collective* being a loaded word in some parts of the world, it does resonate with the condition in the UK. For a while we looked into cooperative structures, but in the UK, that has a stronger political understanding about how you organize and what your attitudes are. When we began, we were not bonded by that, we just recognized that working together collectively could produce the type of work and investigations that interested us. However, that did not necessarily mean we were signing up to this entire world of thinking collectively and aligning ourselves with some ideology. Therefore, we started using the word *collective* as a means to describe to other people what was a weird, amorphous group of individuals that kept changing. It is easier to say "we are a collective," and people potentially do not interrogate what that means. And it stayed with us. The notion *collective* might also work against you, because now it is almost like a brand. Often clients expect ten people to show up and they are disappointed when only one or two people come. Here in the UK, over the last ten years it's important, because there has been a frustration with the way in which the environment is produced. As a consequence, there are particular clients interested in finding alternatives. Most people come to us because we get behind this idea of the word *collective*, rather than trying to hide from it. It is something which represents our way of working. And how do you stay truly collective? We have got junior staff now, much younger people in our studio who are technically employees. There are these implicit hierarchies that we recognize. It feels like we do not really safeguard collectivity as a political idea, we just use it to describe how we work together, which we like to say is not hierarchical, but the actuality of that is probably quite different.

For us internally, it is more of an attitude and, externally, it is more of branding, unfortunately. But it changes over time, which I think is quite interesting, and I am sure everybody here has this story of how they see their practices and understand what they do and why they do it. Has this changed a lot?

Collectif Etc, Théo Mouzard: In France, the word has become really popular within the architecture community, and many students want to create collectives. Ten years ago, we wanted to be a collective so hard that it is even in our name, Collectif Etc. Ten years later, much has changed. What we are interested in is to stop the authority, work on individual emancipation, and not give orders to each other. It is important for our group, because that is what we want to do in architecture. For us, being an office or a collective was not the question, but what really interested us is to create other ways of producing architecture. This might be something that connects all of us, to be more interested in architecture than architects, at least we are. Therefore we wanted our collective to become a wider collective, and when we work on a project, we work with the inhabitants and other people outside our collective and pay them to work with us. We are a big collective during project time, and it lasts for a few weeks. Stopping authority and creating spaces of individual emancipation is at the heart of our practice.

Both the learning process and the need of giving attention to each other are the important sides of being a collective. We are only familiar with many collectives within the French context, however we believe the situation might be different in other countries. So that is a question for you in other countries in Europe, how is the collective movement looking like there? Are there many collectives with an interesting way of working? In the French context, there are some collectives of only one person, however they still define themselves as collectives. And, Jane, regarding the fact that Assemble starts to have employees. Sometimes we ask ourselves if we want to have employees, but this is a border that we decided to never cross because we feel it would break our collective way of organizing authority in our group.

(ab)Normal, Marcello Carpino: The Italian situation is very similar to the French one. There are numerous collectives, especially in Milan. As a student, you feel that creating a collective is favorable rather than having a normal office. During my experience in the Netherlands or in Switzerland, working collectively was something completely different. People could not grasp what we mean by *collective* or they only portrayed it as an office without income.

CNCRT, Marson Korbi: Collective probably differs from one context to the other. In the south of Italy the collective has a strong relationship with the university context. As many of you said, the idea of being a collective starts from university. Here in Bari, many students find themselves working for free for professors, therefore the collective now became a phenomenon. People suddenly reunite into groups and start doing projects for themselves, instead of doing them for the professors. And even if the collective does not rise from a political question, it is often a response to how labor is organized, and this accounts also for the way of doing architecture. If someone works for someone else, and this someone else decides for you and for the project, which is actually what happens in an ordinary office, you become the CAD-monkey, the one who executes what someone else is saying. The collective offers the opportunity instead to work in a cooperative term, and in that moment the project transforms into something able to give us personal pleasure. This personal pleasure perhaps might only be achieved within a collective. I believe we should discuss what kind of relationships are established within the collective, how they differ from the hierarchical office organization and how they offer an alternative.

constructLab, Licia Soldavini: I am here representing constructLab, but I have been working in the last ten years with different collectives in France, Germany, Italy, and Portugal. I was wondering if the rise in number of collectives has to do with the way our clients work—not just cultural institutions, but even more local governments, councils, and cities—and the way they develop their projects nowadays.

If there is more demand for such forms of flexible organizations, different ways of doing, and bringing values into the work, is there not more offer? Regarding constructLab, we are scattered around Europe, and we do not call ourselves a collective but a network. However, we can call ourselves a collective once we think that our main interest is to approach projects in a different way. We found each other because we either looked for an escape after our studies, or we were searching for alternative methods of designing space. Our organization, the way the decisions are taken, the way we share responsibilities on projects, depends on the scale of the project, the country, the people involved, and these are always variable.

constructLab, Sébastien Tripod: Licia was talking about how we function, and as she was saying, we are more of a network rather than a collective and have different levels of action in our cooperative work. The network helps regulate ourselves financially, although we always try to work and share ideas. We meet once a year in a place connected to a project. We meet for a few days, and we discuss our network problems. It has been a couple of years now that we are trying to develop ourselves locally in different places with local associations, because we realized that being global means being vulnerable in terms of action. We have been creating associations in Berlin, in Ghent, in Fribourg. We are entering a new phase by approaching a more local perspective. However, the construction moments on the building site still remain a way to come together and be active within the network, and we invite people from our network to join. The issue of being collectives is also connected to responsibility. We can collectively be responsible for doing the dishes, but maybe not up to the structure of the house. The work does depend on tasks, after all. We are different generations working within this network, however we reject this notion and are permeable. It is also important to be open to new people—for this reason we are growing. Some people are less active, some people more. This is how we function.

constructLab, Bert De Backer: The challenge for us is how to combine the horizontal structure of decision-making with the way of operating within a group of people scattered around the world. Every project for us is a way of creating a group that exists out of people that we know very well. But we are not there together to decide how projects evolve or initiate. The decision of how to structure the team is taken at the beginning, and it is very important and challenging. From that moment on, that newly assembled group from our network is in charge and responsible, all involved at an equal level in the growth of the project. If we go into a territory that is new for us, which happens very often because we are locally anchored only in a few places, we come there with a set of people and embrace the horizontal feeling created by a situation which we are all new to. And we seek ways to investigate this and grow into it, looking at it as research.

Lacol, Carles Baiges: When we started ten years ago as a students, we used the word *collective*, not only because people called us in that way, but also because there was the network Arquitecturas Colectivas, which connected groups around, mostly in Spain, but also in Latin America, Italy, and France. The word *collective*, which I do not think is so politically charged, felt old and also, as some of you already mentioned, it was misused by groups of one or two people. We then got connected to the cooperative system in our neighborhood, from which we learned a lot. Five years ago we founded the workers' coop and decided to start using the word *cooperative*, which is more defined and limited. We have also been dealing with some of the topics already mentioned. We just started having employees, and we had the same discussions on how the system is not horizontal anymore. But at least in Spain, the workers' cooperatives are very limited. There is a limited amount of workers that you can have to keep democracy inside the company. In this definition, we feel more comfortable. When we started ten years ago during the economic crisis, there was a sudden trend of collectives. Still, most of the people wanted to be starchitects and individuals. In the last five years, mostly in Catalonia, but also in Spain, there has been a growth in workers' cooperatives also and inside which there are mainly architects. Suddenly there was an explosion of this model, which created an occasion to rethink what models and ways of working are valid.

    We do all have similar questions. In our case this year, we were doing some work on how we communicate internally and work together. We found out that the collective was even a bit oppressive to the individual, there were some moments that the group was putting a lot of pressure on some individuals. It was interesting to see how sometimes a group can be oppressive and how we can be still hierarchical even when we are a horizontal group.

false mirror office, Filippo Fanciotti: Do you all know each other?

Lacol, Carles Baiges: Yes, we are not such a big cooperative, we are fourteen. We started as twenty, then once we created the club, only fourteen of us remained. We have been very focused on how to be efficient, how to make the company work, and how to pay our salaries every month. So we have been trying to have less people in the projects. We have once a week the collective workshops where everybody can join and be involved in a certain project. However, when the projects have two or three people, we try to balance the main roles within the projects. If you lead one project, you will be working in another role in another one. Regarding the start of our talk on the type of projects, we discussed that with our colleagues for a few weeks, because we do very different projects, from small installations to architecture to sociology. I also work on social issues, in big housing projects. We have clients that come to us because if they have regulation problems, budget problems, collective work problems, they know we can solve it. I find it an interesting way to define the type of work we do.

Collectif Etc, Théo Mouzard: In France we see many initiatives coming from a political background, led by many self-managed initiatives in construction, architecture, and in urban planning involving farmers and other people. They organize talks, and we are surprised to see that their discourse often matches with ours, European collectives. Even during the yellow jacket movement in France, many people went to the local roundabout and started building shelters and pop-up stores. These initiatives are close to what we can define as the top-down-bottom-up way of designing cities: open projects about collective construction. Therefore, as a collective, we are now asking ourselves where we should be on the political chessboard. Some of the collectives in France are involved on one side in political programs, on the other side in institutional projects, balancing between the two. In other contexts, for instance, the political background is closer to the collectives. I am thinking about the project of Assemble, the Granby workshop. It started from people fighting in the neighborhood, and it turned out to be a ceramic factory in the end. However, at the beginning, it was very political. Do you feel that in your countries within your collective, do you question political values and how radical you are with your projects?

Assemble, Jane Hall: Within our group, everyone has their own political beliefs. Collectively we do have a sort of shared idea about where we sit. We are not outwardly political in terms of how we frame the work, even if some of us would like to do more active political work. The project in Granby to which you are referring was working with a community land trust which had been formed after twenty years of collective activism to try to save their homes in an area in the north of England, called Granby in Liverpool, from being demolished. And this was set against the backdrop of race riots in the 1980s, the Blairism New Labour, the government of the 1990s that managed the decline of the area. The individuals who stayed on were greening the streets as a form of resistance against the demolition of the houses, which never happened. The entire area was full of unoccupied buildings. They managed to acquire ten of them and wanted to refurbish them. They imagined that a traditional architect would not be interested in the story. And we were suggested to them as people who might look at it differently. It was a really early project and made us think who we were as a group and how we were working together. At the same time, the community land trust was dealing with the same situation: we were two groups trying to work out what we were doing and why we were doing it. It ended up being just the standard refurbishment of these houses due to economical restrictions. The ceramics industry business that came out was a rejection of this, as this community had campaigned for so long to save these houses. We made an orangery studio, where a series of products could be built from scratch in the back garden of these houses, using waste from the site to give character and speak of its story. That evolved into setting up the whole ceramics workshop, which is part of an ongoing strategy in the area to introduce industry. The political nature of our work potentially is about staying with our projects. We sit on the board for three projects that were set up and we continue to play an active role in how those projects are organized, how they are managed, and how they run. So the design element is not the only one. The architectural, spatial, and material part is only a really small facet of how we think about our projects.

As a group, we are interested in the idea of architects swimming upstream. You get involved in decision-making, policy, and business planning before the architectural brief is put out into the world, and we really struggle in conditions where a brief is handed over to us. We often do not perform well when we have to produce something. The product is a total world, and it comes with a positioning, which I would like us to be more explicit about. Once you have been working together for so long, you definitely share some sort of—not center politics, but center ground.

There are a lot of talks about architects being more political in the UK. Institutions are quite dangerous organizations in the UK. The governing bodies are supposed to promote architecture. However, architects have no agency in the UK. It is much easier to be confident in a political position if you identify yourself as somehow Other. And I think that is where the term *collective* has been quite good for us. We can be more explicit and take more risks in that sense, and I hope that is felt in the work that we do. Does anyone else feel the difficulty to behave or act in that way, take risks, or is it made easier by this "collective" banner?

Lacol, Carles Baiges: The Spanish situation was peculiar five years ago when in the local elections there were municipalities and city councils where some representatives of the political party Podemos, with a lot of people coming from social movements, were elected. In certain areas, these political representatives did not want to work with the collective they had been working with until that moment because they were afraid of being accused of nepotism and favoring their friends. Here in Barcelona, we had the occasion to work with other municipalities, and most of the experiences ended up being positive. We could see the risk of corruption when they were working with us and were asking us to not be critical or, on the other hand, to publicly support them. When somebody that you openly oppose is in government, it is easier to be critical, to create alternatives and unite with other people who are also against them. And this happens on all levels. I have a similar feeling with the Architects Association in Catalonia, which is now run also by a group of people who are closer to us and have a similar mind-set. They try to incorporate us and hear us, whereas before we had to protest because they did not listen to young people, collectives and cooperatives. However, things are still not changing the way we would want. Indeed, how do we fight against the people who are incorporating us? Sometimes it is even more complicated.

Natalie Donat-Cattin: Many of your works incorporate a will of going back to action. In the 1960s, architects acted through images, and now it is more of a physical action. Many of you come together on the construction site or in other ways. This is also a political statement.

CNCRT, Marson Korbi: I will try to answer your question by also connecting to the yellow jackets episode you mentioned, Théo. We should not see them as radical, but episodes to learn from, if we analyze their cooperative methodology and forget what they wanted to do and where they come from. By wearing these yellow jackets, they identified themselves with a symbol. After two years, we still talk about them, thanks to this symbol. Today we have been discussing the idea of how we work, how we organize ourselves as collectives and what is our relation with clients. This conversation makes us somehow similar to the way these yellow jackets were organized or tried to organize each other. And this is also a political problem. If we compare ourselves to the phenomena of the 1970s in Italy—thinking of Superstudio and Archizoom—we are different from them. They were very influenced by certain texts of Mario Tronti. Indeed, the way they were trying to put their project in relation to their active work was very interesting. And we can learn from them when thinking of how to structure ourselves.

This is something that we try to do in our collective. The idea of the institution, of assuming a symbol to represent ourselves, is what we actually do in CNCRT, because we try to understand ourselves as individuals and as part of the collective. And we try to find that archetypical form which represents better this new form of working together, which is a collective.

baukuh, Andrea Zanderigo: We do not do any action, we are traditional in that sense. Our specialty is the project and the project is a condensed space of negotiations. The sheer number of people involved in a collective already makes you aware of how to tackle negotiations outside of the group. Even within the group you are constantly trying to convince someone else that certain ideas are key and the potential of transposing them into a project. Is that political per se? Good architecture should always try to do that. For me it is difficult to understand if what we do is political per se or if we are simply political and social beings.

raumlabor, Markus Bader: We are very much action-based. The book we made was called *Acting in Public*. This idea of going out there and creating a sphere of common action was, and still is, fundamental to how we describe our work. It is part of our architecture, even though our buildings are not permanent, but in terms of discussing spatial questions, access to the city, notions of empowerment, questions of who is able to speak and who is able to design. It is also about opening processes. We are involved in more long-term processes that are tiring and intense negotiations in itself. One is Floating University in Berlin, where we are trying to develop a site differently, and one is Haus der Statistik, a collaborative and collective site development in a central spot. Both of them are two attempts to find different and collaborative modes to the question of how can we make the city and project development different?

Earlier on the term *client* was mentioned. We do not believe in this client-architecture relationship so much. A second line of thinking I would like to offer in this respect, even though we talk about architecture, we also like to use the term *urban practice*. We are still testing this term, to see to what extent it would be helpful or not.

But as we are placed between architecture and some other arts, being performative or fine arts, we feel that *urban practice* is an interesting term that incorporates some of the participatory, some of the public space and some of the collective. And it is probably more accessible to everybody than this exclusive term *architecture*. Architecture in many respects is associated with a certain expertise, and people sometimes do not feel invited to this kind of conversation and to action. Indeed, would you feel *urban practice* is a term that could be helpful for what we do?

X=(T=E=N), Scott Lloyd: Urban practice in the sense that there's a publicness to the work? Until now all of our works are public and accessible and that has automatically a vulnerability, but also an openness to critique and sharing. That is probably to the urban side of our work. This is a good term to use, because *urban* is not just about master planning. It is about engaging. So I like that better.

Assemble, Jane Hall: Just to add something to the idea of action and notion of publicness. We have always found architecture to be quite abstract and it is hard for people without architectural training to feel like it is something that they can or should engage with. Many of our early works began with thinking about investigating or embracing amateur knowledge and practices and making that part of the project. A lot of work collectives do, especially on temporary projects, can be misunderstood as social practice and have some sort of social agenda and be benevolent about engaging people, when actually it is valuable knowledge. When architects or designers re-organize that the way they work is about trying to create structures that enable an interaction and an exchange of knowledge. Action enables that—making something visible and seeing changes happen rather than waiting for a year to see some product which seems totally alien to you. A question within our studio is, do we only work locally? And what does *locally* even mean? How do you create methods which make your approach and your way of thinking actually valuable to people? Not urban practice but *action practice*. But both are interesting ways of framing it.

Natalie Donat-Cattin: On the level of the city, regarding urban practice, many of you act in remote areas of the city or voids. Markus, the site of the Floating University, was it an active choice?

raumlabor, Markus Bader: For those who do not know the site, it is quite special and very central, but it looks like a completely rural setting.

The discovery of the site was the discovery of an underused opportunity in the city, which happened at a time when Berlin was rapidly filling up. The former condition, with lots of empty lands and spaces of potential, very much transformed. The open spaces became building sites and then residential areas. It was a beautiful discovery to find this place trapped in time that offered itself as a space for experimentation.

Going back to the urban, I agree with Jane, when you say *action practice*. The second part of urban practice is the practice, and it focuses how we are doing things. So how do we practice space? How do we practice architecture? That is a question we are discussing a lot. An open statement.

Collectif Etc, Théo Mouzard: In our collective we are talking about remote areas as a space of potential, and we are trying to work in rural areas and small villages as an opportunity to create something. For instance, we are working on the rehabilitation of a former factory in a small village in the mountains in the south of France. I saw that Assemble is working with a farm in London. As we are very much focusing on urban spaces, I wanted to know if you guys are sharing our questions on the remote areas and rural territories as new potentials for developing our methods, types of practicing, and creating projects.

Assemble, Jane Hall: I suppose not. The architectural discourse is very much focused on the urban and the city as conditions. The farm is on the edge of London, so it is not explicitly rural. But what does *urbanity* mean? Nothing more than a geographic location. Coworking in Granby, for its intents and purposes, could be more of a rural condition because there is no population left in an entire area of the city, which is however entirely inhabited. What constitutes the urban question? Is Assemble an urban practice? Are we even based in London? We have a few people who live in different cities across the UK now and a lot of people in the group do not want to be living and working in such an expensive place so far from their families. So we have been looking at moving the entire practice outside of London, which would also fundamentally change our interests and the types of work we do. It is no coincidence that we are interested in these neutral spaces, typologies or questions in the city, because we work every day and live ourselves in the city. Maybe other questions might become more prominent to us if we ourselves were based in another location, which comes back to this idea of being a local practice or a global one. The globalization and conditions of cities make it easier as practitioners to work in other cities because there are many differences, but also many characteristics that are shared by a similar spatial condition. Whereas the rural or the countryside is a foreign land.

Collectif Etc, Théo Mouzard: I am asking the question because our collective is moving from the city and we are going to buy a big house all together in the countryside. We want to move our practice out of the city, which is something completely new for us. We can see that in Europe, the huge cities are less and less comfortable for people. With the Covid-19 virus, in Paris a million people left the city to go live in the countryside because it is more comfortable. So we are going to do this in the next six months. And we are really looking to live it as a practice collective.

Assemble, Jane Hall: Have you found somewhere to go? Where are you going?

Collectif Etc, Théo Mouzard: We are going south of Marseilles, where we have this project of a factory. It is a new project to us because it is a restoration project, which is a more usual way of looking at architecture. It is a three-thousand-square-meters project. As many of us wanted to go live in the countryside, we decided to move just nearby the project and we found a big house with a huge garden at the bottom of the mountain.

The garden will be a territorial project itself. In Mediterranean context, there are many interesting places that are being built up with local communities. We are setting a European project to go in the south of Italy and in Greece to meet these people and work with them. Living in the countryside is part of moving our way of practicing and the objectives we are dealing with. That was the essence of my question, are many of the collectives born in the last decade moving to other places and getting interested in other things? Maybe that's another point we have in common with the 1970s imaginary.

Natalie Donat-Cattin: To round up the conversation, how do you foresee the next phase? Will these experiments, which still remain marginal within the architecture world, even though they are an alternative, take over? Will architecture change its way of practicing? We are entering an interesting period now, especially with Covid-19, which is already challenging our way of working and living.

X=(T=E=N), Scott Lloyd: I do not foresee a trend, I am aware that there are new ideas of approaching architecture coming up, and I do not think that is going to be any large movement. It is great that this project has come up, because it has been interesting for us to look around to see what other people are doing. We are going to continue finding new ways, we have already made adjustments, and we have tried to make many more. It is good to be inspired by new ways of approaching architecture. What is the future of architecture? It is nice to be able to pick it up, take it and try to learn from it.

Assemble, Jane Hall: The architectural discourse has been rather stagnant. And it is inspiring to see so many collectives globally and especially in Europe. It is not a thing in the UK. It comes naturally to me to be talking about networks and collectives, spread across many countries and working across them, whereas we are naturally isolated. Our challenge is how to break out of that and expand, now that we have a solid ground and way of working together. It is about the individual and the collective, what does it mean to continue as individuals to find areas of particular interest, which we want to push? How can we kind of be less collective, but use the collective support and understand it as a support structure to enable us to actually be more radical and take more risks in the future? How do you keep it interesting and relevant? Moving to the countryside is a great idea. Assemble might be coming to the south of France for our annual trip. We do an annual trip together.

Collectif Etc, Théo Mouzard: You are all welcome in Marseilles in our workshop. Four years ago, we tried to invite some Spanish collectives. And recently we have been working with the Italian collective orizzontale. There are many European bonds to be created. We are interested in two scales: one is the local scales, how the community can be involved in projects and how we can work with them, but also how that can be linked to a no-border spirit. Working at the European scale is very important, otherwise our local projects would stay local and only work in small places, becoming nationalist episodes. So we have to work on both scales. We tried to set up a meeting between collectives in France to create more solidarity between them. Can we be more powerful if we stand together as collectives? And maybe we can create a bigger voice, especially saying that alternative architecture is not only about small initiatives, but it can be broader, not a movement, but something that we stand for. Can we be together and powerful as collectives without making it just smooth and without differences? How can we come together sharing our singularities? I think we should do that from a European perspective. The modern movement had this International Congress of Modern Architecture and we should do the International Congress of Alternative Architecture. And I will not be Le Corbusier, do not worry.

Natalie Donat-Cattin: We should organize that. It is time to close it off. Thank you everybody for a great debate.

Proposing
Ways of Practic
in the

Discussio
Pioneers: bau
and Z

lternative
g Architecture
000s

 with the
h, raumlabor,
loark

Monday, January 27, 2020, 14:45 PM
baukuh's office in Milan

baukuh Architecture as a Collective Operation

Natalie Donat-Cattin: How did baukuh get together?

Andrea Zanderigo: In 1999 in Italy they were launching the Villard, an architectural traveling seminar, which was selecting ten students in every university participating to the seminar. Every fourth week, the students would go to a different university. In 1999–2000 the universities participating in it were Rome, Turin, Pescara, Palermo, Ascoli Piceno, Genoa, Milan, and Venice. We were all doing a project for a big area in Palermo. From the IUAV in Venice we were four friends: Paolo Carpi, Vittorio Pizzigoni, Francesca Torzo, and I. From the Genoa gang, there were two guys: Lorenzo Laura and Pier Paolo Tamburelli. And that is how we met each other, through the program. Pier and Lorenzo had traveled to Palermo by boat and brought a car, so Paolo and I were given a ride in their car and they were listening to an Italian underground band we all liked, called Massimo Volume. We did not only have an architecture connection, but also the same taste in music: it made it easier to bond. In the next three/four years, we did a couple of competitions together and helped each other with our respective diploma projects. In 2001, we participated in Europan 6 in Marseille and did a housing project. Nobody was an architect, so we had to ask an architect friend to sign for us. We rented a small place in Genoa to do it, as it was a cheaper city than Venice. We traveled there by train with the big monitors of our computers, the Apple with the big handles and semitransparent plastic.

In those years the people we were working with were continuously changing, and we were split between Genoa, Venice, and Milan. At the time, for example, I was working for Stefano Boeri at the University of Venice. However, in December 2003 we won Europan 7, and it was eight of us who took part in it, the six from Villard plus Silvia Lupi and Giacomo Summa from Genoa. That made the group. We applied for two sites, which is the maximum you can do. We won the first prize in Amsterdam and the second prize in Budapest. It was not decided that it would be these eight people, it just happened. There was no big decision behind it, it was just life. With the money we won in Europan 7, we suddenly had the possibility to do something together and we decided to take the risk of creating an office. When you are younger, it is easier to take that risk. With some of the money, we decided to rent an office in Genoa, as the city had been in a crisis ever since it had lost a third of its population since the 1950s, and had plenty of empty spaces as a result. Indeed, it was easy and cheap for everybody to find a place. Therefore, in summer 2004, we moved to Genoa. For the first two months we used a disco as an office, as it was closed for the summer, and some of us knew the owners. I still remember how sticky the floor was, I think they had not cleaned it in a while. In September we found a proper office space.

Everyone joined at the time, but a year after that in 2005, Lorenzo Laura left the group and moved to Milan to work for Citterio. One reason was economical, but I think he also wanted to leave Genoa. After that also Francesca Torzo left around 2007–2008. We remained six and we still are.

Natalie Donat-Cattin: What brought you together ideologically at the start?

Andrea Zanderigo: We might say generation, but *generation* is always a tricky word; at some point you start sharing a discourse and topics, a universe of some sort. If we think of when Superstudio or Archizoom were born, it is a very precise moment, 1968. It was an extremely ideological period. For us it was not about ideology, it was about conditions. It was partially related to the condition of the Italian market, which was completely saturated, as so many buildings had been built in the 1970s, '80s, and '90s; this combined with the fact that the economy has not been growing consistently in the last twenty years. So, once you enter the market, there is no market, which means that you have to find other ways to express yourself, to conquer a bit of visibility, because if you cannot build in Italy maybe there is the possibility to build somewhere else. For this reason, we were so prolific in terms of conceptual production and competitions, which is simply related to the fact that we had time to do it and we thought it would be a good way to get known outside of Italy.

Natalie Donat-Cattin: How did baukuh develop throughout the years?

Andrea Zanderigo: At the start, everybody was working in the office as much as possible, apart from Vittorio, who was doing a PhD, and Pier Paolo, who was enrolled at the Berlage Institute. Everybody was working a hundred percent, in fact a hundred and fifty percent, in the office. Nobody worked with us in the first years, then we started having a couple of employees. Over time things changed. In 2011 we moved to Milan, but we kept the office in Genoa, and some partners remained there. We never managed to build anything in Genoa and after a while we decided it was better to go somewhere else. Milan was more convenient as a city, also in terms of being well connected within Italy and Europe. There were and there are more opportunities, it is easier to find specialists of any kind. Silvia also moved to Burano after a while. What started as a collective experience within the same office space, is now more tentacular, meaning we meet with everybody every two weeks. We still take most decisions together, but it is true that sometimes it is less of us taking day-to-day the decisions.

At the beginning, everybody was doing the same job, and then after a while you understand who is better at a certain task, which does not mean that there is more power in one role or another, but it certainly means that you need to realize what you are good at doing and what makes sense to do. However, we do not have a hierarchy, but we know who would qualify best to undertake a certain task. When working together in a number of six or eight, on the one hand, you need to be willing to share the projects, and also be ready to lose time discussing with everybody in order to convince them about your ideas. On the other hand, you need to be open to accept everybody else's ideas. To do that, it takes an extreme amount of openness and flexibility. The moment you feel like a project is only yours and you need to have the last word on any decision, then it becomes impossible to work together.

Natalie Donat-Cattin: When it comes to projects, is it always the six of you working on it?

Andrea Zanderigo: Ideally everybody works on all projects, however, not everybody can be project managers. But we often discuss in groups of two or three, and even of six in some cases. You try to share as much as possible, and sometimes it is not possible. In architecture certain things happen in a very long time, but other things happen in half an hour, for example when there is a problem during construction.

Eirini Peraki: Are all of you involved in the academic world?

Andrea Zanderigo: There are four of us involved. Pier is teaching at the Politecnico di Milano, I am now at the Royal College of Art, Vittorio is teaching in Genoa and Paolo is currently not teaching, but he was teaching before and he just finished a PhD on demolitions.

Eirini Peraki: Was this PhD topic also a common obsession?

Andrea Zanderigo: Yes, demolition was a common obsession. It started to be of interest for us when we did an exhibition in Genoa. We made a huge drawing in a space called Pink Summer. As I previously mentioned, there is a lot of empty space in Genoa and half the apartments are empty. Demolition is a real opportunity, but with the current protection of property, it is sadly only a fictional opportunity.

Natalie Donat-Cattin: What do you think about the current Italian situation? Would you be more for acting in the context or for stepping back and conserving?

Andrea Zanderigo: In Italy the heritage protection system is crazy. Everything slightly old is considered untouchable. Instead of judging case by case, what is possible and what is not possible, what is good to do and what is not good to do, the Italian system simply blocks everything. And the other countries are evolving in this direction. In Belgium the control was very light and now it is becoming tighter and tighter. We do a lot of projects on existing stuff, because we like it and because—it is slightly ideological—we pretend that modernity never happened. We still believe that it is possible to treat the city and its building as they were treated for example in the Renaissance. So it is possible to continue working on existing architectural matters and modify, refine, adapt, give new meaning to these constellations of objects, which is exactly what modernity at some point decided was not anymore the case. Indeed, the hyper-protection of contemporary heritage is a reaction to the disruption of modernity, to the danger of tabula rasa.

Working with the existing is something that we have to do or at least consider, especially now with the issue of the climate crisis. Is it necessary to throw away something or could it instead be reused and refined?

Eirini Peraki: In the southern countries, also due to the crisis, we are more used to not building. And now because of the ecological crisis, this attitude is also being considered in other countries. However, it is still a taboo for architects to not build. And we are not taught alternative possibilities in the academic environment.

Andrea Zanderigo: I like drawing on a tabula rasa if I have the opportunity, but again, this is partly a problem dictated by modernity. For Bramante, for example, it was perfectly acceptable to work on something which was already there and trying to transform it. Often big buildings were the result of accumulations over centuries, with many different designers involved. For example, in Santa Maria presso San Satiro there is this small building on the left, which is a paleo-Christian building and which was falling down when Bramante got the commission. First he built a big wall around it in order to prevent it from collapsing. Inside there is still the paleo-Christian space and outside you see this big wall, which is from the Renaissance, and then he constructed an oversized lighthouse on top of it, which changed the scale of the building from outside and brought light to the dark interior. The Renaissance was about light and definition of volumes, and Bramante basically injected this new light into the building. It is an ancient building and, at the same time, it is a Renaissance building. Indeed, it has even to do with the concept of authoriality, which is a modern invention. Before the Renaissance, we know of a couple of architects, but very few. It is only with the modern era, starting from the Renaissance, that individual authorship becomes important. However, many of the Renaissance buildings were collective productions, for example the "fabbrica Vaticana." Everybody worked there: it starts with Bramante and ends with Borromini. Two full centuries. It is not like a Gothic cathedral, where at a certain point you do not even know who is the author anymore. In the case of a Gothic cathedral, the project at a certain point starts moving by itself, and the decisions become obvious. The people are changing but the general plot is there, because the canon is there. In the Renaissance, instead, the canon is being continuously discussed and refined and that is where the individual comes into play, interpreting a canon, and that is how, by the end, the building appears as a weird combination of individual decisions and of a general tradition. And the production happens throughout an extended amount of time, under different powers and influences. However, it is still about authorship and authoriality.

Natalie Donat-Cattin: What do you think about the word *collective* itself? I believe the word was not associated with architecture until just a bit ago.

Andrea Zanderigo: It is a word, so it depends what you project on it. It is certainly a word coming from politics, linked to the left wing and to a post-Marxist view. I am a bit reluctant to talk about collectives in architecture because the moment you use that word, at least for me, you are immediately projected in a political sphere. The relationship between politics and architecture is extremely ambiguous. What does it mean to make politics as an architect? As an individual it is easy to state your political position and try to be consistent with it, but then doing politics in architecture is like saying you are doing politics while being a doctor. However, there are moments when your person as a political being and your person as an architect completely collide, and then you can take decisions which are entirely political: for example, a bit ago, someone we know proposed us to do a project in Saudi Arabia, and we said no.

I strongly believe in architecture as a collective production. Absolutely. Architecture is by definition a collective operation, because it is made for people and by people. And it survives authorship. At the same time, I do not think we are a collective, because our main focus is not politics, but architecture.

Eirini Peraki: Does this also come from the fact that since you are Italian you also experienced an extreme politicization of architecture? There is this theoretical and ideological impulse as an architect, however the architecture studies are very much apolitical. And even some of the architecture we admire, often go against what we believe in.

Andrea Zanderigo: The environment in which you grow up is fundamental. For example, if you come from a humanistic background, like the humanistic gymnasium in Italy, you are mainly interested in architecture as a cultural expression, and then you might get caught up in history and theory. For us, however, it is very important to build, and in that sense we are only partially successful, but obviously we would not build at any cost. Of course, unbuilt projects do not get lost and there are plenty of unbuilt architectures which arrived to us. However, you cannot deny that something built is always more powerful, because it becomes part of the heritage of a city or a territory. It starts to be not only yours, but part of humanity. It has a stronger and long-lasting effect, both on a conscious level for the specialists, but probably also on a slightly less conscious level for everybody else. Whereas unbuilt architecture is only for specialists. It is only for architects. Built architecture is for everybody, and that makes a big difference.

baukuh produces architecture. Designs are independent of personal taste. No member of baukuh is ever individually responsible for any single project, each of which is the product of the office as a whole. Working without a hierarchical structure or a stylistic dogma, baukuh produces architecture out of a rational and explicit design process. This process is based on a critical understanding of the architecture of the past. The knowledge encoded in the architecture of the past is public, and starting from this public knowledge, any architectural problem can be solved. baukuh is: Paolo Carpi, Silvia Lupi, Vittorio Pizzigoni, Giacomo Summa, Pier Paolo Tamburelli, and Andrea Zanderigo. baukuh was founded in 2004 and is based in Milan and Genoa.

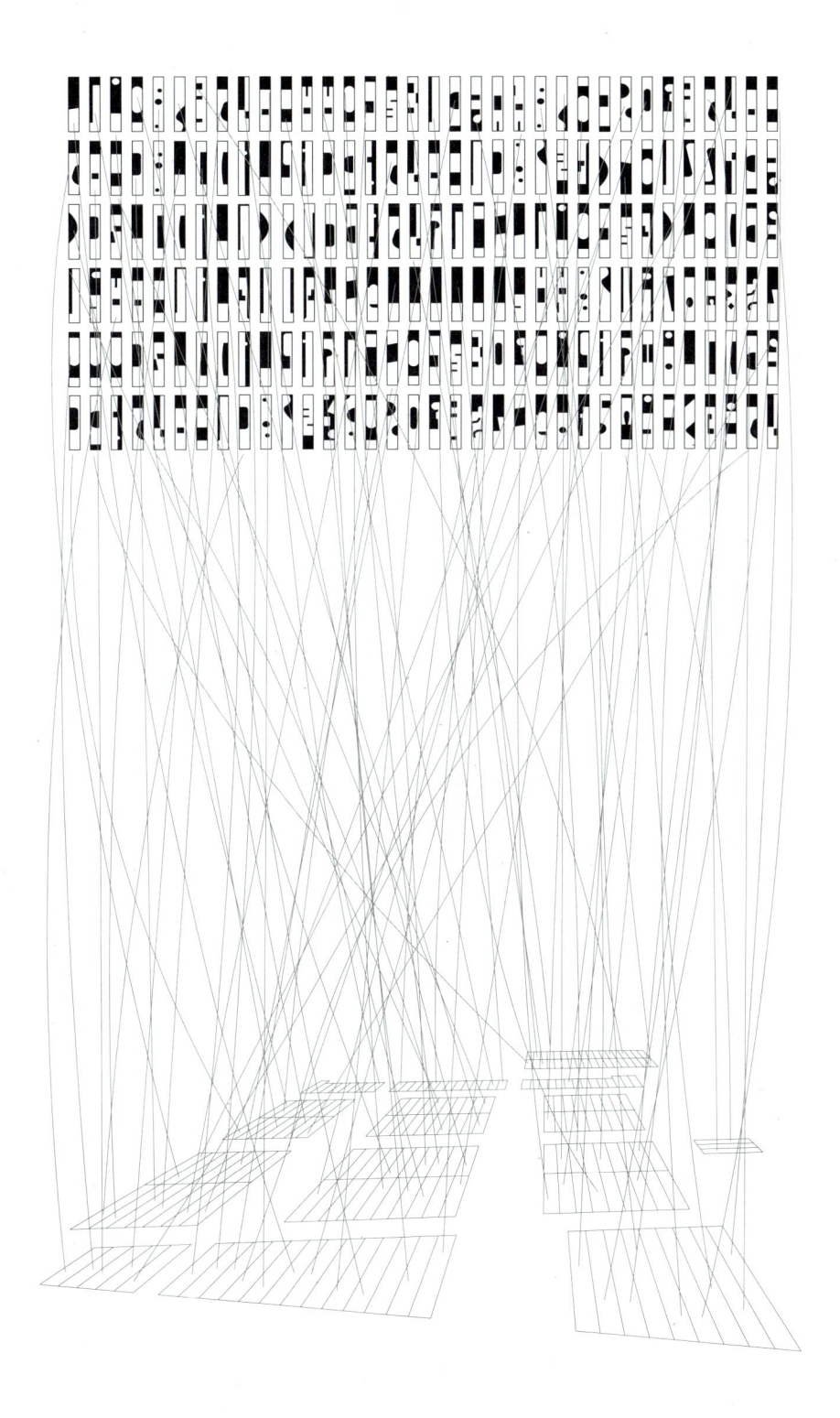

baukuh, *Cassius*, winning proposal of Europan 7, Amsterdam, 2003

Friday, March 27, 2020, 5:30 PM
Joining Skype

raumlabor Engaging the Public Eye

Natalie Donat-Cattin: Hello.

Markus Bader: Good day. Good morning.

Natalie Donat-Cattin: Where are you now?

Markus Bader: I am working from Berlin, we have a studio not so far away, which we now try to minimally equip with people. The other context is the University of the Arts, also in Berlin. But the university decided to completely close facilities. Not even the staff is allowed to enter. Given the unique situation that we have with Covid-19, I am trying to see it also with curiosity.

Natalie Donat-Cattin: I contacted you, as I am researching on alternative forms of practicing architecture. My focus is on groups of people working together horizontally, which I define as *collectives*. There are many shades of it, already the word *collective* has different connotations for everyone. Generally speaking this research goes from the etymology of the word *collective* to what it means organization-wise in the practice.

Markus Bader: We do like the term *group* more than *collective*. Whenever we discuss the political question of how we are organized and how we relate to each other, it is how we call ourselves. We understand the term *collective* very much with the imperative of equalization, which we always try to avoid.

    Our way of organizing is driven by the idea of accommodating difference rather than agreeing on a common. We do not set up rules which everybody has to obey. Somebody recently described us as anarchists, which came as a surprise, since we are still into form, organization, and defined outcomes. But to a certain extent, the term could be appropriate because we do love nonorganic, nonfixed organizations. We seek openness in order to react to new questions and situations. Trust has been the base of our relationships so far, more than any given set of rules. It is not a professional way of organizing, but it is a very personal, private way of being together. It is also important to mention that our group of nine is actually composed of around twenty people at the moment.

    Many of us (talking about the nine founders) met during studies and had a disinterest in going straight into an office career after studies. We wanted to safeguard an open collective space, where it would be possible to extend some of the ambitions that were there during studies and that are not accommodated in a professional office or in the straightforward architect-client relationship. Therefore, this idea of having a space for ourselves was very much the beginning. Our first space was a shop front: it was important to be on the ground floor, to have a door to the street, to be able to use it for events, to invite people in, to discuss, to drink together.

Between 1999, which is an official founding date—even if it had actually started before—and 2001 there was a process phase where we understood how we wanted to operate and how it seemed feasible to do it. This has to do with finding the link between cultural production and architectural questions. Looking at the city and combining it with an engaged way of doing a project.

Natalie Donat-Cattin: I read your participation to the book *Towards New Commons for Europe*, curated by Flavien Menu, where you mention your way of looking at architecture as something broader than just architecture and city planning. The relationships you weave with cultural institutions and other entities become key to the project. Even the shop front you mentioned enters this discourse: using a space as an off-space, where friends are invited to curate exhibitions and bring their ideas in the space, broadening its purpose. You mentioned that what brought you together was a common will to not venture on the traditional architecture path, what did you envision as your goal at the time?

Markus Bader: This takes us back to Berlin in the late 1990s. We went through our studies with mixed feelings. It was the time of the very large competitions, where conservative designs would win and experimental designs would come second. I am talking about the competitions for Alexanderplatz and for Potsdamer Platz or the new government district. We were observing that very closely to understand how the architectural discipline envisioned the future. There was a marked position of opposition between these conservative designs, which were winning, and the potential feeling that also the proposal coming second could win. We realized that there was a window of opportunity for the city to be shaped in different ways.

The political scenario was also shifting to a very conservative approach. This is linked to Hans Stimman, who was the director of the building department of the city, who had a very clear idea about the so-called European city as an ideology to be implemented. Another influential situation was the Internationale Bauausstellung, the international building exhibition, of 1987. Many of us started to study in 1989 and came to a city where this international building exhibition—based on small-scale interventions on the road, working with the people, exchanging ideas, and developing schemes from the context—had just taken place. We very much engaged with this mind-set during studies.

Berlin was not a normal city at the time, because of the system change. There were many properties where no one knew who the owners were, leading to a lot of in-between spaces, therefore more accessible and less defined. They held a huge potential, and people were taking action and reinventing it on a one-to-one scale. In the meantime, we were studying a discipline that was talking about large-scale planning with a different mind-set. We wanted to combine the knowledge coming from the situated, local, engaged work with the larger scale, in order to create definitions of plans for possible futures. This was imagined as a more colorful, more lively, more heterogeneous city than the European city proposed by the general planning director. The architecture policy of the time allowed us to come together and express the joy of being able to create something when mobilizing energies together.

Looking back, we know that it was a temporary absence of capitalist city-making regimes and a temporary window of opportunity for these practices. Now, we live in a city with a high rise of property prices, which led to a transformation of the question of accessibility of space.

Natalie Donat-Cattin: Would you say that, because of this, your work focus or your way of working had to transform over time?

Markus Bader: I think yes. Our two latest large projects, the Floating University and the Haus der Statistik, are a reaction to that. In a time when places were accessible but not so contested, we pushed our approach toward the temporary project and invited people. Now, in a time when spaces are contested, we are interested in finding ways to engage with this question. Therefore, we look at mid- to long-term ways of running a project.

Natalie Donat-Cattin: Your core group is composed of nine people, however you were saying that realistically you are twenty. What is the relationship with the other people in the group? Are they employees in the office or are they artists or other experts coming in for the purpose of the project itself?

Markus Bader: Yes and yes. There are people that have been working with us for some years now, in a situation not based on friendship, but on a professional working relationship. Although, also old friends join projects based on their talents or interests. They would never define themselves as being part of the movement.

There are also students working with us. We see it as a mix of learning and working. Many of them are happy to join in the process for a while and then go back and continue with other experiments in their lives. It is a temporary engagement of people between three months and half a year.

Natalie Donat-Cattin: Regarding the main nine members, are you legally bound or did you have to constitute a legal office structure or are you still freelancers?

Markus Bader: Juridically, we do not exist, it is just a name. People agreed to contribute to this common form in a specific way, and that means paying rent to the common office space, being in charge of acquiring jobs and not only keeping your own projects running, but also investing something extra into this nondescript common form. It is a commitment to take care of whatever this collective thing is. That is how we take care of the website or the coffee machine or toilet paper. It is something like an extra project. In this way, all of us can rely on a sort of infrastructure.

Natalie Donat-Cattin: And in terms of projects, do you create your own brief? And are single people responsible for the project and asking for help from other group members in case they need it? Or how does it work in terms of project and organization?

Markus Bader: In our neoliberal times, to organize things by project means that you can actually organize. Our organization is built around the idea of the project. A project has a team, an economy, and a time span. There is also a critique of the project because it is temporary, it is not necessarily sustainable, and its time frame engages you and feeds you while you feed it. It is difficult to bridge the time when the project ends and, therefore, organize everything around projects. As with many practices, there are a multitude of projects running at the same time and you try to create a beautiful confluence of projects happening, then raumlabor and everybody in it can survive. This type of long-term commitment, like the Floating University, the Haus der Statistik and my teaching engagement, questions how to escape the dream of the project. The beauty of the project is that it is so nicely contained, and we are the ones to create a set of relations, of answers, of proposals contained within its frame. The part-time project is very ambiguous, in the sense that it does cut off a big side of reality and the problems related to it. Regarding the question of how do we work inside these projects and how do they come to us? Do we "invent" them ourselves or do we respond to invitations? Again, we do both. Larger projects are usually self-initiated. The Floating University was a proposal coming from us. More specifically, it came from Benjamin (one of the raumlabor members) who sort of discovered the site and thought to do something. The idea was to combine the potential of the site with another line of thinking and practice that we had developed in raumlabor: the open raumlabor university, following this idea that raumlabor is also an educational instance. Then of course, a process of three years of convincing the city, finding funding, writing concepts, writing applications, inviting artists in, inviting other experts in, building a network of relationships around it, carried out by many of our group. The project started to exist in the spring of 2018. This is very self-initiated.

But other projects like the festival center for the Ruhrtriennale, which is an ever-changing temporary architecture that appears in many sites across the same area every year and involves interesting elements, like a former military plane that is dismantled and reconfigured every time, this can be called a commission. There was a conversation with the artistic director about their interest in having this kind of in-between space, which could be a festival center.

For many as what I see as collectives, there is this interest of not just waiting for a competition to come out—a set frame asking a specific question—but rather finding a way to inscribe ourselves in the world, for the joy of living or doing, imagining that we can ask questions ourselves and propose answers.

Natalie Donat-Cattin: Are many of you involved in the university environment?

Markus Bader: More or less half of the group, but two-thirds have a history in teaching.

Natalie Donat-Cattin: Regarding research, are your researches always aimed at becoming projects? Or do you develop research that will not have a physical outcome? As a practice, are you grounded more in the real than the ideal?

Markus Bader: Yes, we lean towards the project. However the interest of the open raumlabor university was to think of raumlabor not just as a productive entity that produces these frames from where spatial interventions come out, but also to open it up toward research protocols. Every project has a very experimental side and we try to not be repetitive, but rather develop our ideas. Therefore, there is a research interest, but not in the sense of academic research. A more action-based research.

Natalie Donat-Cattin: Then would you define your work as a totality? Is it a process where every project evolves into the next one or suggests the next first step?

Markus Bader: There was never something like the Ten Commandments, the manifesto describing everything and setting up rules. We see it from the beginning as an evolution and everybody follows their individual interests. When we match interests, we create groups of people working together. This is also why we still exist, because it is not a set frame, but we develop, change, and modulate according to interests. We are always responsive to new environments, new questions, new influxes.

Natalie Donat-Cattin: In that regard, is the client public or private?

Markus Bader: Who is the client? If he is the one funding, then it is 99 percent public funding. The client also involves the relationship of somebody asking for something and the architect being a helper or a provider of this question in order to answer it and implement it. The projects that are based on public funding are more application-based, so it is not really a client relationship. A client relationship for me, it is more a discussion with the critical public, with the media.

Natalie Donat-Cattin: Would you say then that the community is who you do architecture for? Or what is the focus of your architecture and the direction in which you take it?

Markus Bader: Another interesting term, *community*. We live in highly individualized times and people who engage, enjoy something and become part of it, they usually do it for a limited time. I am not sure if the community idea is helping us much further, but let's call it the public eye for now, because that is more anonymous and open. But it is still a term to group people in.

Natalie Donat-Cattin: Are all of you based in Berlin?

Markus Bader: We are very mobile, but everybody has a bed in Berlin and sort of a living situation here at the moment.

Natalie Donat-Cattin: When a project comes externally, do you have a sort of board meeting where you decide to accept it or not? And do you accept all kinds of projects, or is there a sort of selection process that comes from all of you?

Markus Bader: Yes, there is a very strict protocol. Whoever says yes to something has to stand in front of the rest of the group and defend his or her approach. So as I said earlier, it is very much based on individual trust between each other and on the decision of the individual. So when there is a project request coming to the board and nobody is responding, then that is a way of saying no. And on the other hand, if one or two people feel like doing it, then they are free to say yes. And whatever you do, there is no way of stopping you. The rest of the group members can just give you a hard time and tell you off. But you can still do your things the way you like it. There is no general collective response policy. And we trust the others, knowing that everybody makes good decisions for the group, even without discussing it.

Natalie Donat-Cattin: Maybe another two questions. One is the question of authoriality, like, what role does it play in raumlabor? And more of a down-to-earth question regarding the organization, do you have group meetings every week or every now and then to check the status of what everybody is doing and what you are doing in general as a group?

Markus Bader: Second question first. We have been testing different protocols on that. One very radical approach is interest-based, you can always walk around the studio and ask the others what they are doing, as you would probably only ask this question when you feel it is important. We also have a protocol of reunions between the nine partners every three months, to have a space where we discuss where we are. We had a time when we were doing it every two weeks and it was horrible, we were boring ourselves with organizational issues. Therefore we stopped. There is also a freedom of accepting that we do not need to talk to each other about the organizational issues too much because all of this is inside the project and it is taken care of by the project team itself. So we can focus on the results of the projects and discuss that. What was your first question again?

Natalie Donat-Cattin: What role does authoriality play within your group? You were mentioning how individuality is very important.

Markus Bader: In this regard, we are also self-contradictory. On the one hand, we believe in the importance of common naming that is also operating as an authorship. Each one of the nine partners takes their decisions and they are not controlled by each other. And it is risky, but beautiful to observe. There is always something happening inside this shared authorship that is beyond your control. On the other hand, we all have an ego and a special love for the project that we do and invest time in. Therefore on our site, we identify who was involved in the project. This is why we are ambiguous, we love this common framing and the common form, but we also like to know who has been doing something, because we are also individuals. Other collectives are more about a "stamp." It is a symbol and then you do not know who it is and everybody can represent it, perform it and own it. I think we tried to with the common name.

Natalie Donat-Cattin: Does it happen often that you all work on the same project?

Markus Bader: No, never. There was a trauma in the beginning where five of us were doing a project together and we ended up doing three projects, you know, because we were not agreeing and having all these different ideas. In the end, only one project was presented, but we invested a lot of time in discussions. Having this in an early phase formed us. We were invited to Venice, and with the current situation we do not know if we are able to go. However, when something like this comes we are opening a discussion for everybody to join. So we do not work on projects together, but if it is about presenting raumlabor, it is an incident to pull everybody in and go back to the first questions where you found yourself in 1999.

Natalie Donat-Cattin: To go back to the first question, was the word *collective* already around at the time you formed the group?

Markus Bader: Not as much as today. There was definitely a culture of doing things together, not defined with the term *collective*, but with loose forms of association, constellations with different agendas or different styles of doing things. You would rather be a member of multiple groups: for instance, one running a bar, one doing a gallery, one trying to be a different architecture office, one performing theater action. And then raumlabor emerged as a constellation that sustained.

Natalie Donat-Cattin: does the name raumlabor, on top of its direct meaning, come from the will of showing collaboration?

Markus Bader: I think so. It was in 1998, it was four of us and we wanted to give it a name. We had a discussion about this, and raumlabor was voted best. And of course we like it because it has the sort of experimental side of the laboratory, the space and the big claim: we are the space laboratory. So we stick to it. The looser form before was *Mit Hertz*, with heart, which was stickered on the window of the shop front we shared with many people. And the group using the shop was referred to as Mit Hertz group, but this was even looser. There is a 2003 ARCH+, which was published in two editions on "off architecture." One is called "Scenes" and one is called "Networks." In the networks, there is a long e-mail interview between the raumlabor people, but also between the wider frame of people that were part of this shop. Everybody discusses what they think raumlabor is, how they relate to it, what they want from it, and you know what the commitment is. I should say good-bye now, we will reconnect another time and wrap it up.

Natalie Donat-Cattin: Thank you and good-bye.

(...)

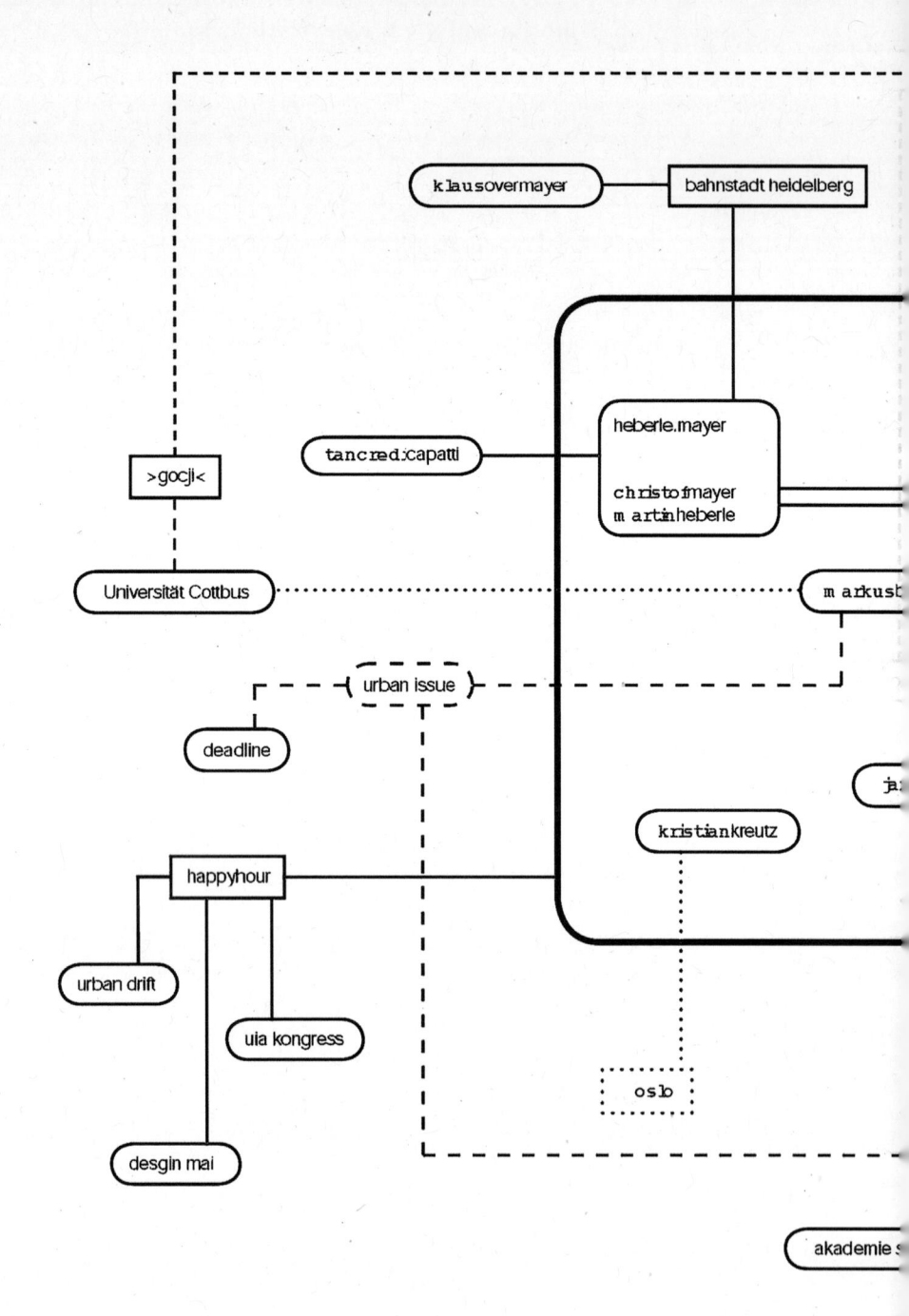

raumlaborberlin, Organigramm of raumlaborberlin and network, published in *ARCH+*, no. 167, "Off-Architektur 2," 2003

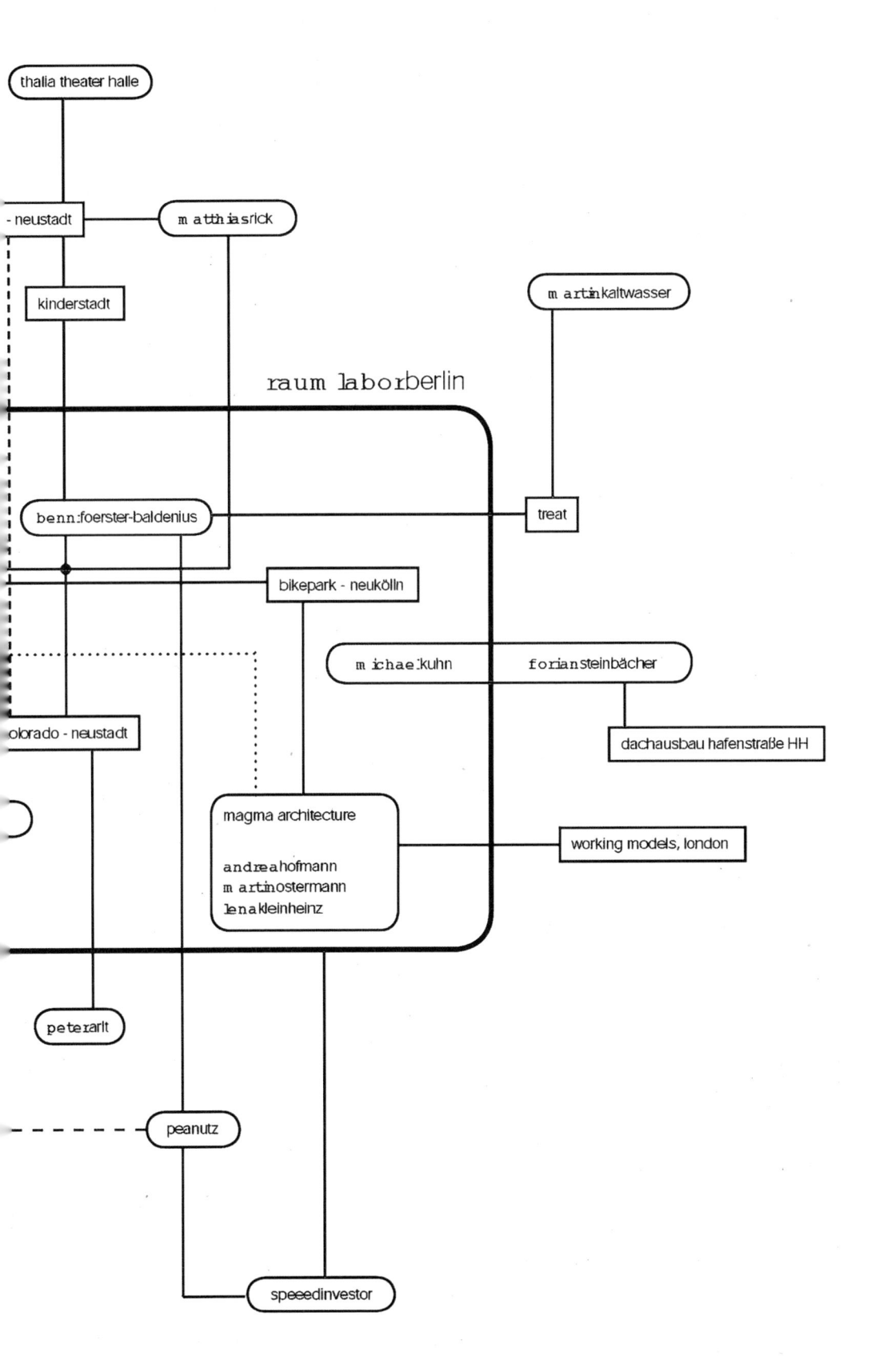

- thalia theater halle
- neustadt
- matthiasrick
- kinderstadt
- martinkaltwasser

raum laborberlin

- benn:foerster-baldenius
- treat
- bikepark - neukölln
- michaelkuhn
- foriansteinbächer
- dachausbau hafenstraße HH
- olorado - neustadt
- magma architecture

  andreahofmann
  martinostermann
  lenakleinheinz

- working models, london
- peterarlt
- peanutz
- speeedinvestor

Markus Bader: Hello again.

Natalie Donat-Cattin: Hello, how are you doing?

Markus Bader: Good, spring is here.

Natalie Donat-Cattin: Here too, it is very difficult to be inside now. I wonder if the current situation will change our way of being, because it does question the way we work.

Markus Bader: It would be interesting to see to what extent this crisis will be used to produce change in favorable ways. Our university reacted very dramatically: everything closed, and we cannot do anything. Now the question is, how do we come back? How do we prioritize between the full scope of university activities, which are the ones transferred online now, and the activities that come aside and within the academic system? No parties, no informative gatherings, no festivities, no cheers with a Prosecco glass after your master presentation. The social side is completely eliminated, but the productivity side is kept alive. And that is a very strange type of university.

Natalie Donat-Cattin: Indeed. During the last time we spoke, you mentioned another special situation—very different from the one we are in now—not just in Germany but in the entire Europe. When you started working in 1999, everything was moving, and borders were starting to be open and fluid to a certain extent. How much of this ideology—the European ideology of sharing a given ground—is coming into your practice?

Markus Bader: We do not use the word *ideology*, but we very much embrace the idea of open borders and free movement and see this as the basis for the citizen-emancipated spiritual practice that is not based on nationalities. On the other hand, we do not actively promote anything European.

Natalie Donat-Cattin: In my generation we look at Europe as something larger than just being Italian or German. There is a sense of sharing in it. I do not see it as something political, but more as the wish to embrace the ground that is given. Last time you talked about how it was a very specific moment in Berlin when you started, just ten years after the city was reconnected. In a larger sense, however, the city was already part of Europe. Therefore I wondered how much that influenced the start of your work. And on the other hand, now that borders are again becoming stronger with the pandemic and incidents like Brexit, we do question everything again.

Markus Bader: I do not have an answer to that, but of course it is important. The arrival of easyJet, I think it was 2004, was quite a remarkable incident, before it was more expensive to travel. But this also has to do with Internet accessibility. That also shaped the practice. Thanks to e-mails we are able to work in different places and we can still very quickly exchange ideas and stay connected, which was not possible before this amazing media. I mean, now we look at e-mail as something very natural and very old. But it is a connection that is timeless, that is not timed, but is very instant.

Natalie Donat-Cattin: It is interesting that you talk about technology. What role did technology play in raumlabor? When I talked to other collectives, they mentioned Dropbox as their main tool, or Skype, or Slack. It is interesting that you say that it was e-mail for you.

Markus Bader: Yes, it was e-mail. And of course, other technologies as well. But if I would have to stick to one, I would keep e-mail.

Natalie Donat-Cattin: I read your description on your website, your sort of manifesto, you talk about openness and complexity, and at some point you mention that you wanted to change the world. I was wondering, is this change more of a stall for you? I find your work very forward-looking, because instead of wanting to do something new and to say it in your words "change the world," you just gave space to people and allowed them to use it. I see your work as something creating a pause, allocating time, in this fast-paced society. Can I describe it like that or is it wrong?

Markus Bader: It is a very beautiful description or observation. If it is about stepping forward or acting toward the future, then the architectural examples that we all have in our minds are Superstudio, Archigram, and other similar groups. They were using their imaginary powers of drawing or collaging to impress statements toward the future. What we do different is that our plots are actually inhabited and their narrative is more open. There is a certain ideology, but also a certain understanding that the future is created together.

And that with this pause, as you call it, this moment of practicing something different together, which we do not know, is related to the statement "BYE BYE UTOPIA." The goal is to create a narrative made by people and not a narrative made by narrative. Bye Bye Utopia. Or Hello, Utopia. Or Let's Inhabit this Utopia. Let's test it. Play it out. Be part of it. Indeed, some of our works are romanticizing and neglecting some of the difficulties of society and therefore they could also be called utopian. So it is not against the term. It is a claim that reminds us how the actual actions are what we are looking for.

Natalie Donat-Cattin: It is very beautiful what you are saying. So I would like to talk about a topic maybe not so distant to this idea of inhabiting: the working space. In these collectives or networks, the working space might be the construction site, a meeting room or a traditional office. In other cases, it does not even exist, it is the virtual network. From the Bürolandschaft to the nonoffice.

Markus Bader: I observe that there are more networking groups, relying less on fixed spaces but rather on shared protocols. For instance, to meet they organize a congress once a year which I think is amazing. constructLab has also a singular approach to it, because they are so distributed and have annual gatherings that are not about a project, but more about themselves.

Natalie Donat-Cattin: Yes, they were saying that for them, the construction site is their office or the only place where they all come together, while building the project. Otherwise the proper working space, as we know it, does not exist, apart from different associations they have in different places.

Markus Bader: It is nice to create links. It is always a possibility to link the different groups through a moment of reflection. And that is nice.

Natalie Donat-Cattin: Yes, I thought about organizing an event and if due to the current situation this is not possible, it might need to be something different. Maybe even just an exchange of questions from one to the other.

Markus Bader: Why not? Keep me posted. Good-bye for now.

Natalie Donat-Cattin: Thank you again and good-bye.

raumlaborberlin, Floating University poster, Berlin, 2018

raumlabor berlin is a network, a collective of 9 trained architects who have come together in a collaborative work structure. They work at the intersection of architecture, city planning, art, and urban intervention. They address city and urban renewal as a process in their work. They are attracted to difficult urban locations. Places torn between different systems, time periods, or planning ideologies, places that cannot adapt. Places that are abandoned, leftover, or in transition that contain some relevance for the processes of urban transformations. These places are sites for experimentation. They offer untapped potential which raumlabor tries to activate. This opens new perspectives for alternative usage patterns, collective ideals, urban diversity, and difference. raumlabor members are: Andrea Hofmann, Axel Timm, Benjamin Foerster-Baldenius, Christof Mayer, Florian Stirnemann, Francesco Apuzzo, Frauke Gerstenberg, Jan Liesegang, Markus Bader, and Matthias Rick († 28.04.2012). raumlabor was founded around 1999.

Monday, June 8, 2020, 7:34 PM
Joining Jitsi

Zuloark A Liquid Professional Framework

Juan Chacón: Hi, nice to meet you.

Natalie Donat-Cattin: Hi, thank you for your time. I am contacting you regarding a research on collectives. I am concentrating on Europe to understand what is happening in the collective environment and am looking at how practices like yours organize. There are publications that are about new young offices but it is rarely mentioned how they function. Many architecture publications focus on the product rather than the process.

Juan Chacón: I am part of this network of networks: Zuloark. Everybody is Zuloark, it is not a defined group. It is a network, an economic structure. Some people work full-time, others are the so-called satellites, spread all over the world and not always involved. There is no vertical hierarchy, but small hierarchies, ever changing. It is an ongoing process. In every project there is one person responsible and other people with less responsibility.

Natalie Donat-Cattin: How did you decide to create Zuloark? How did it start?

Juan Chacón: We were a group of friends, having the same classes between 1998 and 2001 in the ETSAM, the school of architecture in Madrid. And we started to ask each other questions about authorship—it was the time of Guggenheim, Zaha Hadid, all this star architecture. Zuloark is born against the concept of authorship, shaping a collective system and rejecting this egomania "starchitecture." The school was pushing us to become influential architects, so we thought about creating an entity which had the power itself, and the people behind it. At the beginning we joined together to do the school projects. It was a moment when students in Spain would not work in groups, they were working at home alone—things like that nowadays are unthinkable. There was not much collective knowledge. And then inside the school, we had the idea of making Zuloark an entity itself, with nobody knowing who was behind it and, at some point, in Madrid there were forty people signing their projects as Zuloark, and not with their personal names. We had a lot of issues with the university. We were talking about authorship, anonymity, working together. There were also other collectives in the university at the same time as us. We started to work together between 1999 and 2000, but the first action signed as Zuloark was in 2001. It was in September in reaction to the Twin Towers attack. In the following years, other collectives pushed in the same direction. Between 2006 and 2009 we turned the academic collective into a professional one. Many people connect collectives to the crisis situation, but collectives were born before it, like us and raumlabor. We were already organized in this way, which is what we define as a liquid professional framework, and this is Zuloark.

Natalie Donat-Cattin: You mentioned how the collective is not a product of the crisis, but something different...

Juan Chacón: Yes, the collective reflects the crisis of identity, the crisis of architecture. It is a different way of doing cities and architecture, against the star-architect system.

However nowadays it is probably different as people are always connected, so they create even less-fixed networks. Sometimes even just individuals who connect through projects. It is a normal evolution. The crisis of 2008 is therefore related to the start of some practices, but not with the way of organizing, which is connected to the era of the Internet.

Natalie Donat-Cattin: You mentioned that when you founded Zuloark you were around thirty members, that is a big community. How many are you nowadays?

Juan Chacón: We are eleven. Plus other people that are part of the larger network, however they are not Zuloark.

Natalie Donat-Cattin: Therefore, when you work with other entities, there is a name that gets created out of this collaboration, and then the authorship dissolves step by step.

Juan Chacón: We are active in different places, we have four headquarters, in La Coruña, Berlin, Bologna, and Madrid, and we are recently opening two new potential ones in Bogotà and Athens. The idea is that if we move, the collective comes with us. The collective is defined by the life of the people. And in any case, we believe that new locations offer new possibilities. We are very community-oriented. Networking is something extremely interesting for the architectural world, we tried therefore from 2007 to link with other entities, with the idea of creating a platform where we could meet. It was also the time when Facebook and these social media were rising. We were also doing competitions like Europan. That was also the moment we changed the structure into a more professional one, an income-oriented structure, and so we managed to create a cooperative. However, the network becomes the author, not Zuloark.

Natalie Donat-Cattin: And in terms of structure of Zuloark?

Juan Chacón: We want people to feel good in the working environment. We have a clan-like structure. We are horizontal and advocate for a freedom of movement, however we do need a structure and tools to measure what we are doing, what we are working on, and economic matters, like the salaries. There are problems of inequality when people feel that they have more, or less, than others. Therefore we started imagining a network that defines our relationships, both on a collective and on an individual level. A sort of matrioska. We do have internal agreements about how we deal with the money and the projects. Six years ago, we started to define a Zuloark boundary, inside this people have more responsibilities and are also more protected economically.

Then there are the *satellites of love*, people attached to the structure and collaborating with us regularly, but not directly inside Zuloark. There are institutions, public and private, and clients. It is an all-round participatory design. Internally, we work with a Google Drive, where information is accessible to everybody. Transparency is something very important for us. We also use Slack for direct messaging. Now, we are also working very often in Jitsi rooms when we do not have other meetings. Somebody can play music and even if we are in the virtual space it is like being together. Coworking together but online.

Natalie Donat-Cattin: How do you deal with coordination within Zuloark?

Juan Chacón: Each one of us has around ten to twelve projects every year, it is a huge amount of work. Therefore we need a system of coordination. For this reason we reorganized the collective in three areas: governing, economy, and communication, and there are two people responsible for each of these three areas. And what we are doing now is implementing a system of rotation. So each group develops strategically. This is directly connected with the collective itself.

Natalie Donat-Cattin: It is a rhizome within the horizontal structure. In terms of general meetings and decision-making, how does it work?

Juan Chacón: We meet twice a week. Every Tuesday, one hour to organize projects. Every Friday, which now became the Zulo-School, we meet to learn together about topics which we are concerned with or we talk about topics we are worried about or we just talk, as we are in different places. It is a space of meeting between all of us.

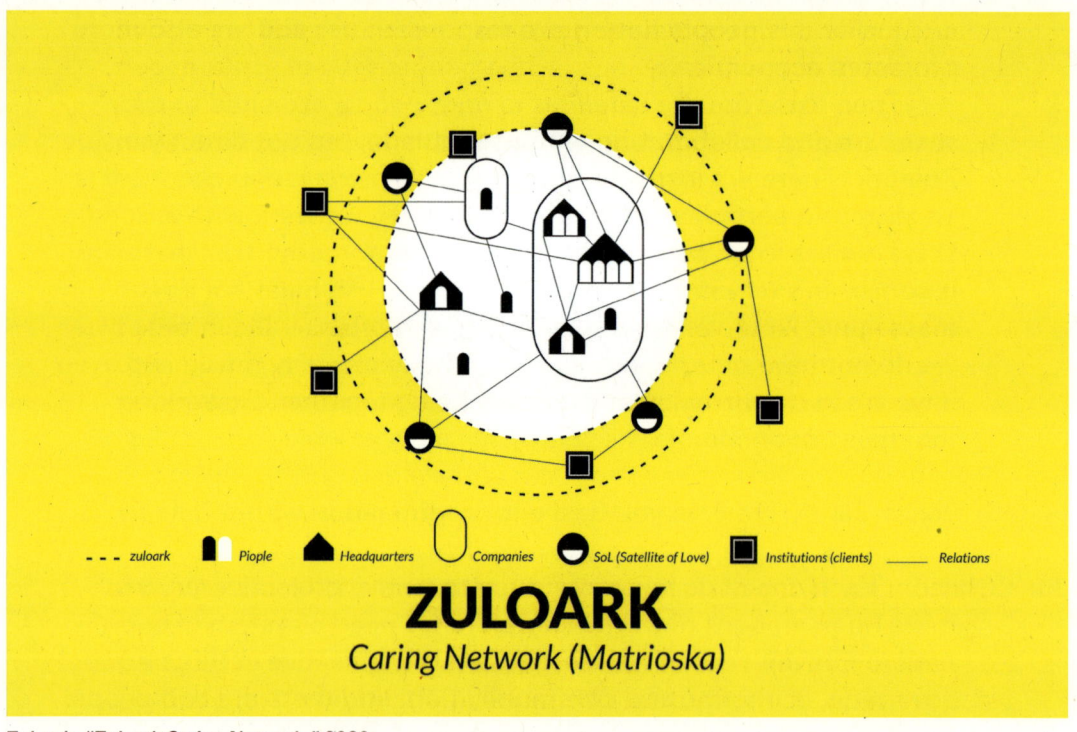

Zuloark, "Zuloark Caring Network," 2020

And then we have an annual conference. We already did eight. It is a way for the eleven of us to meet for a week. At the start it was very informal and not structured, now it got formalized and we always meet in January to plan the year. We are trying to implement the same in summer. In winter it would be more related to our structure, and in summer it would be more related to a project that we could do together for the span of the week.

Natalie Donat-Cattin: There are many positive sides of how you work, however it is very complex to make the machine work on a larger level.

Juan Chacón: There is a balance within our group: everybody should feel free to do whatever he/she wants, but in collaboration with the community, to create a space that is safe for everyone. That is why we started to create tools that help us to measure ourselves and, for instance, how much time we spend on a project. All this is a way of developing our entity.

Natalie Donat-Cattin: In a more practical sense, when someone joins Zuloark, is he/she automatically part of it? How does it work?

Juan Chacón: It is a very organic process, there are people close to us and they start collaborating with us, at some point, it becomes a more permanent collaboration. That happened sometimes. Sometimes it happened through an internship, however not often because we have economic problems and we rarely take in interns. In order to come in you also need to know one of the members, who can act as the godfather or godmother of the newcomer, as the structure is itself very complex.

Natalie Donat-Cattin: You have quite a fixed form within Zuloark of how someone can be welcomed into the core group. It changed very much from the start, when everybody could use your name, and then you had the need to structure yourself following certain rules...

Juan Chacón: We are really slow. It took us eight years to create this cooperative. Now we have faster ways of decision-making. Before all the decisions needed to be taken in an assembly, where everybody had to agree. And now we developed a frame of rules where people can move freely inside and if there is an issue we talk about it and fix it.

Natalie Donat-Cattin: In terms of projects, how does it work? Do you have mainly self-initiated projects or clients coming to you?

Juan Chacón: Most of them are self-initiated. Some self-initiated projects within Zuloark. Some other self-initiated projects within our network and then some clients. However it is rare for a client to come to us. Now we are doing some private housing projects. We are also doing some competitions. We are also part of different universities, which gives us a long-term income. Everything we earn goes in the common economical pot. We also have projects for public institutions.

Natalie Donat-Cattin: The clients are people related to your network? Or are people looking for you?

Juan Chacón: Both. We do not close ourselves into a specific type of work. We are doing everything from participatory urbanism plans to artistic interventions, to festival setups, to private housing, competitions, consulting for companies, etc. So our clients change compared to our area of work. We have seven design areas. I am also curious about what is happening now. People are connected to each other and no longer really related to labels. People want to be multiconnected…

Natalie Donat-Cattin: I am exactly interested in this evolution. raumlabor and you are a previous generation of collectives when a different technology was available. And the more the technology advances, the more possibilities in structuring the group. People do not necessarily need to be in the same place. Even the working space becomes debatable because some people, as you mention, see Jitsi as their meeting spot.

Juan Chacón: I feel like today people have the general tendency of coming together. Together it is easier to find projects. However the many open competitions also give possibilities to different individuals. It is also important to acknowledge that this collective idea is often just an image, a banner. Some people pretend to work horizontally and within a large group of people, but realistically there are still some individualities behind it and a strict hierarchy. We are so into this, the collective, that is it hard to really understand what is going on.
I think it is interesting to have a voice outside the picture analyzing it.

Natalie Donat-Cattin: I do think that being a collective is also a life choice. I am interested in what you said about authoriality and the ego. It is a process humanity is undertaking, reunderstanding how to live in a community.

Juan Chacón: Europe is undertaking an opening process and going towards an interesting direction. Everything is becoming more feminine. In the Istanbul Biennale this year there is a group of women curators. In general we still live in a masculine world, and there is a big influence of that in our society. We still have the myth of heroes that are individuals. There is also still a strong level of competition. However, this is a conversation for another time. Wish you all the best with your research, let's keep in touch.

Natalie Donat-Cattin: Thank you very much and talk soon.

Zuloark is a distributed architecture and urbanism open office, founded in 2001. Developing flowing and collaborative professional working models and building coresponsibility environments through shared authorship projects ever since. As a distributed architecture platform, Zuloark is currently based in La Coruña, Berlin, Bologna, and Madrid. Their activities are involved in different contexts such as El Campo de Cebada or Inteligencias Colectivas. Zuloark is materialized in every achieved project and it is redefined while it grows. It's a living structure thought and constructed as a "critical object." Zuloark never equals Zuloark.

Widening th
Architectur

Seven Questi
Contempora
(ab)Normal, A-A C
CNCRT, Colectivo W.
constructLab, f
Fosbury Architect
n'UNDO, orizzont

Spectrum of
n the 2010s

s to Fourteen
 Collectives:
lective, Assemble,
ehouse, Collectif Etc,
se mirror office,
e, la–clique, Lacol,
e, and X=(T=E=N)

Introduction

These collectives were all founded in Europe between 2009 and 2019. Despite their variety of intentions and their heterogeneous architectural production, the desire to analyze them according to a common yardstick reflects the ambition to outline a European collective panorama of the 2010s.

A number of common questions gave rise to a virtual dialogue between the abovementioned collectives:

1. How is a collective formed?
2. Is there a founding act of the collective?
3. What are the key references behind its architecture?
4. How is its working space?
5. How is it structured?
6. How has it changed since its foundation?
7. What is the key aim of its architecture?

The different answers, which follow one another in a banal alphabetical order, take precedence over the collective entities, while highlighting similarities and tensions. This process toward collectivization turns out to be fragmentary and eclectic in its declinations.

The way in which each collective is formed, develops, and creates—its beginnings, references, working space, organization, ability to evolve, and architectural aim—is interconnected with the architecture evoked or produced by it, be this a vision, a building, or a space. In architecture, there is the tendency to concentrate on the product while forgetting the process behind it. Here, the focus is on the process to offer a wider understanding of the product.

Sunday, November 8, 2019, 8:40 AM

1. BEGINNINGS
How to Get Together and Why

Contemporary problematics—be they social, political, or economic—create favorable conditions for people who share the same vision to aggregate. With the advent of the Internet and the easy accessibility to transportation, the human network is proposed as an alternative to the pyramidal system: a connective supersurface offering new possibilities and heterogeneous collaborations. If individuality leaves room to the personalized community—rich with different nuances and architectural impulses—anonymity replaces authoriality. The collective aims to become a mini version of society, in which participants come together to exchange ideas, to interact and design. They act under the same veil and are not bound to one another, rather they are enveloped. The collective might not have a defining form, but it understands the need of restraining rules and common intentions. It is envisioned as a network of people trying to escape the archaic and hierarchical office structure, an in-between embracing both academic and professional ideologies. "A new form of cooperation is what we experiment [with]. An alternative to the office-cooperation-labor. No bosses. Our cooperation is still invisible. Cooperation is what makes this possible," says CNCRT.

Therefore, the stories behind the formation of these collective practices highlight a contemporary spirit of aggregation. People move around cities or countries and meet at university or in an office. Friendships are strengthened through a project. Enthusiasm and shared ambitions give rise to opportunities. These beginnings appear here as fragments of conversations I had with the different collectives, recorded, and then transcribed. They are a series of individual anecdotes, as personal as they are universal.

From: Natalie Donat-Cattin
To: (ab)Normal, A-A Collective, Assemble, CNCRT, Colectivo Warehouse, Collectif Etc, constructLab, false mirror office, Fosbury Architecture, la–clique, Lacol, n'UNDO, orizzontale, X=(T=E=N)
Subject: How is a collective formed?

> Sharing a working space during university time.
> The chance. The moment.
> The unexpected project.
> Not just architecture.
> A university. A friendship.
> A shop front window.
> A certain office. A common path.
> An ideal. Europan.

From: (ab)Normal
To: Natalie Donat-Cattin
Subject: How is a collective formed?

> Although all of us studied at Politecnico di Milano, we first met each other in Rotterdam in 2016 at OMA. After some collaborations on competitions and call for papers, we started (ab)Normal at the beginning of 2017. (ab)Normal did not start as a project, rather it began as a common diary that collects our obsessions through architectural representations. Thus, at the beginning [we] did not have a clear message to propagandize, it is more like a therapy that unleashes unexpressed fantasies. Obviously it supported a clear critique against a certain type of photorealism that affects the communication apparatus of architecture nowadays.

From: A-A Collective, Furio Montoli
To: Natalie Donat-Cattin
Subject: How is a collective formed?

> Switzerland was the meeting point. Srdjan, Zygmunt, and I met in Mendrisio. After studying I moved to Paris, and then to Basel, where Srdjan and Martin were both working and where they met. Zygmunt in the meantime had moved back to Poland. It all started spontaneously because Martin had his own art studio and occasionally did some art and design projects with Srdjan. When everything moved more towards architecture, Zygmunt and I started collaborating with them, too. The first project we did together was the pavilion in the park. There is no precise chronological line, which is why defining the foundation year is difficult for us, there was never the idea of really working together at the beginning, we all worked freely with other people and then at a certain point with the Warsaw Square project, it all got consolidated. When you win a competition, everything becomes more official. The official year of the foundation, let's say from a legal point of view, is 2018, as all four of us got legally bound due to the Warsaw project.

From: Assemble, Jane Hall
To: Natalie Donat-Cattin
Subject: How is a collective formed?

> Part of the reason why we started was to create more of a form of resistance or a set of tools to describe a form of resistance, rather than itself a proper model of practice, a completely thought-out

alternative. It was more of a methodology to find an alternative, a different way of practicing, because what we do now and how we organize, we could not have come up with when we started working together. The misconception potentially in the way we are talked about or situated is that we represent a legit alternative model for architecture practices, which is clearly not true, because in many respects we are quite a traditional practice, day-to-day. However, a big reason why we came together was the interest in the self-built, which is not necessarily the same as other practices.

From: CNCRT
To: Natalie Donat-Cattin
Subject: How is a collective formed?

> The first projects were carried out by only three people. At some point last year, the network expanded, creating a network of people who worked with Martino Tattara and Vittorio Aureli at DOGMA, as the projects were increasing and as there was the desire on the part of the three to do a more collective experiment. When we were already around ten people, we all worked together on the first project, *We Are Beautiful*, an ode to the multitude and coworking.

From: Colectivo Warehouse
To: Natalie Donat-Cattin
Subject: How is a collective formed?

> Our story starts in 2013. We were still at university and shared the same interests. In particular, our main focus was to stay in Portugal. However we were facing a huge crisis and there were no jobs in architecture in Portugal. But somehow we decided to give it a try, and we rented space. At the beginning there were ten people involved. We did a little bit of refurbishment in the space. And then we started doing some competitions and some small commissions. We had many requests from people who wanted us to make products for free. When we talked about payment, the answer was often "we do not have any money." Then we actually met several collectives in Portugal because there was the Capital of Culture in 2012. There was a great energy, and a number of collectives gathered in Lisbon, like EXYZT and constructLab. That is when we met them and had the opportunity to join them in the construction of Casa do Vapôr. It was a new way of doing projects. After that we managed to do our first big project, together with another Lisbon collective, ateliermob: a community kitchen made from the wood leftovers from Casa do Vapôr.

From: Collectif Etc
To: Natalie Donat-Cattin
Subject: How is a collective formed?

> In Strasbourg in 2009, a group of architecture students took over the school's car park, where they cobbled together an unusual set of urban furniture—thus revealing a living space where people used to simply store their automobiles. [...] The students realized that there was merit in acting collectively: they decided to form a collective under the name of "Etc."
>
> Thierry Paquot, "Tour, Detour, Retour," in *Détour de France, An Education off the Beaten Path...*, ed. Collectif Etc (Marseille: éditions Hyperville, 2015), 18.

From: constructLab, Sébastien Tripod
To: Natalie Donat-Cattin
Subject: How is a collective formed?

> There is not a clear founding date, but it was a project—Casa do Vapôr in Portugal—which created this new network level. The self-initiated project brought together many people. There was no money, there were only people who were motivated. Indeed, all of a sudden, a whole resource of wood came from another project and so the potential of being able to do something.

From: la–clique
To: Natalie Donat-Cattin
Subject: How is a collective formed?

> We are a group of friends that formed during our studies between the EPFL and the ETH. Throughout our student years, we often collaborated either by working in teams or simply through informal discussions around our projects. After graduating, everybody spread all over Switzerland and started working in different offices. Gradually, we started to miss the spontaneous exchanges and productive energy of collaboration from our student years. In order to hold on to that feeling, we tried to keep doing small projects together. At first, we were not sure how it would develop: it seemed like a youthful dream to be able to combine friendship and professionalism. Some of us started discussing the possibility of forming a collective with the name la–clique. The project for Manifesta in Marseille became the occasion to give it a go. After being selected, everything happened very quickly: suddenly, we had to create an association and set up a bank account to enable fund-raising. One

month after the selection, we organized our first general assembly, and that was the moment that la–clique was really formalized as a collective. Ever since, la–clique keeps evolving as something flexible and dynamic. For each project, the constellation changes and so, too, does the way of working together.

From: orizzontale
To: Natalie Donat-Cattin
Subject: How is a collective formed?

We started the collective while we were still university students at Valle Giulia, faculty of architecture of La Sapienza of Rome. The idea of founding orizzontale came from Jacopo and Juan. In March 2010 a public action was carried out on a sidewalk of Pigneto, a lively district of Rome, called le Orecchie di Giussano. That project was the start to a series of meetings, discussions, and actions on the subject of community space. Between 2010 and 2011 the group was not fixed, as it expanded and decreased, going from 12 people to 7. orizzontale collective has seven founding members. The choice of forming a collective was driven mostly by a natural attitude and will of doing things together without a rigid hierarchy. Working together can be difficult, especially in decision-making. Meetings sometimes can be very long! We debate and discuss many aspects of our practice, as we are different individuals with personal ideas, interests, and opinions. At the same time, we share a general methodology as well as architectural vision and general values that we also want to address with our projects. Apart from being colleagues we are friends, and we enjoy what we do. This is an important aspect that makes us committed to what we do.

orizzontale, "Le Orecchie di Giussano 2010," Facebook repost 2020 and orizzontale, "CIN-CIN compleanno orizzontale 10 anni," Zoom, 2020

From: X=(T=E=N), Scott Lloyd
To: Natalie Donat-Cattin
Subject: How is a collective formed?

The Roman X came from an artist, whom we asked to do a study—it is still in progress after years—and interpret our name in order to develop our identity and our being. TEN was our name early on, but no one was truly convinced with it. The worst part when you have a collective is when you have to come up with a name, and then everyone comes up with different names. It was not getting anywhere and we got stuck with TEN, even though it does not have a strict relationship to us.

Anyway, the artist went on and did some studies, started to write things and do some very large-format drawings. It just kept on evolving. Initially he thought of a logo, however then he started focusing more on the essence of what TEN is, its geometry, its mathematics, its network. It went on for a long time, there was no deadline, no brief, nothing, it was this parallel philosophical but graphic project with no real end to it. It got to a point where we thought that actually the start was quite interesting. We took that: X=(T=E=N)—and left the rest to an endless evolution.

X=(T=E=N), *TEN Boat High*, Istanbul, 2019; Unknown, *TEN Boat Low*, Istria, undated

Once someone asked me where X=(T=E=N) came from and I actually sent them these photographs. It was different photographs of a boat which actually says TEN on it. While everyone was debating what the name should be, someone saw this boat when they were on holidays in Istanbul and then someone else saw the same boat in Croatia. It is the same boat, but because of what is in it, it sinks deeper into the water. We thought that actually that was quite an interesting identity: this container, which is something, and when there are more people in there, more projects, more things happening, it just changes what it is. So that became the story, the official story, but then it changes all the time, actually.

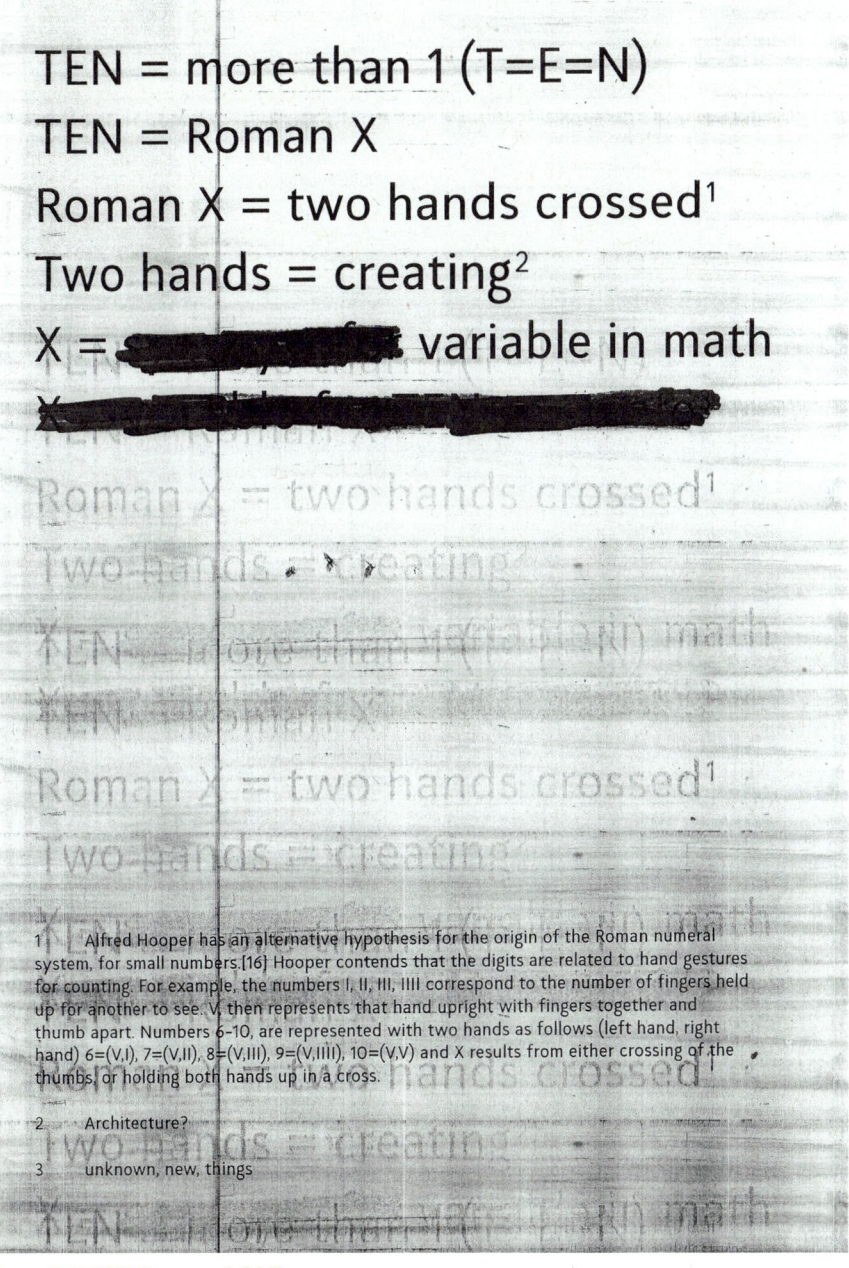

TEN = more than 1 (T=E=N)
TEN = Roman X
Roman X = two hands crossed[1]
Two hands = creating[2]
X = ~~something~~ variable in math

~~X = ~~

1   Alfred Hooper has an alternative hypothesis for the origin of the Roman numeral system, for small numbers.[16] Hooper contends that the digits are related to hand gestures for counting. For example, the numbers I, II, III, IIII correspond to the number of fingers held up for another to see. V, then represents that hand upright with fingers together and thumb apart. Numbers 6-10, are represented with two hands as follows (left hand, right hand) 6=(V,I), 7=(V,II), 8=(V,III), 9=(V,IIII), 10=(V,V) and X results from either crossing of the thumbs, or holding both hands up in a cross.

2   Architecture?

3   unknown, new, things

Simon Egli, "TEN" proposal, 2017

Monday, January 13, 2020, 10:12 AM

2. STATEMENTS
Founding Acts

An act of some sort is needed to come together, be it a self-initiated project or a set of rules to follow. This founding act transmits the essence and uniqueness of each collective: a political statement, a poetic passage, a list, a story, a quote. Some collectives set a simple goal for themselves, others a more complex constitution to follow. In both cases, this allows them to not deviate from a defined path of action, a sort of legacy of the mission, which reminds the different members of the reasons why they started this journey together. In it, from time to time, a series of indications are updated, but others remain to guarantee the integrity of the collective.

For some, even if there are no manifestos or statements of any sort, it remains a common ambition, a friendship, a trust that holds the group together.

From: Natalie Donat-Cattin
To: (ab)Normal, A-A Collective, Assemble, CNCRT, Colectivo Warehouse, Collectif Etc, constructLab, false mirror office, Fosbury Architecture, la–clique, Lacol, n'UNDO, orizzontale, X=(T=E=N)
Subject: Is there a founding act of the collective?

A statement, a manifesto, a constitution,
a set of values, a hymn, a motto.

From: (ab)Normal
To: Natalie Donat-Cattin
Subject: Is there a founding act of the collective?

(ab)Normal is a graphic novel without chronology. Instead, obsolete 3ds and rejected timelines are reconfigured in spatial narratives. Iconographic images describe the allegory of a culture that revolves obsessively around Internet, Gaming, and Religion.

Being the collective idea of four architects, (ab)Normal is firstly an experiment on architectural representation; photorealism is carefully deconstructed and rearranged in illustrations based on normal vectors, avoiding the traditional structure that builds the contemporary visual description of a space. Hence, this project is both scientific in its method and evocative in its thematic background.

NORMALS
Around the American crop belt, driverless threshing machines cultivate the soil with zero tolerance. This is possible only by providing them real-time geometric information: normal vectors. Satellites

floating around Earth's exosphere scan terrestrial soil and return gradient maps that lead tractors' movements. It's a very compelling image, for these slow and constant machines look oddly like an organized army of pachyderms.

Normals are vectors describing the inclination of a nominal fragment of a surface, according to the point of view of the observer.[1] Thus, normals are impalpable characteristics of surfaces, controlling lights and reflection. if natural evolution didn't provide mankind with such a perception, technology did. under the transhumanist perspective, normals become akin to a supernatural sense, the first sense for the machine, the sixth human sense by product.

1. Edmund Husserl, "Der Ursprung der Geometrie als intentional-historisches Problem," *Revue Internationale de Philosophie* 1, no. 2 (January 1939): 205.

A DELUSIONAL REVOLUTION

At the beginning of the 1990s, 3-D printing had been welcomed as the system that would upset product industries. Autarchic utopias, in which the procedural design of an object will become more important than the object itself, in which a diffused society of producers will replace the Fordist top-down routines, started to colonize popular fantasies with uncountable catalogues of user-designed objects. Well, anything similar never took over. While the printing revolution might sparkle in the next future, these replicas remain useless. (ab)Normal collects and arranges them in three-dimensional collages.

INTERNET, GAMING, RELIGION

These three topics, sounding at first unrelated, structured the prehistory of the metadata society. According to Harari,[2] religions are intersubjective reality, conventions trusted and supported without verification by entire communities. Religious dogmas had always represented less the unravelling of a mystical truth rather than the trajectories that channel coexistence among men. The Internet, and the consequent epiphenomena, could be understood more likely under this perspective; HTML and coding in general are complex languages, oddly resonating as religious litany, understood by a very limited elite of the initiated. The constant interactions with communication devices constitute a body of digital rituals reiterated without comprehension, like chanting the Christian rosary. What led us to embrace religions in the past brought us to accept the Internet as the main societal manager. Lastly, if the Internet is a religion, gaming represents its heroic beginning, the rebellion against a preexisting status quo. "In the 1980s, arcade rooms provided a space for cyberfreedom. They were often advertised as spots of youngster rebels who desire to upset the hierarchy. [...] Akintoa Primitive Hut for the digital reduction of the world, arcades became the founding myth of a generation of future technocrats."[3]

2. Yuval Noah Harari, *Homo Deus*, trans. Marco Piani (Milan: Giunti/Bompiani, 2017), 223.
3. GruppoTorto, *Ongoing Research on Forgotten Spaces*, 2017.

From: A-A Collective
To: Natalie Donat-Cattin
Subject: Is there a founding act of the collective?

> We believe that collective thinking is stronger than individual style.

From: CNCRT
To: Natalie Donat-Cattin
Subject: Is there a founding act of the collective?

> CNCRT is a political project and the last scenario of conjunction for individuals like us, grown-up as self-made workers. CNCRT aims to define new working practices that go behind the canonical structure of the architectural office and can be further extended over the disciplinary boundaries of architecture.

From: Colectivo Warehouse
To: Natalie Donat-Cattin
Subject: Is there a founding act of the collective?

> Building community.

From: Collectif Etc
To: Natalie Donat-Cattin
Subject: Is there a founding act of the collective?

> Don't write manifestos, do things!

From: constructLab
To: Natalie Donat-Cattin
Subject: Is there a founding act of the collective?

> Construction is the first step of inhabitation
> a door to the social reality of a particular locus
> an amplifier of an already existing potential
> a balance between individual desires and collective vision

the practice of a collaborative body
an exercise in engagement
open and accessible to all
as a participatory process
Construction is about embracing all surprises
not only a final form
a tool for communication
not only for the shaping of the material forms that surround us;
but our imagination towards different futures
A building site is a learning site
a meeting point
a microcosm
Party

constructLab, Plataforma Trafaria, 2017

From: Fosbury Architecture
To: Natalie Donat-Cattin
Subject: Is there a founding act of the collective?

Human beings, both male and female, have lived in houses for 12,019 years. With houses, they have built cities for 8,000 years. The collective at Fosbury Architecture are not all that certain that all this will continue, but they are sure that if one day the house-form were to be exhausted, architecture would survive its ruins.

They are therefore prepared to provide you with: rolling houses, intergalactic sofas, and sensory deprivation tanks, maneki neko and Barbapapa, but also creations in beautiful plastic, reinforced concrete, and optical fibers, Dazzle Patterns and Dalmatiner, PVC and electrical tape, tree bark or cardboard. They can stick to the rules of the game or deviate from the straight and narrow, winding their way among pavilions and photomontages, competitions and renovations, publishing and the art market, escape routes and floor plans,

RROARK!

ISSUE #01 - OCTOBER 16, 2014 - BILDUNGSROMAN

.01 about the possibility and the opportunity to print a manifesto on a flyer advertising a kebab shop; not to mention the countless misunderstandings that may arise - 25.000 copies printed and distributed for a month.

.02 no boring presentations - We called our group Fosbury Architecture. We have gathered together because we share the same inclination, nonetheless, we definitely did not have identical principles. Because our group is formed, it is a matter of timing, a thing of the moment. We, each one of us, possess desires and passions that we feel we must elevate individually to a degree of objectivity. However, while recognizing what we possess may be occasionally exclusive, we acknowledge the fact that we could not form a group without it. The proof is in the pudding.

.03 how to write a proper manifesto - We have understood that there are four fundamental points to be observed: to deeply believe in what is proclaimed ("Art is art. Everything else is everything else.", Ad Rehinardt, 1958), to deal with the ancestors ("Workers of the world unite!", K.Marx, F. Hengels, 1848), to find a tone adequately bombastic ("I cannot know your name. Nor can you know mine. Tomorrow, we begin together the construction of a city.", Lebbeus Wood, 1993), to identify someone or something to oppose or at least a 'father to kill' ("Cose a cui gli UFO non vogliono tanto bene. I piani regolatori / La speculazione edilizia / I plastici / I professori di storia / ... / I Kennedy", UFO, 1968)

.04 arrogance, pre-formed positions, rigid filters, the 'moral clarity' of the immature: a few things for which we can not be blamed - Since this is our Manifesto, albeit not a very aggressive one, for us no granitic mindset but temporary intuition to run after, no class struggle but apotropaic rituals, no rhetoric but narrative, no enemies but solitude, no innocence but guilt trips, no fathers but grandparents.

.05 in other words - Rroark!, more than an egotistic declaration of intents, it is a kind of collective psychoanalysis in episodes, a 'bildungsroman' in which everyone is participating, willingly or not. From now on, every week for an unknown number of weeks, we will publish a new issue, the nth element of a shared soliloquy. Few issue and nothing more, enough to donate ourselves. Ultimately, no psychologist already knows how many sessions will be needed to heal a patient.

.06 funeral party - Many argued that the 2014 Architecture Biennale curated by Rem Koolhaas sheds light on the death of architecture, or at least on the death of architectural grammar. Someone even argued that Koolhaas himself is 'dead'. Death in Venice. Now that even the 'delirious architecture' is fading, it emerges the lack of masters we have witnessed for the last 40 years. In our attempt to find a noble father with whom to deal, we only find old prophets, whose dystopic prophecies have all ironically materialized. The only route we have to build our path is screaming out loud all our doubts.

.07 haruspicy and birdwatching - We are a group of guys who just graduates and we are entering the world of work, but we believe that the only place to share and discuss ideas is the University. Public university is in ruins, university as the privileged place of cultural production is in ruins. Rather than surrender to nostalgia we decide to take it as an unavoidable matter of fact. This irreversible process opens to the chance of an enormous freedom. Students complain of being trapped in a cage, but the cages are open. The risk is to find ourselves fat pigeons unable to fly.

.08 what "The Fountainhead" is apparently about - Howard Roark in the movie is an intransigent architect that rather than come to terms with the enemy and bend to trends decides to abandon his career as an architect and work in a mine. We know that architecture is something else and it can not help but get its hands dirty with all that it encounters. In a context in which the immaterial wealth is exalted by the financial markets, we have a powerful weapon at our disposal: our immaterial capital. What would happen if we created a speculative bubble?

.09 if you do not agree, please go to Switzerland -

RROARK! IS A FREE WEEKLY PUBLICATION PRINTED BY "MR.POLI KEBAB" IN MILAN - EDITED BY FOSBURY ARCHITECTURE
follow us on facebook | contact us on fosburyarchitecture@gmail.com | current issue on line www.fosburyarchitecture.com

Mr. Poli kebab is not responsible for any content presented in this publication

Fosbury Architecture, "Fosbury Manifesto," *RROARK* no. 1, 2014

lifestyles and orders of ideas, five-year plans and double-decade instability, finely detailed plans for weeds and brushwood, pompous master plans or teeny-tiny rooms. A little bit of everything, but certainly not everything (a poetry of multitasking, but spontaneous and proud, certainly not bound by the laws of the market).

They are not afraid of research and ethical doubts, porous aesthetics and collective actions. They are not ashamed of studying and are ready to travel, but have set up residence in Milan, Hamburg, and Rotterdam, foggy northern spots dense with expectations. They got together in 2013. The same year, Benedict XVI announces his resignation, Queen Beatrix abdicates, a meteorite explodes over Russia, the North Korean regime proclaims a state of war against South Korea, the North Korean army publicly announces a green light for a nuclear attack against the United States, Snowden starts talking, Croatia enters Europe, Silvio Berlusconi is sentenced to four years in prison for tax fraud, Marcovaldo turns fifty, and a new island is born in Japan. Yet the Fosbury team swear that the events in question are not in the least bit connected.

The individual names given to the registry office are: Giacomo Ardesio, Alessandro Bonizzoni, Nicola Campri, Veronica Caprino, and Claudia Mainardi. They steal the name of the collective, however, from the athlete who—first and with mismatched shoes—jumped back-first. Each experiment breaks rules, evokes heart pangs, and casts a glimpse toward the past, but this does not prevent it from taking an unconventional approach to the obstacles at hand, in architecture as in life.

From: la–clique
To: Natalie Donat-Cattin
Subject: Is there a founding act of the collective?

The formation of la–clique can be seen as a desire—perhaps nostalgic—to continue the exchange that we appreciated during our years of studies. We try to confront the disparity of realities experienced by each of us in the universities and practices we're involved in. Essentially, it is a work mode without hierarchy that allows us to grow with and learn from our peers, without a master figure.

We see a fundamental quality of the collective in its pluralistic nature. The projects are developed in a manifold approach rather than a single one, determined each time anew by the respective individuals taking part in a project. This means that we do not want so much to define the outcome of our work but much more its process as a collaborative act, a series of discussions.

The constellation of members involved in a specific project is constantly changing according to each person's interests, skills, and sensitivities, which triggers different dynamics. It is by confronting our multiple opinions that the architectural response is strengthened. The principal product we are working towards is thus not only a good architecture but a way of working in a network, laying the foundation for future collaborations. It is by acting collectively that we will exercise our response to today's issues.

From: **Lacol**
To: **Natalie Donat-Cattin**
Subject: **Is there a founding act of the collective?**

Anna Gran and Lacol, Graphic recording of an internal meeting, undated

We work from architecture toward social transformation, using architecture as a tool to intervene critically in the environments that are closest to us. We believe that the way to transform the city is through the active participation and purposeful action of the people who live in it. The architect's contribution is made within urban movements, as one more piece within this mechanism.

From: **n'UNDO**
To: **Natalie Donat-Cattin**
Subject: **Is there a founding act of the collective?**

It is possible to build more and better by reducing, containing, and well-reasoned declining. Subtraction and renunciation are alternatives for pertinent and necessary interventions:

1. The purpose of architecture is to improve people's lives and to increase the value of its surroundings by its very presence.

2. Given surplus production, overdevelopment, and land deterioration, the following are proposals for actions to be taken: not constructing, reusing, minimizing, and dismantling.

3. Architecture, urban planning, and landscape architecture do not only imply building and producing, but also restoring, maintaining, clearing, and reclaiming.

4. Every territory is a landscape, even the most ordinary and common. Territories must be appreciated and respected since they are fundamental for developing people's lives.

5. Any built configuration, whether urban or territorial, must be thoughtful, argued, debated, and agreed upon according to social, environmental, urban, economic, cultural, and ethical criteria.

6. Reporting and criticizing actions that are harmful to the territory or to the city is necessary for promoting awareness, debate, and (re)action.

7. Architecture and the city are not consumer goods.

8. Much of the (non)architecture that pollutes land and cities is reversible, reducible, reusable, or disposable; these are the actions that should be developed by the discipline of architecture and territory.

9. The permanence and immutability of architecture and the impact of interventions are questionable at times when society's future stipulates flexibility and constant change.

10. Common space and the shared environment are given priority over individual space and private enjoyment.

11. Architecture cannot be used either as a tool to undermine human rights or to replace education, civic values, and common sense.

manifesto n'UNDO November 11, 2011

From: X=(T=E=N)
To: **Natalie Donat-Cattin**
Subject: Is there a founding act of the collective?

TEN talks through drawings
TEN constructs with simple means
TEN affirms territory through form
TEN composes buildings as constellations
TEN annotates projects with many hands
TEN studies relationships between books and buildings
TEN explores variables
TEN practices design by research
TEN reinterprets typologies
TEN works with temporality
TEN wonders around questions of beauty
TEN qualifies the urban
TEN measures precedents
TEN welcomes all from 7 to 107

3. REFERENCES
Question of Identity

The references to which each collective clings as the firm roots of its being appear to be necessary to understand—in an absolute sense—where each collective is located in the architectural world and—in a relative sense—its correspondence to its familiar surrounding context, as well as its relationship to other entities—buildings, works of art, other architects, other collectives, institutions, or movements—present, past, real, ideal, public, or private.

The collective, in the act of choosing its references—in general or while approaching a project—is confronted with its multiplicity and polychromy. It is forced both to accept different individual impulses and to hold on to a common ground (A-A Collective), a Wunderkammer of obsessions (false mirror office) or an imagery in evolution (Fosbury Architecture): a collective space in which to move, evolve, and confront one another; a table around which to sit and be able to discuss architecture or other issues (la–clique).

Finding a collective identity—or rejecting it—is a long process toward the awareness of collective strength, as well as of individual freedom. Collectif Etc, in whose name this idea of continuous regeneration is already intrinsic, in November 2011 left for "Le Détour de France," in search of an "education off the beaten path," a physical and figurative journey toward a hybrid identity, between architecture, urban planning, and civic work.[1]

1. "By adding 'Etc' to the word 'Collectif,' the group acknowledges its state of perpetual reconfiguration and refuses to restrict itself to a specific number of members. Some might join or leave, but they always remain fellow travelers." Thierry Paquot, "Tour, Detour, Retour," Collectif Etc, *Détour de France: An Education off the Beaten Path* (Marseille: éditions Hyperville, 2015), 18.

Indeed, many collectives look with admiration at the simplicity of anonymous architecture, rejecting personal profit and expanding their spectrum to a larger participatory vision grounded in collaboration, dialogue, and exchange between architects, other specialists, and communities. Among the architectural projects to which they refer as models, those encouraging the appropriation of space stand out—as Colectivo Warehouse declares by bringing Lina Bo Bardi's SESC Pompéia building on the table—or orizzontale, by mentioning the informal squat spaces in Rome.

A general underlying condition is this cry for a humanity of architecture through the rediscovery of the simple joy of building, as Assemble affirms; a more introspective architecture focused on its intentions and dimensions, which instead of offering form and functionality, puts the user at the center. As X=(T=E=N) writes, "for this we utilize the act of drawing […], it helps us draw ourselves into place, to locate points of departure and moments to act collectively." Once one, architect and not, realizes it is a small fragment within a multitude of people, all that remains is the possibility to share knowledge, experiences, and desires (CNCRT). To conclude, the references of each collective become central to understanding the architectural project that each one of them, alone or in collaboration with other collectives, wishes to pursue and implement.

From: Natalie Donat-Cattin
To: (ab)Normal, A-A Collective, Assemble, CNCRT, Colectivo Warehouse, Collectif Etc, constructLab, false mirror office, Fosbury Architecture, la–clique, Lacol, n'UNDO, orizzontale, X=(T=E=N)
Subject: What are the key references behind your architecture?

A building that has inspired you or a historical period, a contemporary necessity, a social problematic, a reaction to an architectural movement, perhaps just a work of art, an idea, a concept, a word.

From: (ab)Normal
To: Natalie Donat-Cattin
Subject: What are the key references behind your architecture?

I like to think
(and the sooner the better!)
of a cybernetic meadow
where mammals and computers
live together in mutually
programming harmony
like pure water
touching clear sky.

I like to think
(right now, please!)
of a cybernetic forest
filled with pines and electronics
where deer stroll peacefully
past computers
as if they were flowers
with spinning blossoms.

I like to think
(it has to be!)
of a cybernetic ecology
where we are free of our labors

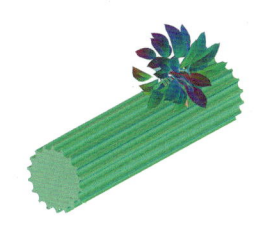

and joined back to nature,
returned to our mammal
brothers and sisters,
and all watched over
by machines of loving grace.

(ab)Normal, "All Watched Over by Machines of Loving Grace," 2020.
Poem by Richard Brautigan, 1967

From: A-A Collective
To: Natalie Donat-Cattin
Subject: What are the key references behind your architecture?

Is not an easy task to define a precise architectural reference for a collective formed by four individuals. Some of us studied in the same school or worked in the same city, but still different backgrounds and interests lead to a broad range of various fascinations and models to aspire to. It is therefore impossible for us to have references to follow dogmatically.

Instead of any precise historical period, style, or charismatic figures, we could state that we are interested in any architecture that bravely deals with the reality where it belongs, architectures that represent or react to their surroundings, history, political situation. Exactly for this reason a very important part of our working process is to prepare a common ground for all of us at the beginning. This is mainly done through research, where we gather all sorts of information about the place where we are going to project. Whether it is about history, contemporary facts, social problems, relevant architectures in the surroundings, particular natural ecosystems, we try to bring everything together to have a big picture of that specific reality.

A good example of this process is our project for the Central Square of Warsaw. Studying the vibrant urban evolution of the city made us aware that the square was hiding an immense invisible richness of stories: urban life, tragic dramas, ideologies, and the demonstration of power. Once we got aware of this, the "only" problem we had to solve together was how we were going to tell these stories. In this project our approach is made even more clear by the presence of the Palace of Culture, which was a "gift" from the Soviet Union and was designed with the Moscow State University building as a model. This no-context building makes the perfect conceptual counterpart to our square that instead could not be more site-specific.

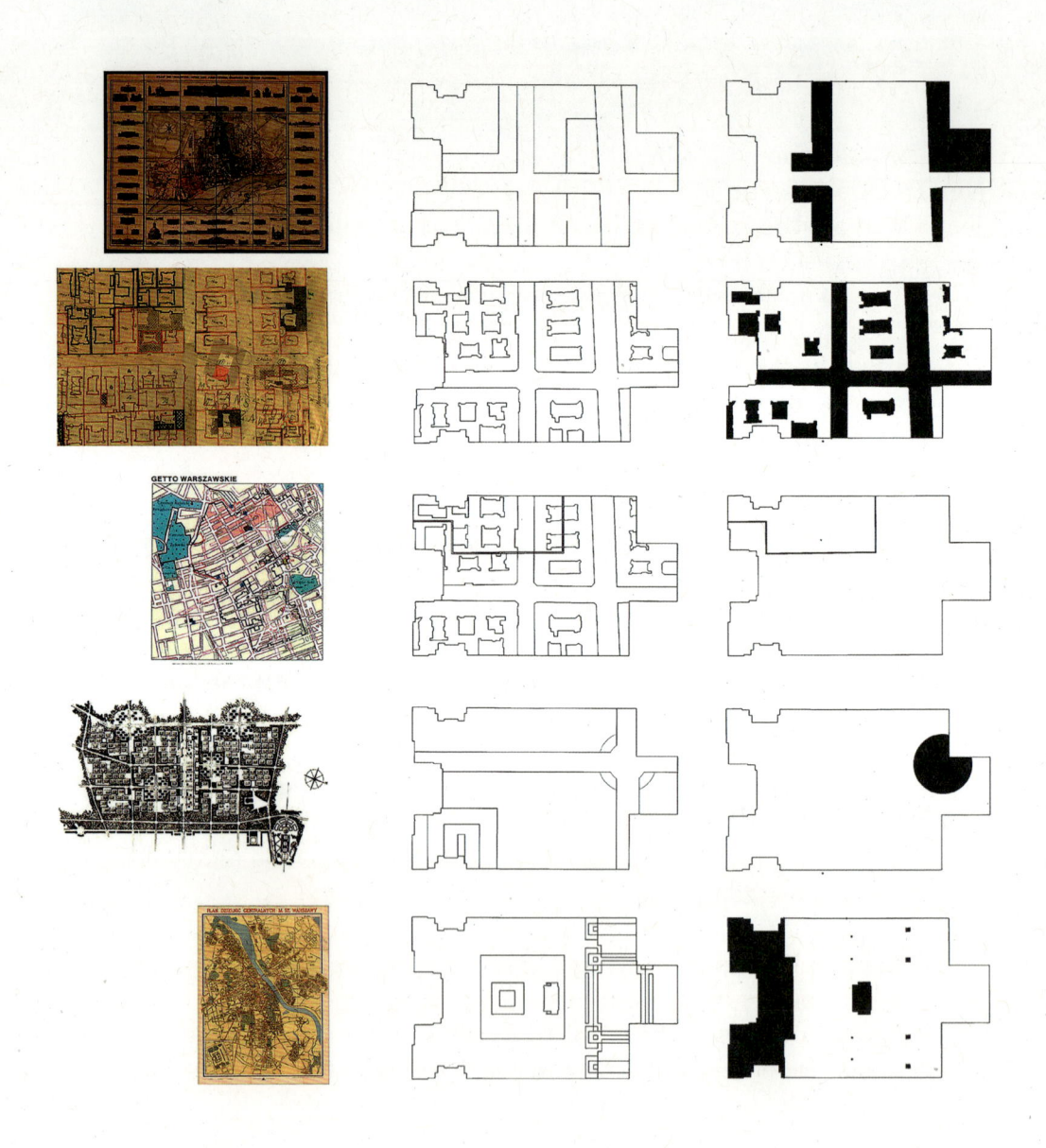

A-A Collective, Warsaw Central Square–historical layers, 2019. 1: First half of the nineteenth century; 2: First half of the twentieth century; 3: Borders of the Ghetto line 1940; 4: 1945; 5: 1955

From: Assemble
To: Natalie Donat-Cattin
Subject: What are the key references behind your architecture?

> Assemble cannot really be characterized by one thing. Perhaps the most significant project was our first, The Cineroleum, as that is what brought us together in the first place. The joy of simply building something collectively and by hand was an exciting experience that as newly graduated architects allowed us to understand how the world is made and can be remade with amateur skills and a DIY spirit. It is an attitude that continues to inform our collective work and is probably the biggest point of reference when we talk about new projects.

Assemble, Weekly Assemble meeting held at Tavistock Square while working on Folly for a Flyover, London, 2011 / Morley von Sternberg, The Cineroleum, London, 2010

From: CNCRT
To: Natalie Donat-Cattin
Subject: What are the key references behind your architecture?

> A Life Question: Our Productive Process
> 1. DIARY OF COMMON LIVES
> The diary is the first form of intellectual production in our lives. A diary collects daily events, affective memories, words, sketches, tears, and smileys poetically given form in a book of white sheets. It accumulates wishes, knowledge, and imagination. Writers or not, poets or not, talented interpreters of plays or not, having to write a diary or not, everyone does collect all those thoughts somewhere. Once within the labor market, as adults/students and workers, what we discover is a multitude of common diaries: us. Same books, same authors, same architects, same teachers, same stories of lives, same city, but born in different ones, different references, different individualities, individual visions, same material problematics, same employers, same mentors, same places in life, such as libraries and universities where all this process took place. What we do is put in common these knowledges, experiences, and wishes.

CNCRT, Diary of Common Lives, 2020

From: Colectivo Warehouse
To: Natalie Donat-Cattin
Subject: What are the key references behind your architecture?

>I just understood what "appropriation of the space" means when I saw SESC Pompéia by Lina Bo Bardi. Some people were sunbathing on the ground, others were comfortably sleeping on the sofas in the exhibition room, kids were running along the concrete walkways. And everybody spoke about the architect calling her by her name. I thought "If one day I will get to do just 20 percent of such a powerful thing, I could die happy."

Markus Lanz, SESC Pompéia, São Paulo, 2014

From: Collectif Etc
To: Natalie Donat-Cattin
Subject: What are the key references behind your architecture?

We are receptive to our obvious contemporary emergencies: needs for self-management and sustainable ways of life, fight against abuses and lies from politicians and insatiable private profit.

We are sensible to historical backgrounds: utopias from the 1960s and the '70s, with their load of thrilling images and their bunch of people without fear building autonomous structures in the desert, Young Lords in the suburbs of New York occupying churches, free market in public spaces organized by the Diggers, revolution in architecture schools in '68 in Paris, Lucien Kroll in Brussels promoting self-built environments and Bernard Rudofsky questioning architects with his exhibition *Architecture without Architects*.

Collectif Etc, "On ne veut pas débattre, on veut décider," 2020

Architect collectives are not new, they do not innovate. They are and could be part of a counterculture's history that takes place in collective acts and awareness—things we can feel nowadays. All these utopias are coming back to life—and these inspired actualities are breathtaking. We are inspired by our contemporary friends' work, too. We hope that one day we will unite into the International Congress of Alternative Architecture in order to defend a social, democratic, sustainable production of spaces, places, cities! We guess it will be far away from the previous CIAM's visions.

From: constructLab
To: Natalie Donat-Cattin
Subject: What are the key references behind your architecture?

Dylan Perrenaud, *Caillasses*, Geneva, 2020

constructLab develops the concept of the projects remotely, therefore there are several methods. They do prefer developing a project around a table, but this is not always possible. Doing it by pixels also brings something general. There is not one clear vision, rather multiple ones.[2]

2. All responses to the questions were collected during the residency of constructLab in Geneva at the embassy of Foreign Artists, while developing the project *Caillasses*. *Caillasses* was our point of encounter, therefore a visual journey through its different phases accompanies the written answers.

From: false mirror office
To: Natalie Donat-Cattin
Subject: What are the key references behind your architecture?

Whether you call them inspirations, obsessions, references, love at first sight, or you simply define them as models, the universe of forms, images, structures, techniques, materials, and words that constitutes the cultural background of each member of our group plays a crucial role in our way of designing architecture.
    For us, the model has nothing to do with the personal erudition or an intellectual statement, but it is a fundamental component of a creative process that considers invention as a collection of pieces ready to be reassembled to generate new compositions and narratives. Ours is a universe of anarchist, heterogeneous, and unfolding models. It is anarchist because when it looks at architecture it cannot bear any choice; it is not passionate about one style but loves them all; it looks at the past as well as at the modern, rejecting every form of "new sobriety." It is heterogeneous because it is understood that architecture cannot be an intimate and tragic

discourse about itself, but it must be a kaleidoscopic discourse that includes all aspects of our society, with its high cultural values along with what is most licentious in its secret belly. It is unfolding because it loves the *polisindeto* and the enumeration, it is always willing to renew and enrich itself, without being ashamed of contradiction. Ours is a universe of models that, if it were to be designed, would look like a Wunderkammer (or a sort of luxurious off-scale jewelry box) in which to display a collection of models that, transformed into objects of worship and affection, have lost the memory of their origin and yet are still waiting to take part in a new play.

false mirror office, Jewelry Box, 2020

Ours is also a universe of references that if it were simply to be told would sound like a banal catalogue of the type: "Things that false mirror office loves so much: the giant ducks, the Red obsessions, M¥SS KETA, *St. Jerome in His Study*, the dollhouses, kitsch reproductions of Padre Pio, *pulcini vivi*, the Bürolandschaft, *phallophoria*, the Teatro del Mondo, PLAYMOBIL®, the domino structure, Nintendo Game Boy, the Chrysler Building (only if anthropomorphic), the Teatrino, Pop-Op artists, Venetian *altanes*, the decorated shed, an operating table (only if combined with a sewing machine and an umbrella)."

From: Fosbury Architecture
To: Natalie Donat-Cattin
Subject: What are the key references behind your architecture?

Fosbury Architecture is a collective that was originally formed gathering people with different backgrounds and aspirations. Lacking a shared interest around which to structure the practice or a manifesto that could have oriented the work of the group, it has been necessary to share references and ideas, heroes and villains, commonplaces and memorabilia, guilty pleasures and idiosyncrasies, so as to shape a private cosmogony that informs any endeavor that the group undertakes. Rather than a pantheon, it is an imagery in evolution that unfolds and modifies along the life trajectories of the different components.

Fosbury Architecture, *References*, 2020

From: la–clique
To: **Natalie Donat-Cattin**
Subject: **What are the key references behind your architecture?**

la–clique took the decision not to answer questions with texts but to approach them in the form of discussions. And so begins the "anatomy of a conversation."

The only rule is that a minimum of five members are involved in answering each question, and that each member participates in at least one question. From the tablecloth here below, to the *cadavre exquis* (answering the question "What is the key aim of your architecture?"), through Zoom and Slack, we wanted to keep the spontaneity and sharing that defines our collective, and so to preserve its quality of an independent platform for exchange and experimentation around architecture.

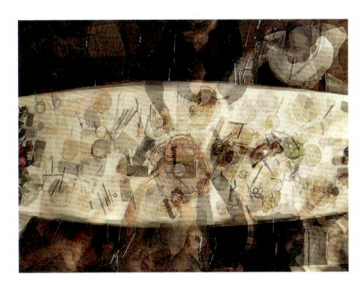

la–clique, A tablecloth, 2020

**et là la–clique est arrivée et elle a dit:
avant moi le déluge!**

la–clique, "Avant moi le déluge," 2020

From: Lacol
To: Natalie Donat-Cattin
Subject: What are the key references behind your architecture?

Socially we are very influenced by the organizations and cooperatives in our neighborhood, Sants (Barcelona). Architecturally it is hard to say. Many are very inspired by what was done in the 1970s, especially in the Netherlands and England. Closer to our days we mainly look at what is done in Catalonia and Spain, but also Belgium and Switzerland are a source of inspiration. Our beginnings were related to the network Arquitecturas Colectivas.

Anna Gran and Lacol, Graphic recording of an internal meeting, undated

From: n'UNDO
To: Natalie Donat-Cattin
Subject: What are the key references behind your architecture?

If we auto-refer to our book *From Subtraction*, there are many: Epicuro, Basho, Whitman, the Internationale Situationniste, Lefebvre, Jacobs, Stravinsky, Cage, Messner, the Brundtland report, Harvey, LeWitt, Long, Jouannais, Bohm, Malevich, Klein, and many others who have previously approached the concepts of not doing, emptiness, silence, undoing, and subtraction; but we really think the idea of a master or reference to follow, which is very much accepted as the only way to do architecture, has to be torn down: "Kill your idols" will be our advice.

Richard Long, *A line made by walking*, England, 1967

From: orizzontale
To: Natalie Donat-Cattin
Subject: What are the key references behind your architecture?

> As references we looked at the Italian radical architecture of the 1960–70s as well as the *estate romana* of Renato Nicolini. We learned from the experience of EXYZT, raumlabor, by Recetas Urbanas of Santiago Cirugeda, Todo Por La Praxis, ecosistema urbano. We exchange knowledge and collaborate with collectives from our generation like Collectif Etc.

Gonzague Lacombe and Serena Cerillo, Osthang Project, Mathildenhöhe, Darmstadt, 2014

Part of our work has also been strongly influenced by the informal active squat places of Rome in which we prepared the first interventions for some public spaces of Rome, when we didn't have our own working space. The fact that we stay in a shared space with professionals from other fields gives us more points of view with which we can question our approach. We also like to use references that are not part of the architecture field. Books, movies, art pieces, historical facts, materials, political movements are a vibrant resource for our projects. Staying in an interdisciplinary context continually gives inputs to the research. We like to form our personal view and language in architecture.

From: X=(T=E=N)
To: Natalie Donat-Cattin
Subject: What are the key references behind your architecture?

We are interested right now in how architecture comes together and how we can expand its discourse from the present fixation on the completed image and quantitative solution. Our design research seeks new modes of challenging this and thereby contributes to common architectural knowledge. We do this with full imagination, not fancy. The world of images is pervaded by imagination and requires our own imagination, in turn, to offer a sense of orientation. For this we utilize the act of drawing and the potential this has to state the actuality and potential of an architectural language. In other words, it helps us draw ourselves into place, to locate points of departure and moments to act collectively.

In the spring of 2017 we conducted a series of experimental and collaborative drawing workshops with architecture students from Serbia, Croatia, Germany, and Switzerland. The aim of the workshop was to investigate and structure the inspiration we draw from the works of Serbian architect Nikola Dobrović and the spirit of West European modernism. The workshops resulted in the production of a set of drawings investigating two seminal projects by Dobrovi, the first being Villa Vesna, designed in 1937 and constructed two years later on Lopud island in Croatia, and the second being the unrealized project for the architect's holiday house designed some thirty years later. Documentation of the Villa Vesna was studied and reconstructed in axonometric format following individual thematic programs. This exercise established knowledge of the methods of Dobrović's architecture and was used to elaborate and project the spatial and construction possibilities suggested in the few drawings documenting the holiday house. This resulted in a type of archaeological reconstruction through the act of drawing. Systematic reviews and exchanges allowed the knowledge from the previous exercises to be shared in the form of common drawing notations by all students. The notation process raised a number of questions surrounding the authorship of drawing and the trajectory of the drawing production process. Such a collective and at times contradictory act also undermines the certainty of completion and thereby embeds the drawings within a fresh dynamic. The works were exhibited at the Cultural Centre of Belgrade between April and May 2017.

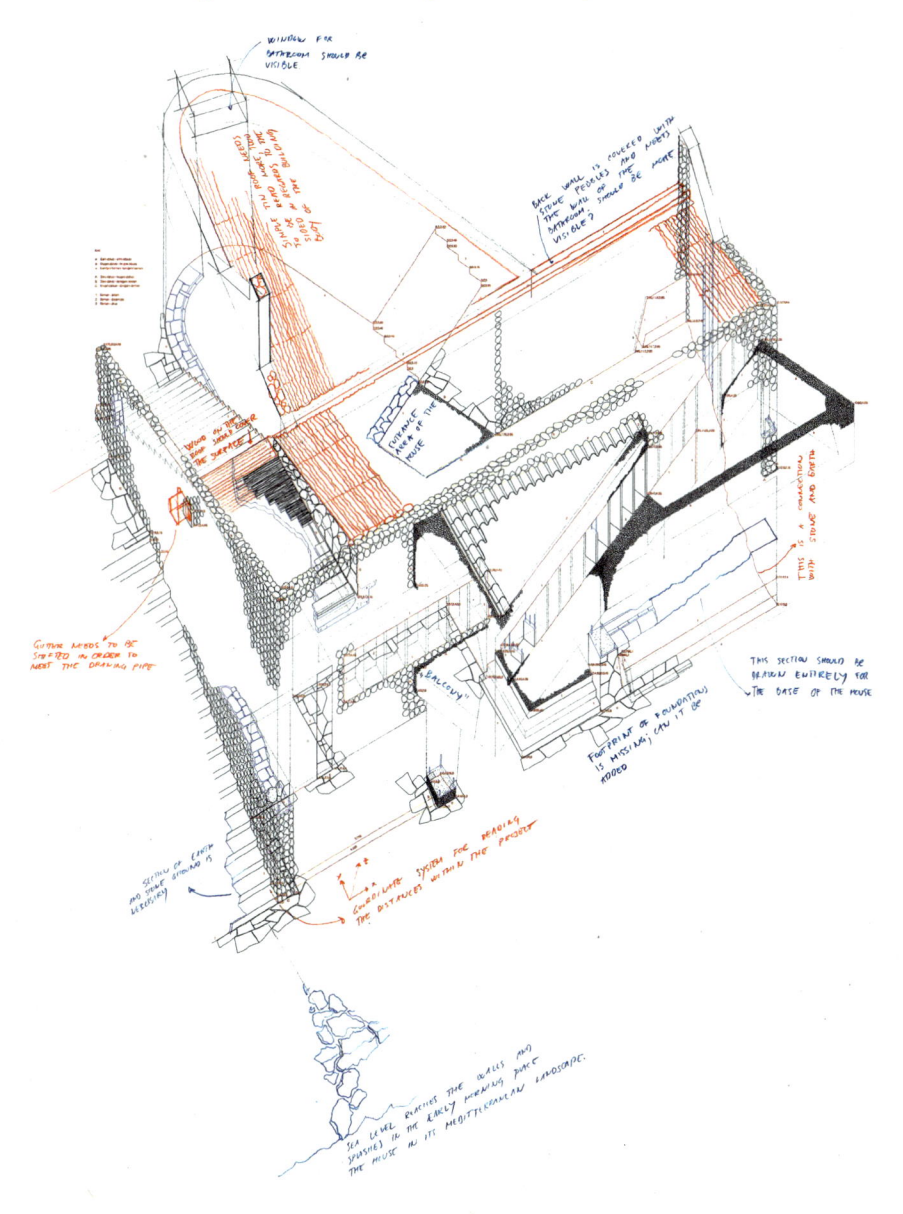

Nemanja Zimonji, Ljiljana Blagojevi, and Jana Kulić (student),
Stitch, X=(T=E=N) drawing workshop *Annotations on Nikola Dobrovi*, 2017

4. WORKING SPACE
Space of Interaction

The working space is a project.
The working space is just a meeting room.
The working space is the living space.
The working space does not exist.

The history of the working space starts from the studiolo, evolves into the room, and turns into the Bürolandschaft, or open space. Today a progressive abstraction of the workplace is occurring and nowadays we experience a hybrid condition: from the traditional working space to the web. As Jennifer Sigler says in the *Harvard Design Magazine* n. 46 *No Sweat*: "The boundaries of the workplace are shifting in place and time [...]. The workplace is everywhere—or is it nowhere?"

The Covid-19 virus has brought these questions on how we work and where we work to an extreme condition by erasing, during the lockdown, the physical workplace and replacing it with the home. This might be just a passing crisis, however the question remains: where is the workplace and what is our work organization?

"Working penetrates within the personal intimacy of the domestic sphere, turning it into a productive space and isolating any possibility of collectivity. Not many choices are permitted within a room which seems an office rather than a place of beautiful creativity," says CNCRT when describing their project *We Are Beautiful!* The personal and professional space no longer seems to have a precise limit separating them, especially in the case of some newly formed collectives or some collectives who are scattered in different countries. The room becomes the office. The office becomes the room. In other cases, the construction site becomes the workspace, or simply a place of gathering, where not only the creative energy of the project is released but a whole community within and beyond the project. Throughout the three months of residency of constructLab at the Embassy of Foreign Artists last summer in Geneva, I had the opportunity to participate in this process. The garden in which *Caillasses* was developed and the different interventions related to it, as well as the surrounding area of the PAV, transformed into a terrain of opportunity to meet new people, exchange opinions, eat together, read poetry, and observe the tension between nature and the city.

It is therefore true that the work space is everywhere and nowhere at the same time, because in these situations it has the power to morph into a space for play, discussion, and exchange—in many cases a temporary space. The office is a train, a café, a bench, a park: "to do a collective means to get out of this everyday routine of working in the office, at the same desk. Starting our own thing and sitting on the same desk everyday would be a contradiction" (A-A Collective).

An Internet connection, a Dropbox or a drive become, therefore, essential in the organization of labor and to trigger collective discussions: many collectives are continuously hyperconnected. (ab)Normal defines its workspace as a mixture of a WhatsApp group, a Dropbox folder, and a Skype dialogue, not so different from the virtual space its members represent in their renderings. Given the distance of its members, CNCRT and false mirror office organize weekly meetings on different online platforms. Fosbury Architecture, instead, after being itinerant, have just resettled in the same city, Milan. la–clique meets for intensive design workshops, in which most of the members take part, in order to create occasions to meet and design together. X=(T=E=N) creates pockets of physical and virtual space, where its members and nonmembers can meet. Perhaps the most ambitious project of X=(T=E=N) at the moment is to create an online platform, not a simple site, but a space for exchanging information and possibilities, where externals and internals have access to the group's projects and data. A real virtual and collaborative workspace, which offers equal opportunities to its members and nonmembers.

On the other hand, collectives like Assemble, Colectivo Warehouse, Collectif Etc, Lacol, and orizzontale have transformed the work space into a real social project, which offers not only an atelier space for the members of the collective but also for other people who can use the space or gather in it. The physical presence becomes, therefore, an integral part of this ongoing project, however always granting the freedom to some of the members to live elsewhere. The constant contact between the members is also assured through a series of weekly sessions or major occasions where all participants can design and brainstorm together.

From: Natalie Donat-Cattin
To: (ab)Normal, A-A Collective, Assemble, CNCRT, Colectivo Warehouse, Collectif Etc, constructLab, false mirror office, Fosbury Architecture, la–clique, Lacol, n'UNDO, orizzontale, X=(T=E=N)
Subject: How is your working space?

An illustration, a plan, a drawing,
a photograph, or a key element
of your working environment.

From: (ab)Normal
To: Natalie Donat-Cattin
Subject: How is your working space?

Living in different countries, our working space is basically absorbed by a WhatsApp group, a Dropbox folder, and the numerous Skype conversations that we have weekly.

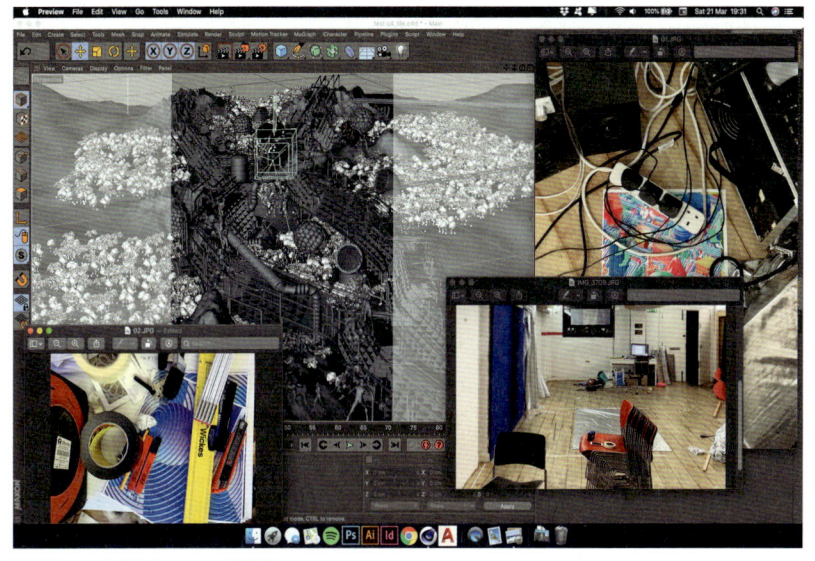

(ab)Normal, Workspace, 2020

From: A-A Collective
To: Natalie Donat-Cattin
Subject: How is your working space?

We can describe our office by showing Google Drive links, messenger chats, and easyJet tickets. We basically work on clouds. We have no main office space and no physical infrastructure. We operate virtually and move where it is needed. We are four partners located in three different countries and that gives us an enormous flexibility and a fair share of nomadic lifestyle.

Part of our practice's agenda is to question the organization of a conventional office and on certain levels probably this is also reflected in our works. (Goes without saying that we are big supporters of the European Union and the Schengen Agreement, which plays a big role in enabling our working method.)

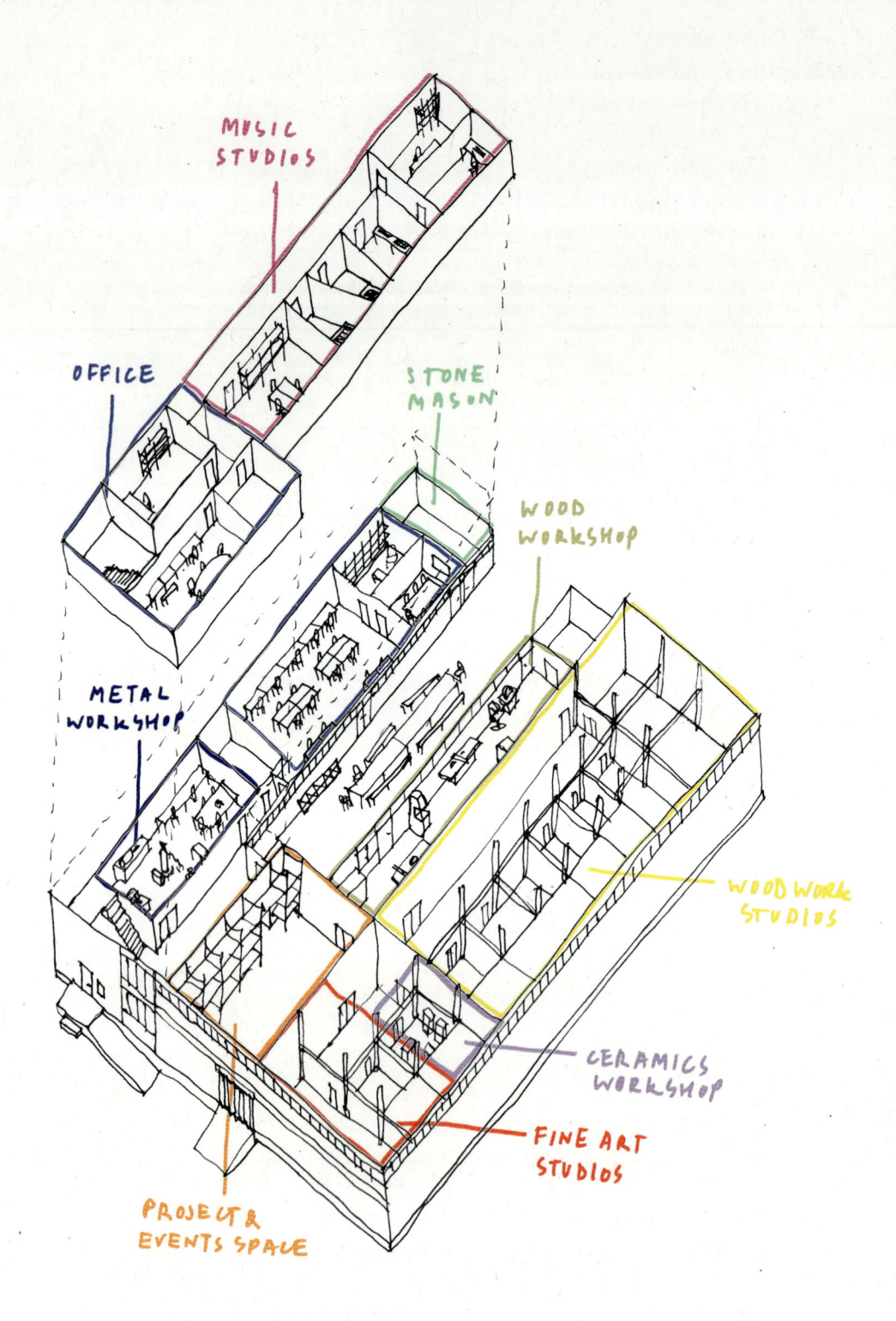

Assemble, Axo of Sugarhouse Studios, Bermondsey, 2017

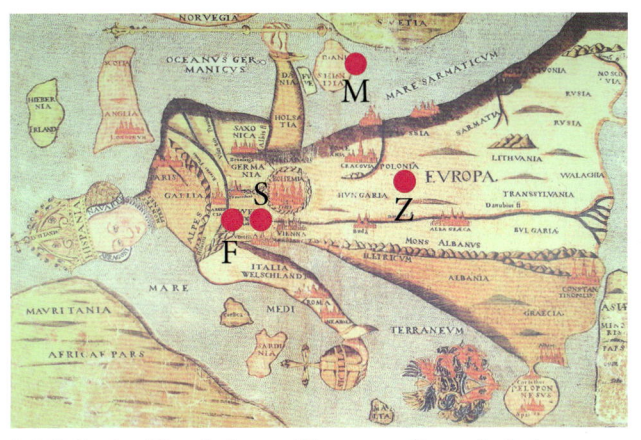

A-A Collective, Historical map of Europe as a Queen, including partners' locations and initials, 2020

From: Assemble
To: Natalie Donat-Cattin
Subject: How is your working space?

> Our studio is called Sugarhouse Studios and is in Bermondsey, South London. The idea is that Assemble shares space with a number of other makers and designers with whom we can work collaboratively on projects. The studio has a number of facilities, a wood workshop, large building space, hand tools, and a kiln, allowing us to build and test prototypes at 1:1 which also means we can be much more experimental in our design process.

From: CNCRT
To: Natalie Donat-Cattin
Subject: How is your working space?

> 2. UNIONIZE EVERYWHERE
> Working together (for us) is possible only virtually—Join the Meeting! Union still seems a utopia today, it is not a syndicate of architects, but it nevertheless happens everywhere. There is not a specific place (it doesn't exist). At home, in different cities, at the office, while taking a train, a bus, while running or walking in a park, while saying hi to a friend, while taking a plane, every moment becomes horribly possible for working and Skyping, WhatsApp-ing, and Slacking with one another.
> After all, without us and others like us working, the city, offices, schools, universities, and airports would have no sense. Right here life itself becomes a productive process. It is enough to have a laptop and an Internet connection to join others elsewhere.

Is this coercion, fun, masochism, or self-responsibility?! Perhaps, yet. Everywhere we move, travel, and change life, others like us are still there, doing the same thing and sharing the same story. Workers of the world... (need to) do something.

CNCRT, Unionize Everywhere, 2020

From: Colectivo Warehouse
To: Natalie Donat-Cattin
Subject: How is your working space?

Colectivo Warehouse, Ateliers da Penha, 2020

Ateliers de Penha is our house.
It is a coworking space to design and build.
It is a creative place we share with other residents.

From: Collectif Etc
To: Natalie Donat-Cattin
Subject: How is your working space?

> We have a couch, a stove, a generous kitchen place, green plants, and personal staff. We have opened our office to friends working in various fields like graphic design. It's like a comfortable home where we feel at ease. We alternately cook for each other in duo, and have some big shared meals for lunch. Our office is a tool for the neighborhood: we loan it to local associations, we organize free sewing lessons, screen-printing sessions, open cine-club, and parties. It's a living place. We have no hierarchy: we spend a lot of time to exchange, share our questions and doubts and be sure that everyone in the group is okay with our choices.

Collectif Etc, Our office in Marseille, with people at an event, 2018

From: constructLab
To: Natalie Donat-Cattin
Subject: How is your working space?

> constructLab does not share a workshop, they are rather a network of practitioners. Everyone has their own practice as a freelancer, the collective moments are the projects. It is all about the energy around the project, there is no real idea of belonging. There are people coming and going.
> They have an address in Berlin which is the address of one of them, Alex; there is also a workshop in Berlin. The people in Berlin manage the finance of the whole network, the website, and the Google Drive. However, they have several centers in other cities: Brussels, Montpellier (in the process of being created), Fribourg, and also a few people in Montréal.

Dylan Perrenaud, *Caillasses*, Geneva, 2020

From: false mirror office
To: Natalie Donat-Cattin
Subject: How is your working space?

Skeptical about traditionally structured architecture offices and well aware of the difficulties in starting a real business, we opted for developing our professional careers independently from false mirror; we even decided to define it as a project. Although we later rebranded ourselves as "office" after we won our first competition, the structure of it remained unchanged: as we still live separately, we also work completely remotely. Once in a while we meet for public presentations taking part in events, sometimes we manage to meet up while hitting the beach during our summer vacation, but we always reunite once a year for a Christmas party.

Being divided between Brussels, Florence, Genoa, Lausanne, and Milan, the location of our office does not correspond to any physical address. What we share is an "ideal" space, capable of collecting and synthesizing different approaches and inputs from each one of us. What appears from the outside as a clear identity is rather the result of the chaotic coexistence of five different minds and their respective obsessions. Our office is in fact a traveling suitcase filled with our clashing personalities, a joyful metaphor of the telework condition we have been relying on for several years. In this teatrino, slightly inspired by Barbie DreamCamper, it is possible to recognize our Wonder Woman—proudly standing next to a phallic totem, reminiscent of certain postmodern domestic objects; Tony Stark observes us sinisterly from the inside of a neotraditionalist *altana*; Milord is intent on the production of artificial dreams inside a colossal lipstick; James Bond, surrounded by mirror backdrops, deceives himself that the radical movement has never ended; finally the Hulk is well protected inside an inflatable structure reminding us that a "home is not a house."

false mirror office, Suitcase, 2020

From: Fosbury Architecture
To: Natalie Donat-Cattin
Subject: How is your working space?

Fosbury Architecture was initiated when more or less all the members were gravitating around the same architecture school in Milan. That was the initial informal gathering space as well as the stage for some of the early projects. With the award of the Europan competition a first working space was rented in Milan. The office changed several addresses: from via Pinturicchio, a basement in the courtyard of an early twentieth-century building, to via Cadibona—another basement, shared with other practices, large enough to host a workshop and several workstations, and finally via Pollaiuolo.
In the past years, some of the members have worked abroad,

whether in the Netherlands or Germany, renting spaces in coworking spaces or informally occupying the workstations of the offices with whom they were collaborating. Today all the members of the collective have resettled in Italy, just in time for the global pandemic.

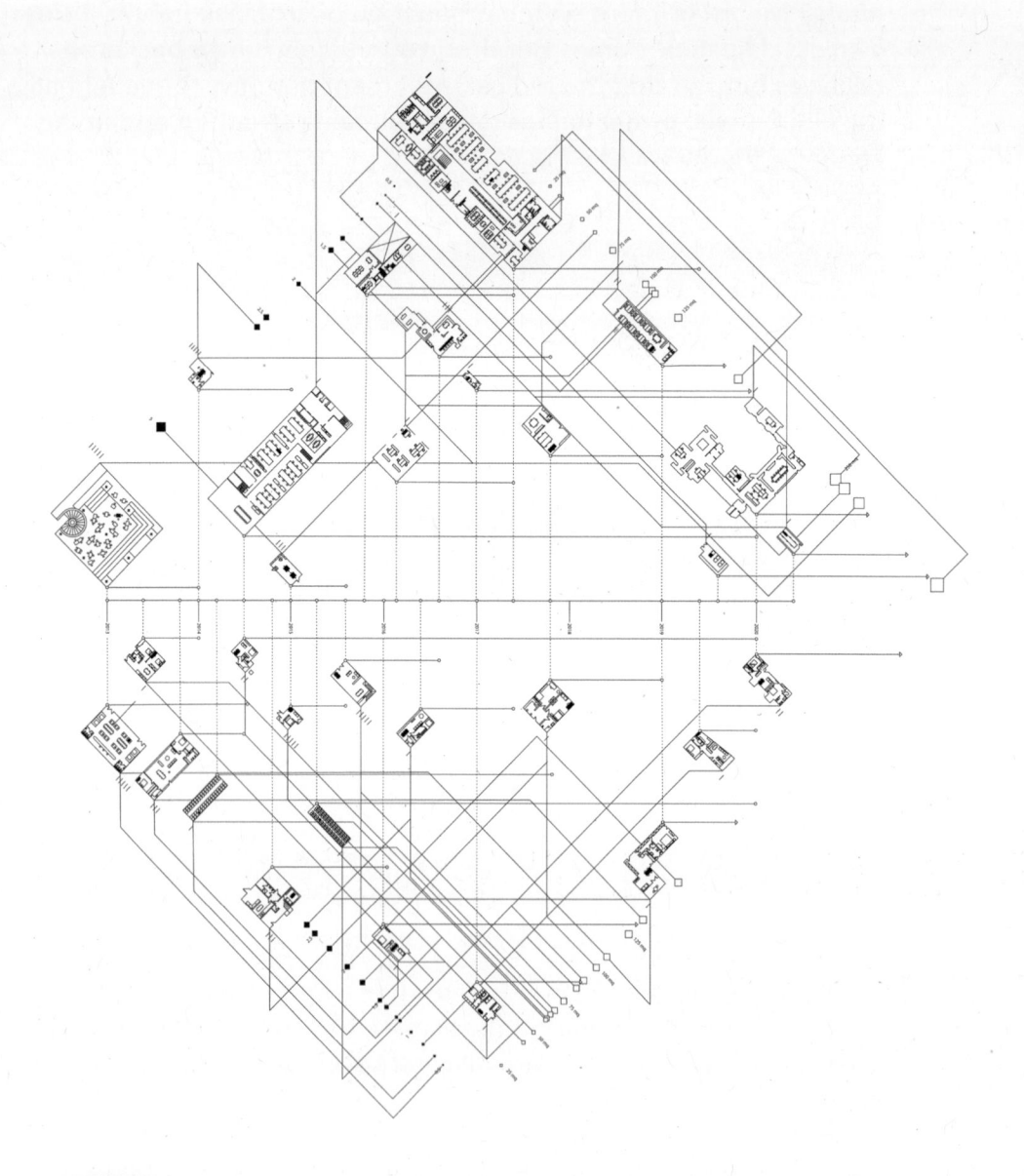

Fosbury Architecture, Working space, 2020

From: la–clique
To: Natalie Donat-Cattin
Subject: How is your working space?

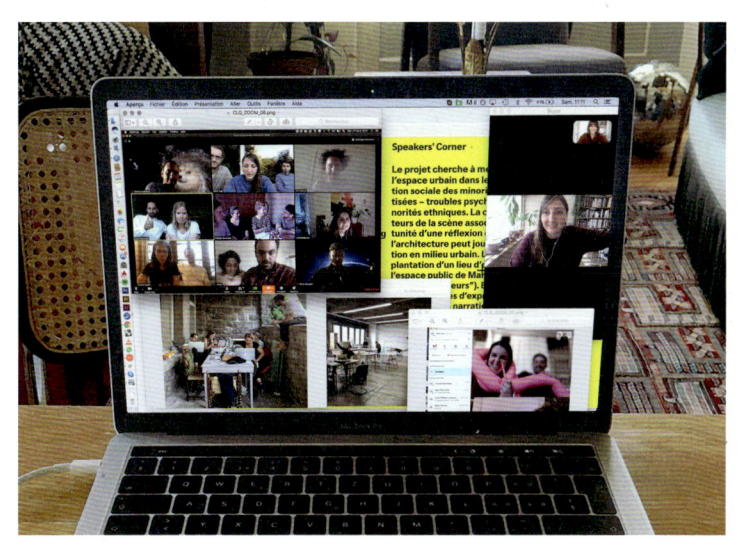

la–clique, F3 Mission control, 2020

From: Lacol
To: Natalie Donat-Cattin
Subject: How is your working space?

> We just moved to a new space, before the coronavirus. It is an old factory we refurbished and we share with eight other cooperatives. Each one has its own space, but we share meeting rooms and other services.

Lacol, Lacol offices in La Comunal, 2020

From: n'UNDO
To: Natalie Donat-Cattin
Subject: How is your working space?

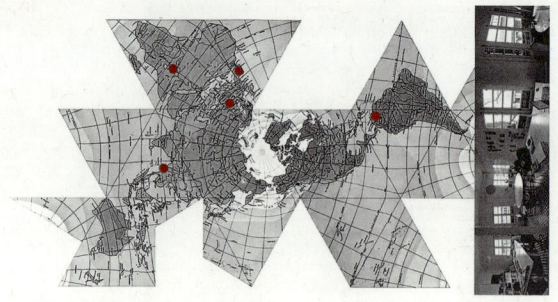

n'UNDO, Working space, 2020

From: orizzontale
To: Natalie Donat-Cattin
Subject: How is your working space?

Our work is developing in a hybrid form. We have both a physical space to work, meet, and develop design and prototypes as well as a network, since some of the members live in other cities and have other work. We have been forming alliances and collaborations with other associations and groups of people. We use various media to facilitate our workflow, since we are often in different places to develop and build projects on-site. The online work has been recently strongly pushed by the pandemic. Usually, we call or meet to have brainstorming sessions or to organize the calendar. We use Drive to share files and as our archive.

orizzontale, Inauguration of La Segheria, Rome, 2013

For us, physical presence is very important. Thus, we organize specific moments in which we are all together to discuss various aspects of the research, the objectives, how to change critical aspects… In this case our tools are the traditional low-tech papers, Post-its, pencils, books, just to name a few.

From: X=(T=E=N)
To: Natalie Donat-Cattin
Subject: How is your working space?

We embrace the uncertainty of working together without always being present in the same space. It means our exchanges are often coded through pieces of work, notations, and quick conversations. It forces us to be more precise with words and sketches. At best it has bred a culture of signifying, annotating, and a kind of Ezra Pound–like shorthand. We recently completed a monks' dormitory in a remote Himalayan valley. One of us was on-site with a good Internet connection, the rest were in Europe responding with drawings and mock-ups. We heard Himalayan rocks being chipped live in our studios. This experience changed something in us. All members in X=(T=E=N) may approach anyone and suggest collaboration, even outside of X=(T=E=N). It is up to these parties to arrange their rituals and workflows and workspaces. We have open studios in both Zurich and Belgrade, and a number of pop-up situations in other locations, mostly related to workshops. We think of ourselves as a record label, mostly because we never wanted to make an architectural office, solidified around the standard infrastructures and spaces that service the architecture industry. In this way, the spaces are interdependent laboratories for architecture.

Forestation is a drawing of spaces within a transforming landscape. It documents the ruins of a city reclaimed by the surrounding vegetation. The remaining pockets of spaces demonstrate temporary resistance, are organized around fragments of form and order, and offer a type of refuge. The drawing was produced in a week-long workshop as a part of our Re:public series, an ongoing program of teaching and drawing research. This was the second in a series of workshops calling for a renewal in the way we regard the city. Re:public references the original description Res Publica—that which belongs to the people, the public realm, the common ground. We see drawing as part of a common language with which architects might better speak to the world at large. To draw things selectively and carefully is an antidote to the illusion of omniscience that GIS+BIM-based mapping promises, as well as the overwhelming volume of information such mapping involves. In the act of drawing, one is forced to make conscious choices about what to show and which methods and means to use. The architectural demand is, of course, that one aims to reveal rather than obscure.

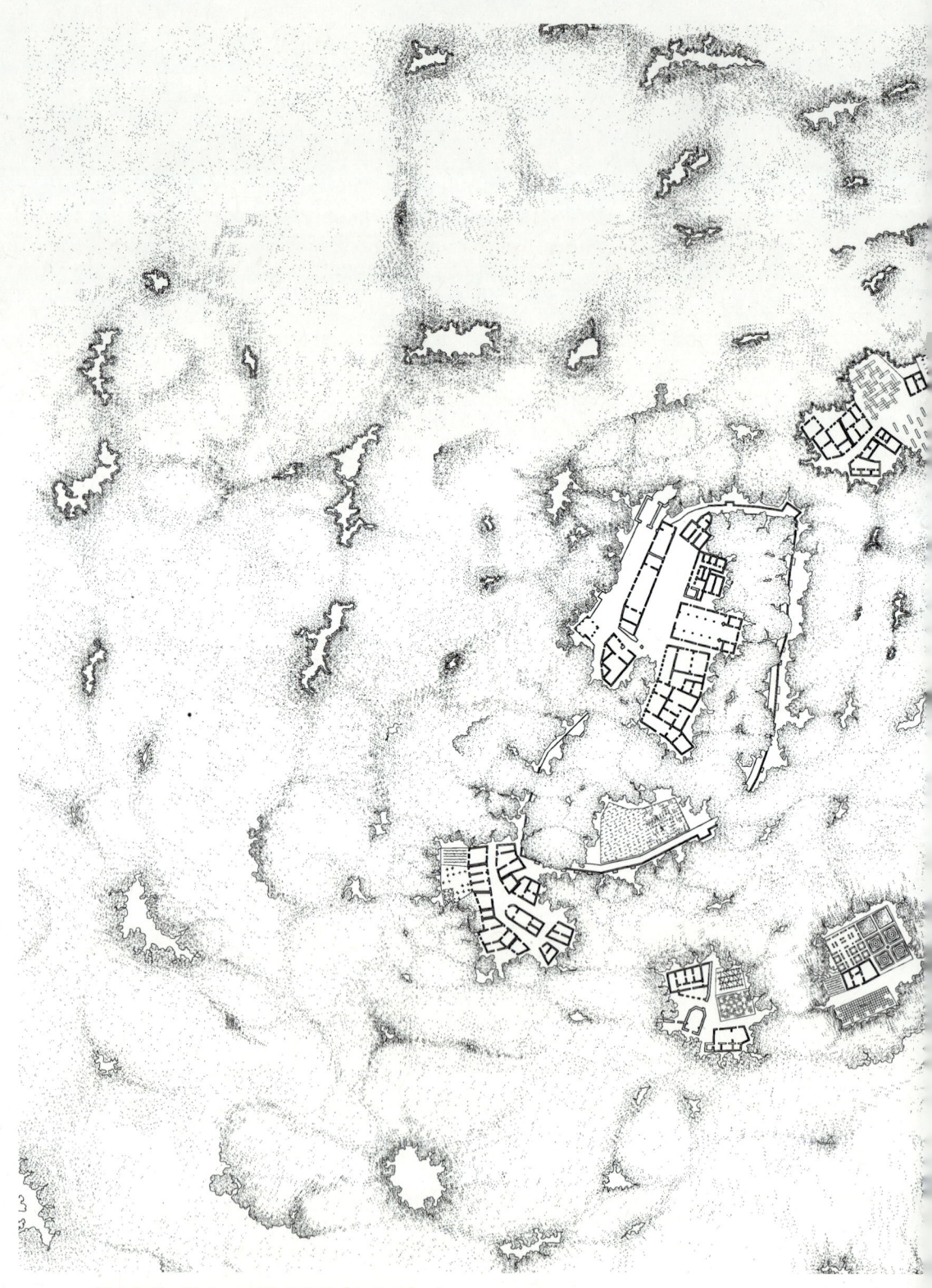

Maksimilian Tasler and Karlo Seitz (students),
Forestation, X=(T=E=N) Re:public Summer School Motovan, 2015

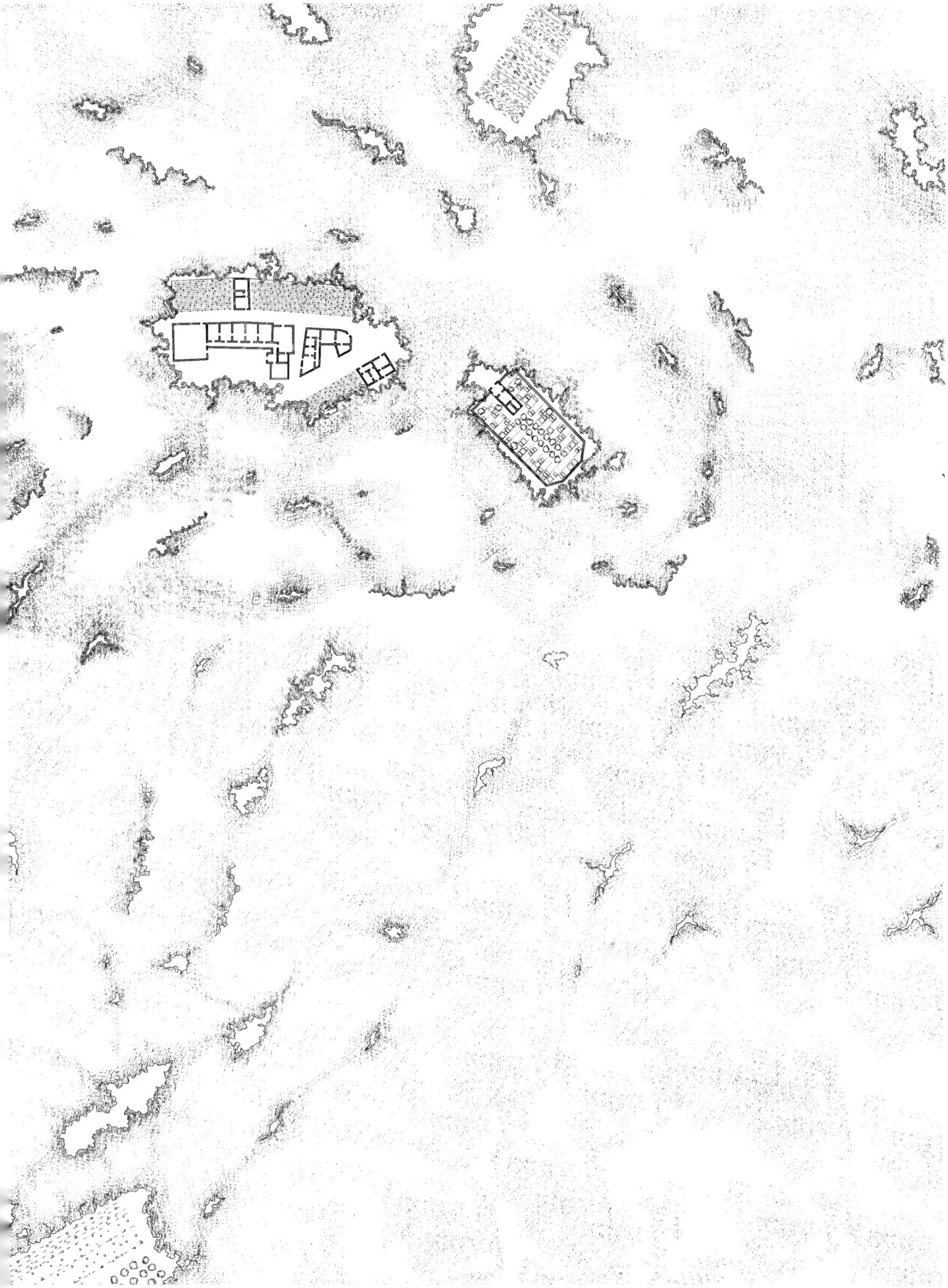

5. ORGANIZATION
Horizontality

Compared to the traditional model based on an office composed of one or more partners, with a variable number of employees, which is usually organized around a pyramidal work structure, the model of the collective is extremely heterogeneous and characterized by a total or almost total horizontality. Given the recent birth of this type of structure in the architectural environment, there is no typical collective structure, and each reality is unique in its kind. However, what many of these forms have in common is an in-depth and self-referential study of how this horizontal structure can work and how it can be transformed into an efficient entity, always respecting the freedoms and rights of its members.

This social environment intensifies human relations, triggering a necessary reflection on the dynamics, which makes possible the development of the collective. These new formats promote personal creativity above the dependence on collective identity, at the same time favoring it. This leads to considering the formation of the collective itself and its research as something expanded. The whole system is based on trust and valorizes the individual and collective intelligence. These diverse ecosystems become especially attractive to individuals who feel locked in what is the traditional way of working. The counterpoint is that, as these forms are not yet fully developed, often a series of negative aspects are added to the benefits. A collective requires an incredible amount of energy and resources, which also demands a high level of investment from its members. The organizational issues, in some cases, become the negative factor preventing a collective from escaping the hierarchy. It is in fact necessary to take time every week or every month to talk all together in order to verify projects and aims: in sessions, not only about design but also psychological, architecture is discussed alongside the general well-being of the entity. The collective can cause discomfort to the individual, such as spending too much time together. It is therefore necessary to find solutions to safeguard personal space, which risks succumbing under the weight and pressure of the group.

Sometimes the work organization is completely horizontal, where everyone is always involved in each project, or at least when the main decisions are taken—Collectif Etc—or in the early phases of it—Fosbury Architecture. In other cases, the members work individually—(ab)Normal—or in small groups of two or three—Assemble, CNCRT, Lacol. In others still, these internal groups mix with external groups—X=(T=E=N), A-A Collective—which bring new knowledge and expertise to the collective. The extreme case is when various collectives unite in collectives of collectives to work together on a project—orizzontale, Collectif Etc, constructLab, false mirror office. On the other hand, projects are often structured according to a temporary hierarchy, which continuously changes from project to project.

As these types of organizations are complex and mutable, it is difficult to insert each collective in a precise organizational box. Even if some are more structured than others, they all denote horizontal, flat, swinging, rhythmic, or rhizomic undulations, not so different from the Paul Klee diagrams used by n'UNDO.

From: Natalie Donat-Cattin
To: (ab)Normal, A-A Collective, Assemble, CNCRT, Colectivo Warehouse, Collectif Etc, constructLab, false mirror office, Fosbury Architecture, la–clique, Lacol, n'UNDO, orizzontale, X=(T=E=N)
Subject: How is your collective structured?

A diagram showing the structure, interaction, and organization— within it and in between participants, but maybe also in the larger network. Are there other people or institutions involved?

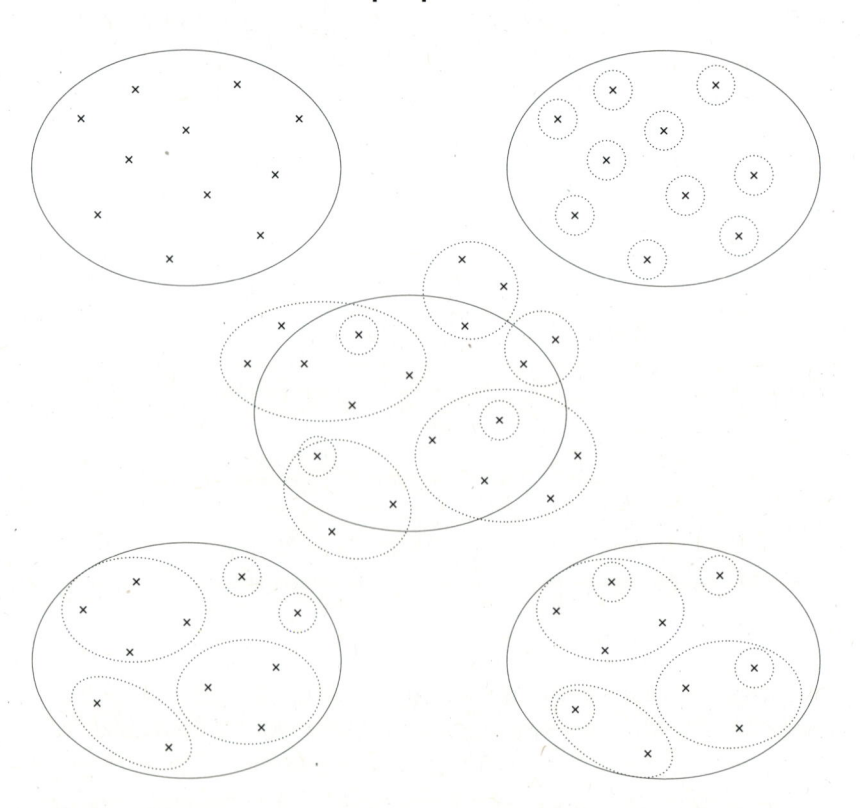

Natalie Donat-Cattin, Graphics of different collective organizations, 2021

140

From: (ab)Normal
To: Natalie Donat-Cattin
Subject: How is your collective structured?

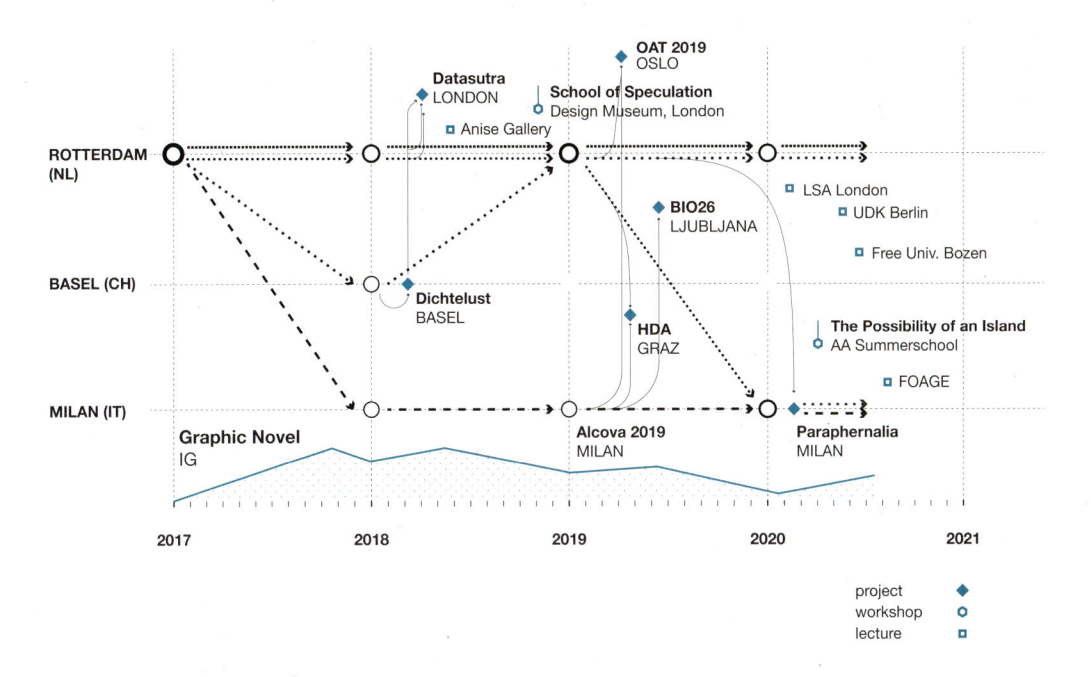

(ab)Normal, Collective flows, 2020

> The four of us share the same background but are currently situated in different cities, often changing location during the years. At the moment, Luigi and Mattia are in Milan, Marcello and Davide in Rotterdam. Although there is no particular structure, generally one of us follows with particular attention a certain project, but the effort is always choral.

From: A-A Collective
To: Natalie Donat-Cattin
Subject: How is your collective structured?

> The structure of our collective is very simple. We are four partners with no vertical hierarchy. This means that we take all decisions in a democratic way. At the very beginning we were even all involved equally in every project at the same time, but slowly this had to evolve in order to be able to deal with the multiple projects that we

have to take care of. Now we divide the workload more systematically and when it is needed we have someone of us who acts as the "responsible one" (project leader still sounds too corporate for us). It still remains fundamental to have periodical meetings where we show each other our work, ask opinions, take decisions together.

We also love to collaborate with external people who bring to the table new knowledge and ideas. Landscape architects, artists, urbanists, and anthropologists are all figures who enhance our vision of the reality where we want to intervene. Cooperation with other young practices of our generation not only helps us on a specific project but actually makes it possible to compare ourselves to other similar situations and share common problems and solutions.

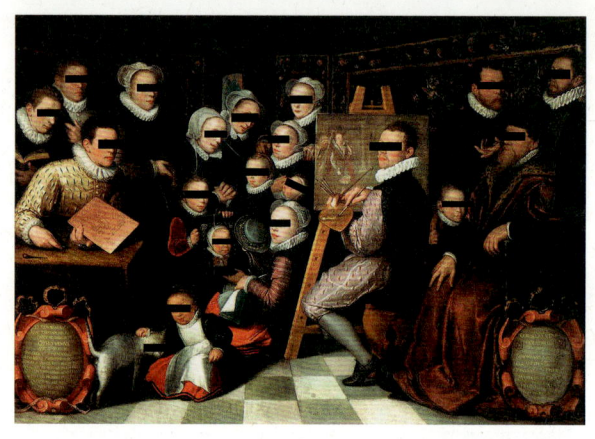

A-A Collective, Collage of collaborators, 2020. Original image by Otto van Veen, *The Artist Painting, Surrounded by his Family*, ca. 1584, Louvre Museum

From: Assemble
To: Natalie Donat-Cattin
Subject: How is your collective structured?

Assemble is organized without hierarchy between a number of founding members. We then have two studio managers and five junior designers who have been with the practice for the last year or so.

The ambition is that they can all become members of the collective over time. The studio environment is very collaborative, however, and we try to create as many opportunities for our younger staff members as possible—having employees has become a necessity, but one that potentially contradicts some of the aspirations behind the practice.

Assemble, Group portrait on the timber frame of Yardhouse, 2014

From: CNCRT
To: Natalie Donat-Cattin
Subject: How is your collective structured?

3. COOPERATION IS...
Cooperation is what structures our productive process. Cooperation is all of us working together, sometimes mixing up, sometimes just 3, sometimes 2, sometimes 1 that wishes 10 or 100,000. (Some of us have never met, while others can always still join, externals, collectives, friends.) Cooperation is also what Capital needs to reproduce itself. Cooperation is the employer orchestrating a team of auto-CADists in his Trump-like office. Everything but an orchestra. Cooperation is Competition. Cooperation starts in the Office. Cooperation is a huge generic room of depressed and anxious, precarious people, sometimes in silence, sometimes laughing, sometimes dining together, still for the necessity of the office. Outside the office, Cooperation is all of us wanting to give a name to what we want to do but still contradict each other.

Contradiction is Cooperation. Sometimes Cooperation confuses with Union, but Union is not office-Cooperation. A new form of Cooperation is what we experiment with. An alternative to the office-Cooperation-labor, no Bosses. Our Cooperation is still invisible. Cooperation is what makes this possible.

CNCRT, Cooperation is…, 2020

From: Colectivo Warehouse
To: **Natalie Donat-Cattin**
Subject: How is your collective structured?

> We are about to start with a new cooperative organization. A platform of multidisciplinary people who want to share knowledge, skills, resources, projects, proposals, visions.

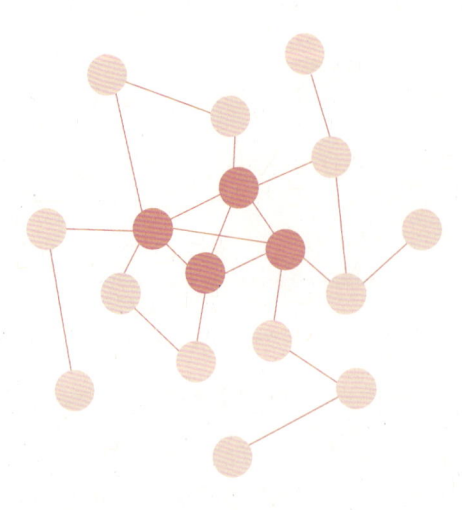

Colectivo Warehouse, Organization, 2020

From: Collectif Etc
To: Natalie Donat-Cattin
Subject: How is your collective structured?

We're now six people. We're very close to each other, and we're bonded with a strong friendship that goes far beyond "working" and "colleagues"—maybe too much sometimes. We make all decisions together, even if there are always duos or trios leading projects. We share all the money we get and we try to be as many as possible when building workshops sessions are involved. We're so close we are trying to buy an abandoned building in the countryside together with our girlfriends, boyfriends, children, and friends! We want to relocate our collectif to a rural area—as we think there are so many interesting things to do there to change our way of life.

Collectif Etc, Open and improvised construction workshop, Val-de-Briey, 2019

We have no experts in our team. We try, learn—and fail—all the time. We have various roles: one day we're welding a structure at our workshop in Marseille, the other we are editing a fanzine, screen-printing a poster in northern France, cutting wood in Italy, having a shared meal with volunteers in a rural area. We go from setting up projects with partners to deal with really basic needs in workshops, like preparing meals and waste management. We have really long but thrilling drives across France and sometimes Europe: we're exchanging, in our truck loaded with tools, what worked and what didn't on the projects and dream of possible futures we hope for ourselves and for society in general.

From: constructLab
To: Natalie Donat-Cattin
Subject: How is your collective structured?

constructLab is very dynamic. During the project on-site, there is a form of hierarchy, linked to the level of responsibility. Not everyone has the responsibility of the project or the experience, either. This creates a certain dynamic. However, this method is questionable and our goal is to understand these interactions. It is not necessarily about horizontality, it is about maintaining transparency and critical thinking. Once a project is developed, a small group will have all the responsibilities and it is always more complicated to flatten hierarchies. Each project brings in new ingredients to develop, it is about human relations. Beyond the practice, there are the human relations, which are not born from a pyramid structure. Behind a collective project, we hide these human relationships, which are sometimes conflicting and generally complex.

Alex Lambert and constructLab, Yearly meeting at Unlearning Center, Fribourg, 2019

From: false mirror office
To: Natalie Donat-Cattin
Subject: How is your collective structured?

As any horizontally structured collective managed via remote meetings and composed of "divas," our office organization is easily comparable to something in between a battle and an orgy, that is, an anarchist organization where tasks are not well defined and where there is continuous overlapping, without a fixed and rigid hierarchical structure, inevitably oscillating between moments of strong conflict and others of desperate love.

false mirror office, Ashtray, 2020

We tried to establish a work method by splitting each time our research topics into five subthemes; each component of the group then develops a part of it personally, collecting them in digital research catalogues we call Quadernetti. If this additive research method has created a sort of harmony during our Monday eve's Skype meetings, when it comes to the design phase, we always dedicate way more time discussing rather than taking decisions over our projects. We often dedicate a great amount of time debating on the theme and scope of our work, relying on an unwarranted capacity of producing quality material in the last stretch. We formerly defined this as an antiprofessional approach: instead of specializing in different research areas, we confront continuously to enrich our shared knowledge on various topics. This aspect is translated in the collaborations that we have with external actors: whether we team up with our beloved Genovan colleagues for a competition or we build a temporary team in workshops, we end up spreading our condition to larger and larger audiences. Last year we applied this approach in a temporary collaboration with two firms in Trondheim, resulting in an international architecture party.

From: **Fosbury Architecture**
To: **Natalie Donat-Cattin**
Subject: **How is your collective structured?**

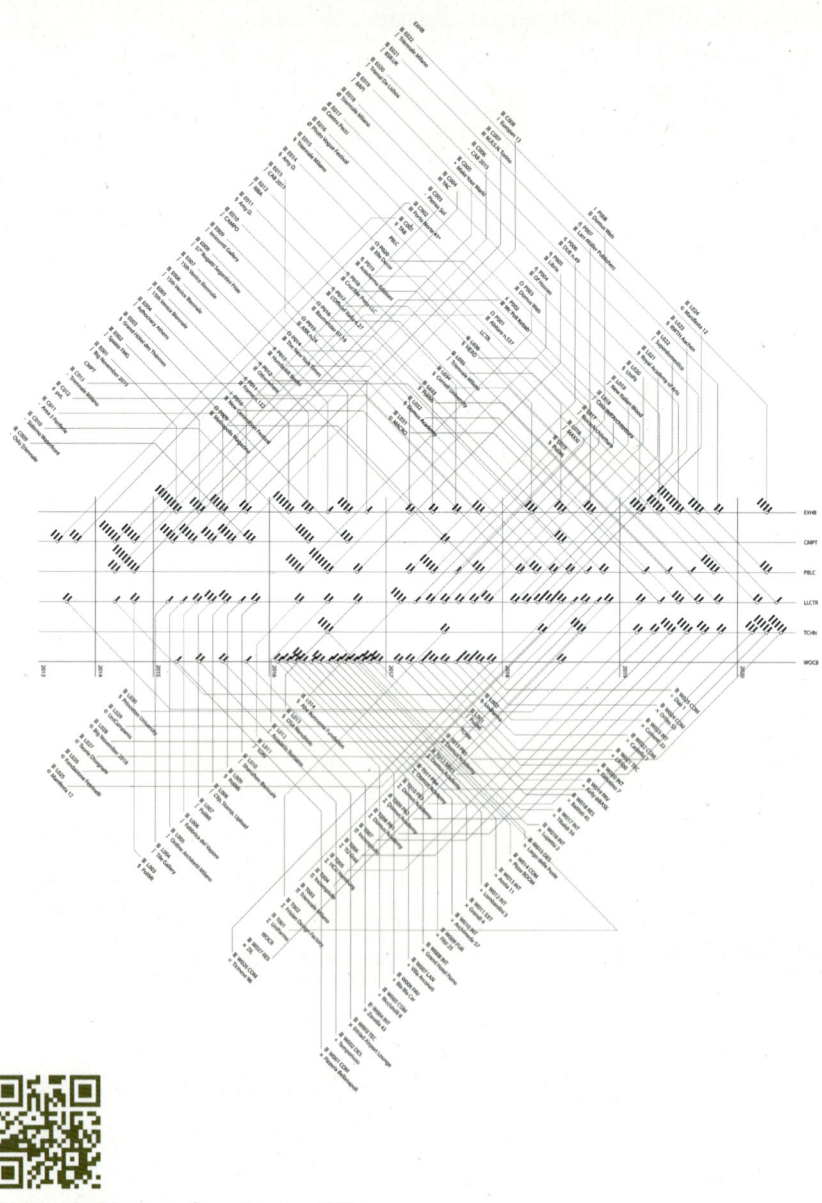

Fosbury Architecture, Organization, 2020

Over time the typology of endeavors undertaken by Fosbury Architecture has changed substantially. If in the early stages spontaneous research, architectural competitions, and drawings were the main activities, in time the spectrum has enlarged to include new architectures, interiors, labyrinths, follies, installations, exhibition setups, and curation together with writing and editing texts and finally teaching. The work is usually initiated collectively, yet normally each member undertakes those tasks that resonate with him the best in a sort of elective affinity.

From: la–clique
To: Natalie Donat-Cattin
Subject: How is your collective structured?

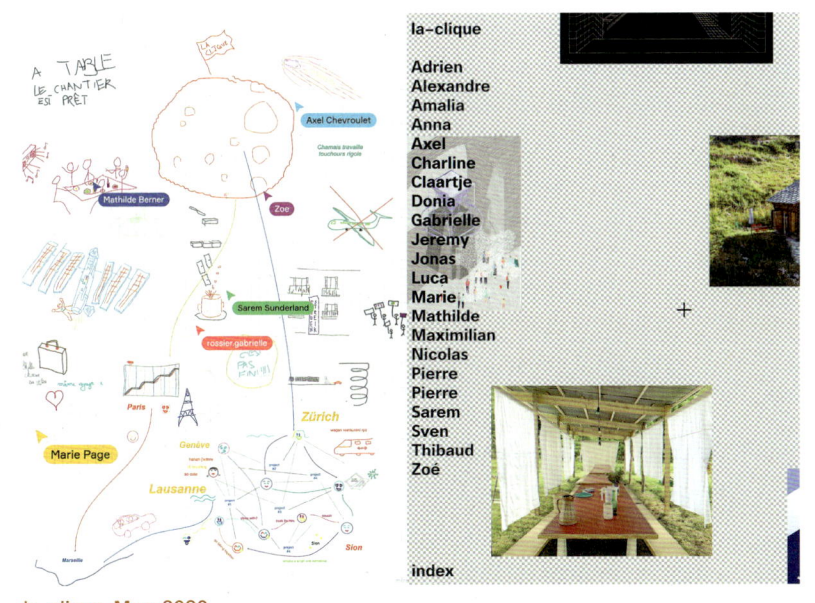

la–clique, Map, 2020

From: Lacol
To: Natalie Donat-Cattin
Subject: How is your collective structured?

It is completely horizontal.

Lacol, People, 2018

From: n'UNDO
To: Natalie Donat-Cattin
Subject: How is your collective structured?

> We refer to it as a hardcore with satellites orbiting and interacting in many ways, going in and out, joining n'UNDO's projects or proposing new ones for n'UNDO to develop. It can also be seen as an onion with many different layers than can be sliced in different ways. These Paul Klee diagrams illustrate the structure.

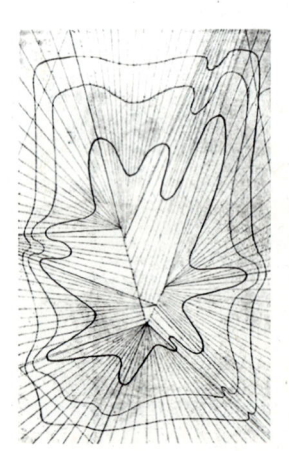

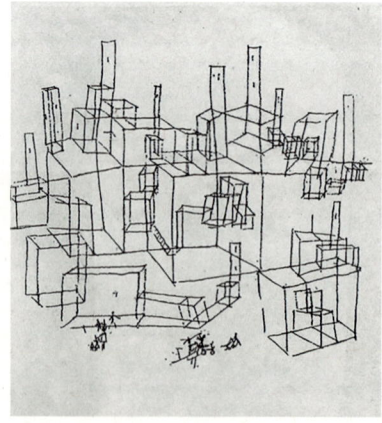

Paul Klee, *Figuration example for an exercise set on Tuesday, 30 October 1923*, 1923, and Paul Klee, *Town with Watchtowers*, 1929

From: orizzontale
To: Natalie Donat-Cattin
Subject: How is your collective structured?

orizzontale collective has 7 founding members: Jacopo Ammendola, Juan Lopez Cano, Giuseppe Grant, Margherita Manfra, Nasrin Mohiti Asli, Roberto Pantaleoni and Stefano Ragazzo.
Four of us mostly work on orizzontale. We have a space located in Rome, Pigneto neighborhood. It's called La Segheria, it's a coworking space that we built together with a group of people in 2012. Here we have an area for office tasks and a space to store our building tools and materials. Three members live and work in other cities and participate in some branches of orizzontale's research and in specific projects.

Since a couple of years, we started to host scholarship recipients. We are used to working in one/two people to manage the projects. Each one of us works on specific general tasks, like archive, media management, administration… We have one weekly meeting for discussions and decision-making, having brainstorming sessions, and organizing the calendar and the projects.

orizzontale, Fuoriporta, Orte, 2021

From: X=(T=E=N)
To: Natalie Donat-Cattin
Subject: How is your collective structured?

Most of us at X=(T=E=N) met during our studies at the ETH, where we later researched and taught for various design departments. In the tradition of the school, these departments establish very distinct positions, and are embedded in an institutional habitus that serves to solidify and canonize such positions. We became aware that a lot of design effort was directed at defending such distinct positions. At the same time we were witnessing a radical change in the way of producing architecture, the way of collaborating on its production and the scope of work and challenges it was directed toward. Outside the school, emerging forms of critical design, applied research, and multidisciplinary practice were reinvigorating a new generation of architects, urban thinkers, and actors. This demanded a rethink of architecture from its first principles and a reorganization of how and who were involved in its making. X=(T=E=N) was established as an open platform to respond to this. Right now X=(T=E=N) is comprised of two entities, a design studio and a design research institute. These two entities strive to fulfill the shared values of X=(T=E=N), to produce work openly and collaboratively, and to make meaningful contributions to the built environment and the social imagination that defines it.

Astro has been extracted from an experimental animation that suggests, rather than describes, the iterations between two moving systems. Both these systems move according to their own internal logic. The larger of the systems circulates on a deliberate consistent path, while the smaller veers more erratically, and beyond the borders of a defined field. Despite the differences, the centers of each system are fixed by a line, along which a point traverses between the two radii. The regular emission from the point creates a seemingly random line that scribes the zone between the systems. We understand this line as a running documentation of the output from the dialogue between the two systems. These are conducted primarily within a field of recognizable and shared values depicted by the broken circle line. At times they also range beyond these set limits, whereby the perimeter of the field expands slightly, adjusting to the new dynamic.

X=(T=E=N), Organigramm, 2021

6. DEVELOPMENT
Fluidity and the Necessity to Morph

It is not always possible to maintain the initial structure of the collective, often linked to a fortuitous beginning. Many collectives are faced with having to continually question their structure and their way of working and this, for some, becomes almost a project in itself. Indeed, this process of change is in most cases still ongoing. Perhaps this is the most interesting side of a collective: its fluid aspect and the unwillingness to fix itself in a form. This is partly a choice, partly a condition: indeed the members often have other jobs either in an office or at a university. "In present times, when each one is carrying out a parallel career in academia, education, or as a practitioner, it has somehow retrieved the initial spirit, benefitting from the different acquired knowledge of the members in different domains," says Fosbury Architecture.

In other cases, the members are fully invested in the collective but they are registered as freelancers. Sometimes, these freelancers are forced to legally bond to carry out a project. And these circumstances can change anytime, becoming more or less permanent.

The collectives with more fixed forms, often brought about by the consolidation of their practice or by legal needs required by a project, are legal partnerships (Assemble), associations (n'UNDO), cooperatives (Lacol), or registered offices (A-A Collective).

Furthermore, some collectives are still formed by the initial core, in others people come and go: it is the very entity of the collective and its objectives that remain. However, for many, the question of bringing in new people is problematic. When the group has already been consolidated for years it becomes difficult to allow new people in at the same level of the founders, and at the same time hiring them risks compromising the horizontality and verticality of the collective itself. Some collectives make use of a transition period, others change into offices with employees. When a collective starts structuring itself, it becomes difficult to maintain the spontaneity of its beginning; for this reason some groups prefer to work as a network, meet during the project and then continue on their own path until the next opportunity. For some, the collective remains a moment in life, an experiment, something that might not last forever and that might continue to change. Perhaps this is the greatest ambition and difficulty faced by a collective.

From: Natalie Donat-Cattin
To: (ab)Normal, A-A Collective, Assemble, CNCRT, Colectivo Warehouse, Collectif Etc, constructLab, false mirror office, Fosbury Architecture, la–clique, Lacol, n'UNDO, orizzontale, X=(T=E=N)
Subject: How has your collective changed since its foundation?

>A diagram showing the structure, interaction, and organization—within it and in between participants, but maybe also in the larger network. Are there other people or institutions involved?

From: (ab)Normal
To: Natalie Donat-Cattin
Subject: How has your collective changed since its foundation?

>Originally (ab)Normal started as a Instagram-driven project, a graphic novel without chronology. Each image we published was accompanied by a short text, an extract of a possible novel taken out of its context and plot. On the occasion of our first exhibitions, at Anise Gallery in London and at S AM in Basel, we opened up our focus beyond social media platforms, getting involved more and more in installations and design.

(ab)Normal, *Paraphernalia*, Triennale, Milan, 2019

From: A-A Collective
To: Natalie Donat-Cattin
Subject: How has your collective changed since its foundation?

>We officially founded our practice two years ago. In architecture this is a microscopic amount of time, nevertheless we had to continuously change in this period in order to be able to react always

to new problems. It is similar to an evolution process of a biological creature that slowly mutates to fit better in the world it lives in. Without any doubt, for a young practice the biggest shift comes when you get a commission, and in our case it was the competition we won for the Central Square in Warsaw.

A-A Collective, Physical gathering of the collective for the inauguration of An Arch for Sønderjylland, Kolding, 2021

It was a critical moment because from a status of relative naiveness we were faced with the complexity of the building process with an institutional client. As was mentioned before, we had to organize ourselves in a more efficient manner, but the beautiful part of this process was understanding that all this effort we put to work better and faster was actually functional to regaining our original naiveness.

Now we are more aware of the importance of the spirit that we had at the very beginning that was letting us taking risks and keeping all possibilities wide open.

From: Assemble
To: **Natalie Donat-Cattin**
Subject: How has your collective changed since its foundation?

We have all stayed basically the same! A few people have moved in and out and we have some younger members, but in general it is the same group of people: When we first formed we organized as a Community Interest Company (CIC) which is a type of organization that allows groups to do work for a social good without the restrictions of being a charity. As we have completed more work and our ambitions have changed, we have formed a partnership.

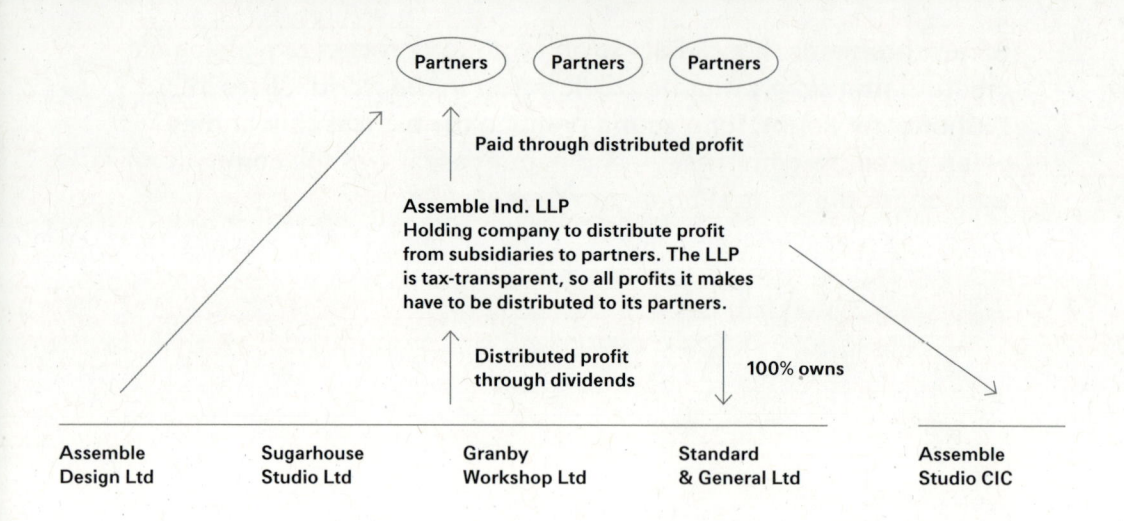

```
                    Partners    Partners    Partners
                       ↑
                 Paid through distributed profit
                 Assemble Ind. LLP
                 Holding company to distribute profit
                 from subsidiaries to partners. The LLP
                 is tax-transparent, so all profits it makes
                 have to be distributed to its partners.

                    ↑                    ↓
              Distributed profit      100% owns
              through dividends

Assemble      Sugarhouse    Granby          Standard        Assemble
Design Ltd    Studio Ltd    Workshop Ltd    & General Ltd   Studio CIC
```

Assemble, Assemble Industries LLP, undated

From: CNCRT
To: Natalie Donat-Cattin
Subject: How has your collective changed since its foundation?

4. STRUGGLE FOR PLEASURE
If work absorbs pure life and vice versa, when will we have to enjoy some moments of pleasure and otium? When will we finally have to do nothing? Once upon a time, bars, restaurants, cinemas, piazzas, terraces were meant for fun, for pleasure and smileys; today they advertise multitasking and long-stay working.

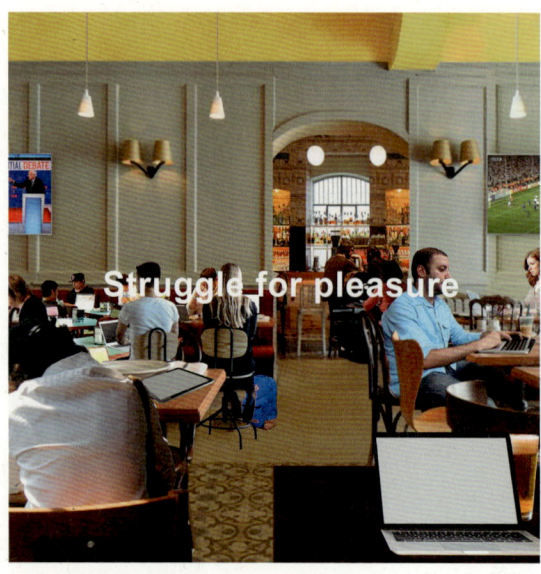

CNCRT, Struggle for Pleasure, 2020

This tautology becomes so banal and horribly cannibal as we think of the shame of an unemployed boy, girl or the discomfort of some young lovers having a drink in a bar full of laptop users. For those of us still emerged in academic life in bars you find crowds of students, freelancers, and new potential collectives. For many of us office workers, after working hours otium is still possible (some call it happy hour); others take public transport and go straight home. Struggling for pleasure means transforming work and the productive process from mere task-obligation to a higher level, closer to art and joyful as creative poetry.

From: Colectivo Warehouse
To: **Natalie Donat-Cattin**
Subject: How has your collective changed since its foundation?

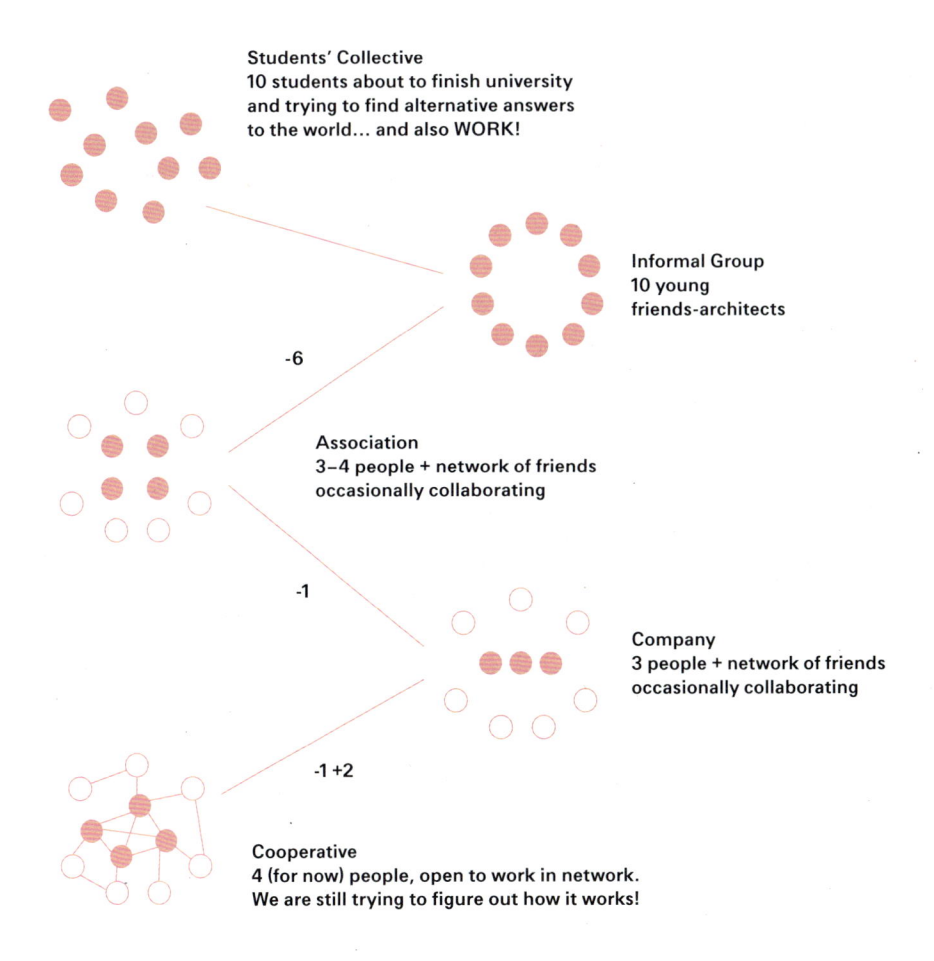

Students' Collective
10 students about to finish university and trying to find alternative answers to the world… and also WORK!

Informal Group
10 young
friends-architects

-6

Association
3–4 people + network of friends occasionally collaborating

-1

Company
3 people + network of friends occasionally collaborating

-1 +2

Cooperative
4 (for now) people, open to work in network. We are still trying to figure out how it works!

Colectivo Warehouse, Development, 2020

From: **Collectif Etc**
To: **Natalie Donat-Cattin**
Subject: How has your collective changed since its foundation?

Our group has changed. People are leaving, some are coming. As we said, we're all friends before being colleagues, and that is how the group evolved. What we have in common is a strong belief that things are not going in a good direction, politicians are lying, the economy is devastating our environment, finance and private interests are destroying solidarities. And we shared a need to build alternative ways of producing architecture—easier said than done!

We thought that public authorities would care more about democratic and ecological issues in city planning, especially by building strong barriers to private profit and thus opening ethical fields for architects. But it turned out that interesting architectural initiatives and projects are more led by civic society than our corrupted and cowardly politicians! We wish for the times to come to meet these motivated citizens who both want to fight against contemporary abuses and build convincing answers on democratic and ecological architectural issues. We have to invent new places and territorial synergies for people to gather, organize themselves, and support sustainable ways of life!

Collectif Etc, "Notre seule patrie, l'enfance," 2020

From: constructLab
To: Natalie Donat-Cattin
Subject: How has your collective changed since its foundation?

Dylan Perrenaud, *Caillasses*, Geneva, 2020

constructLab is a group with a variable geometry. Each one has his/her own role and interests. There are also several generations within the network. We like to preserve its fluid entity. We tell a story, but there is not a real reality. There are several realities and a continuous flow. For this reason the way we present our work is not under the form of a manifesto but as a hymn. The idea was to write a melody. We did not want to describe a practice.

From: false mirror office
To: Natalie Donat-Cattin
Subject: How has your collective changed since its foundation?

Our group has evolved slowly and without great shakes. The fact of being organized in a "collective" form—we always have some problem using this word—made even easier the switch from the initial conformation of six members to the current five. Today, at the exact moment we are asked this question, our development can be described as an uninterrupted journey with a circular trajectory. Recently we seem to be back on those university desks where our shared experience started five years ago.

Our story begins, in fact, in Genoa in 2015 when, as recent graduates of the Polytechnic School and former students of Professor Giovanni Galli, we participated and won the Europan 13 competition in Trondheim. Although, initially, the purpose of false mirror office was only to collaborate in the development of the project that had just been awarded, the long and exhausting wait before getting a real assignment convinced us to develop together more and more projects and activities that were disparate but which were tackled from an aspect that was crucial for us: the preeminence of theory over practice.

false mirror office, Souvenir Ball, 2020

These activities include projects of different types, from competitions in collaboration with other Genoese firms—such as the former office 5+1AA or four young groups, Gosplan, LINEARAMA, Pia, UNO8A—to small artifacts, including pieces of furniture and installations, to tutoring in international workshops and lecturing in different European countries.

In 2018 we finally managed to get our first assignment: the beginning of a series of projects on the future of Nyhavna (the port of Trondheim), which kept us busy until last year. In the last few months, however, our passion for studying and teaching has led us to dedicate [ourselves] to research and writings that contribute, in a new way, to nourish our vision of designing.

From: **Fosbury Architecture**
To: **Natalie Donat-Cattin**
Subject: How has your collective changed since its foundation?

> In the early stages Fosbury Architecture was a platform to realize together those projects that no one would ever be able to carry on alone, and a place to experiment beyond the limitations of a traditional working environment, especially during the economic crisis. Eventually it became a proper office absorbing the entire working day of some of the members. In present times, when each one is carrying out a parallel career in academia, education, or as a practitioner, it has somehow retrieved the initial spirit, benefitting from the different acquired knowledge of the members in different domains.

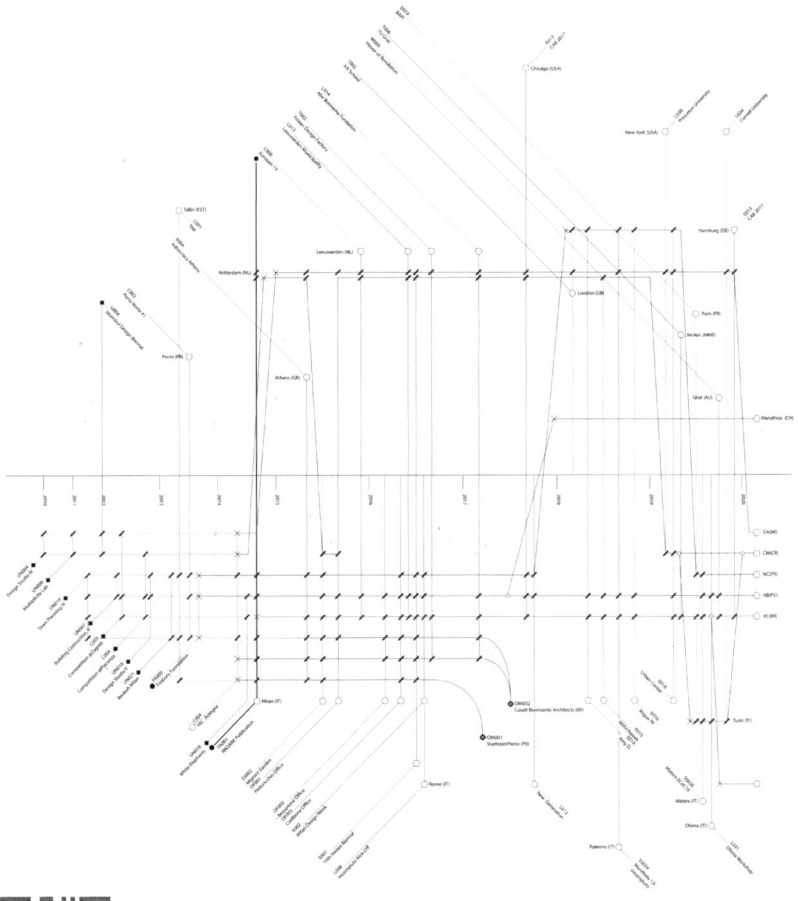

Fosbury Architecture, Development, 2020

From: la–clique
To: Natalie Donat-Cattin
Subject: How has your collective changed since its foundation?

[17:11] her:
time, places and people constantly redefine la–clique

[17:12] he:
I was looking for things that would have changed in this last year; and it seems that much hasn't changed actually. We still have the same optimism, energy, enthusiasm.

[17:12] her:
change is a caracteristic of la–clique

[17:12] he:
and of course what doesn't change
[17:13] he:
Haha quite nice how our two contradictory messages interweave

[17:14] her:
i was thinking exactly the same
[17:15] her:
this make words really pointless
[17:16] her:
actions have much more significations
[17:18] her:
we have to always remind ourself to do rather than to talk too much.

[17:18] he:
Amen

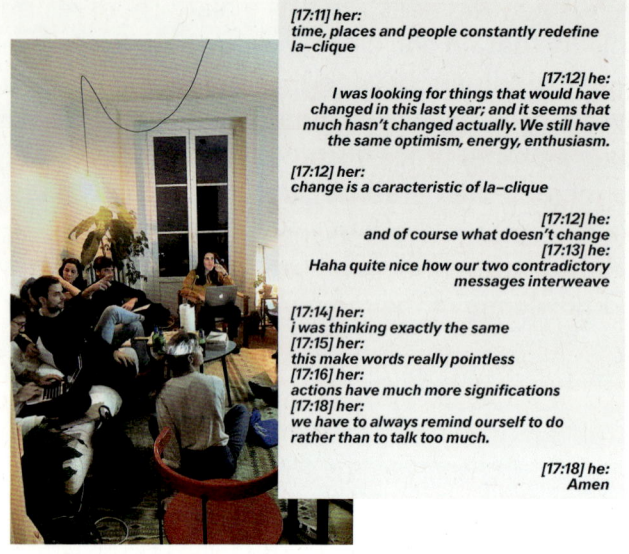

la–clique, "Type a Message," 2020

From: Lacol
To: Natalie Donat-Cattin
Subject: How has your collective changed since its foundation?

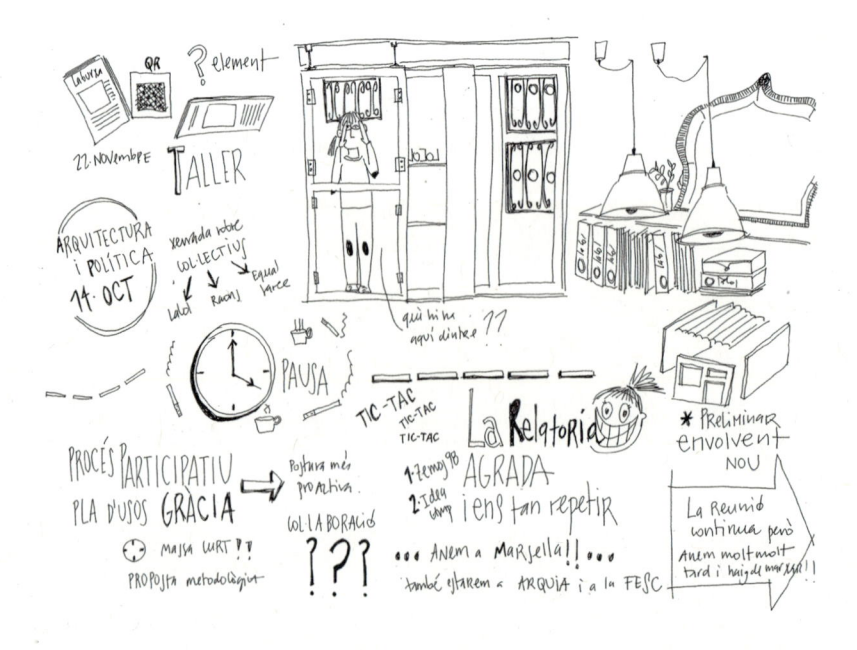

Anna Gran and Lacol, Graphic recording of an internal meeting, undated

We started as twenty-one students sharing a space to work out university projects, then we started doing more activist projects and finally fourteen of us decided to create the coop. The others left the country or didn't want to continue on this venture. Before we had a very loose organization. After that we have a more structured one.

From: n'UNDO
To: **Natalie Donat-Cattin**
Subject: How has your collective changed since its foundation?

We have evolved from the foundational small association (two members) to an actual association with more than thirty-five members and a technical office. n'UNDO as a think tank is the research, teaching, theoretical part, while n'OT the technical office moves into practice and the development of projects and strategies.

n'UNDO, *From Subtraction, Desde La Resta*, dpr-barcelona, 2017

From: X=(T=E=N)
To: **Natalie Donat-Cattin**
Subject: How has your collective changed since its foundation?

Defining the structure of X=(T=E=N) is a live project, one of continuous adjustment, and one that is a serious design exercise. After all we are designing our own models for how we want to work and how we want to live. We know this is missing and there is a real calling for it. For this, we are currently undertaking an evolutive restructure that establishes X=(T=E=N) Studio for concentrated architecture production in a studio environment as a dynamic, creative, and experimental entity, and X=(T=E=N) Institute; an inclusive network exploring the contours and definitions of architecture through research, nonprofit projects, and institutional collaborations. This restructure means redrafting statutes, building templates, charting how, when and why we work with each other and others. In the first few years of X=(T=E=N) we realized which workgroups and themes were more dynamic and immediate and which ones require a different time span—a different urgency. It was important for us to clarify this because the design effort that aims to contribute to real-world enterprise needs a different mode of commitment and is scrutinized in a different way than self-defined speculation or research. In our view, it is all about defining the fields of work and providing the space for different roles, mandates, and capacities to engage with purpose on the production of architecture.

The image is an artificially generated morph sequence spanning two architectural floor plans. The instances between the archetypes are drawn by artificial intelligence software sourcing a database of some four thousand spaces from the history of architecture. All inherently civic in nature and all recorded in floor plan—the primary tool of the architect. The Great Mosque at Shūsh from 850 determined the first floor plan, the second represents both our Zurich and Belgrade studios. After three months of calculations and manual adjustments, the process offered a first glimpse into the way of working with a machine. This makes architects very uncomfortable, especially as the horizons of the profession are changing rapidly.

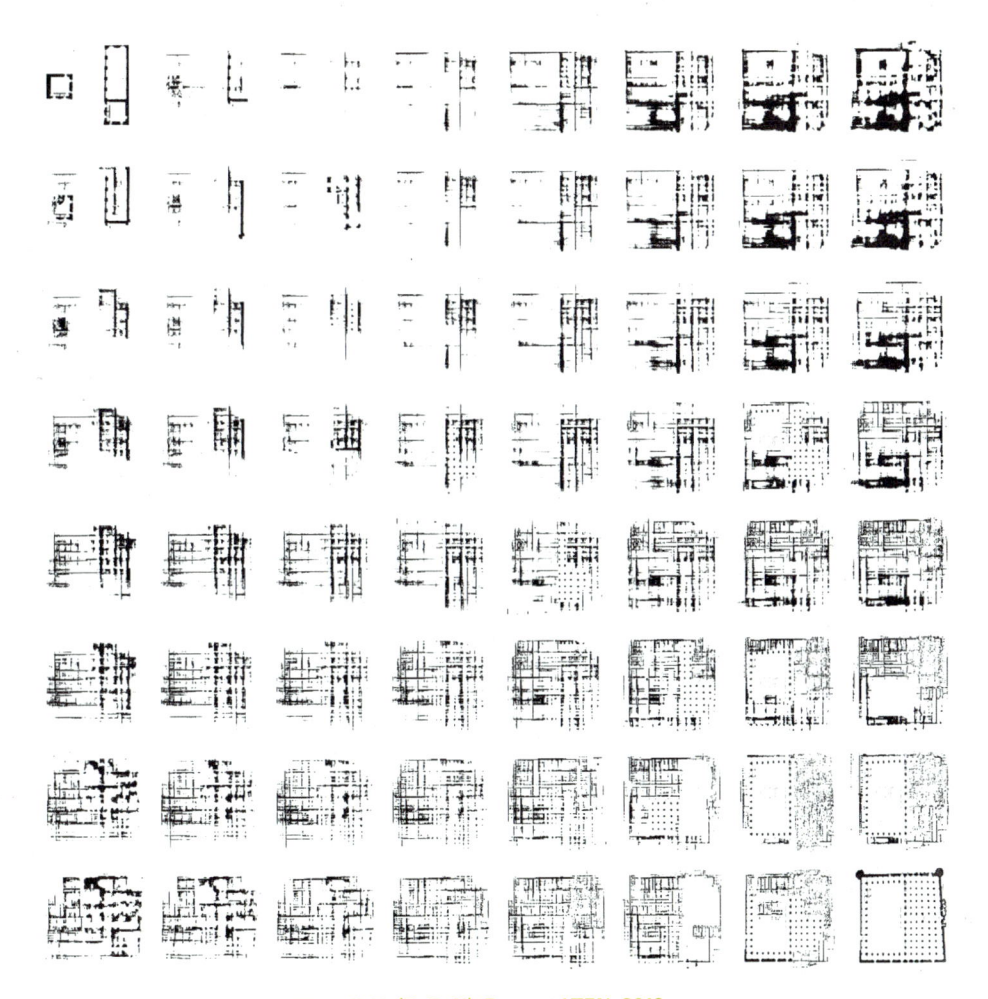

Luka Piškorec and Nemanja Zimonji, X=(T=E=N), Rooms of TEN, 2019

Saturday, November 14, 2020, 6:22 PM

7. ARCHITECTURE
Action for Reaction, Proposing an Alternative

In most cases, this is defined by a mission, by a common goal, by a path diverging from the one offered by today's architecture market or by a contemporary problem to reflect on, such as the theme of sustainability, equality, and technology.

The interactive and horizontal view on the making of architecture becomes a referential element for how to conceive a project, move within it, and further develop it, always in direct contact with the community around it. It is a bottom-up process, as orizzontale says. Placing at the forefront the common needs means transforming them into a project brief. For this reason, having to work locally and in direct proximity to a certain community is the necessary condition to ensure a gradual development of an area of the city over time, as Assemble and Lacol do. Architecture acts not only as a means of social transformation, but as a way to establish a bilateral dialogue with other organizations and cooperatives in the area, with the goal of creating a responsive and active network of people. Architecture holds therefore the possibility to become a space of encounter, exchange, and opportunity, a platform to investigate what it means to work collectively, with the potential of improving people's lives.By offering consultation and research to its clients, n'UNDO shows how architecture can guarantee sustainability by redoing, undoing and mainly not doing, in an effort to slow down the construction industry and the real estate market.

The act of architecture becomes a social act being built, represented, or theorized. Sometimes something physical remains, but not always. Sometimes it is just about transmitting a new vision of space, through the rearranging of reality, as (ab)Normal and false mirror office do. Sometimes it is about approaching a problematic and solving it with minimum means, in the respect of the environment. It is an act of sensibility and poetry: a simple architecture which holds quality and still manages to question the status quo. A way of bringing knowledge and experience.

From: Natalie Donat-Cattin
To: (ab)Normal, A-A Collective, Assemble, CNCRT, Colectivo Warehouse, Collectif Etc, constructLab, false mirror office, Fosbury Architecture, la–clique, Lacol, n'UNDO, orizzontale, X=(T=E=N)
Subject: What is the key aim of your architecture?

Social, ecological, the community. Might be a key project, or a collection of key projects, just a drawing or a collage of the ideal project, or the "building to come."

From: (ab)Normal
To: Natalie Donat-Cattin
Subject: What is the key aim of your architecture?

(ab)Normal is a multidisciplinary collective set to explore different realms: design, architecture, novel. Nevertheless we reserve a particular focus on architectural representation. Photorealism is carefully deconstructed and rearranged through the use of normal vectors, avoiding the traditional structure that builds the contemporary visual description of a space.

(ab)Normal, Mnemonic artifacts, 2020

From: A-A Collective
To: Natalie Donat-Cattin
Subject: What is the key aim of your architecture?

As with the first question, it is hard to have an answer that goes very specifically into the interests of each of us. Exactly because we are a collective, we have very different thoughts and we have the ambition of embracing all of them. We don't want to take shortcuts and hide ourself behind slogans.

As stated before, we aim to have an architecture that has a strong relationship with its reality, with its place, and with its people. At the same time, never as in this period of quarantine and home office is everyone so aware of how important the space that surrounds us is. When you are forced in the same place for weeks you realize how important is to have the luxury of having a small balcony toward a view or how nice is to have a wooden floor to walk on in your socks the whole day. So we also want to achieve architectures that have quality from their fundamentals.

PAP and J. Baranowski, Labor Day celebrations including a model of the Palace of Culture and Science, Warsaw, May 1, 1952

From: Assemble
To: **Natalie Donat-Cattin**
Subject: What is the key aim of your architecture?

Assemble doesn't really have a collective aim for the work itself—we are more interested in changing the way in which the built environment is produced through collaboration. We are working with a shared idea of what we might collectively aim for in any future work, which is oriented around working primarily in a collaborative and ecologically sustainable way. This involves organizing people and resources as much as it involves traditional forms of design. Our work began with a self-build methodology, and we are keen to explore how we can continue to be involved in the construction of our projects as they grow in scale.

Assemble, Illustration of open studios, 2016

We also aim to stay with our projects for a long time. Our work in Granby has been ongoing for nearly ten years now with the Community Land Trust as a repeat client. We also sit on the board of two of our projects: Blackhorse Workshop and Baltic Street Adventure Playground.

From: CNCRT
To: Natalie Donat-Cattin
Subject: What is the key aim of your architecture?

5. INSTITUTIONS OF LABOR

What if we build monuments?! In architecture history, temples, churches, cathedrals, classicism, columns, neoclassical formalism, rhetoric totalitarianism, late-Rossism, statues, obelisks, Krier's Atlantis deliriousness, and so forth, through their language and order of powerful imposingness, were used as devices for the representation of the institutions of totalitarianisms and nation-state capitalisms.

Emerging from the genericness of the city, these architectural forms had to institutionalize specific functions of the State: religion, universities, schools, administration, economy, government, Palace of Soviets, banks, Wall Street, army, kingdom, but never labor or pure togetherness. Taking into account this dialectical relation of architecture and representation (of a ritual/function), what if we institutionalize what we do, our labor and our rituals of being together?

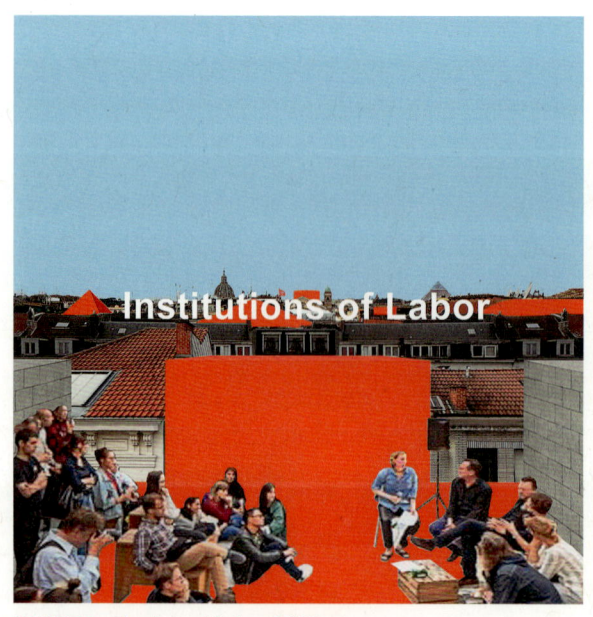

CNCRT, Institutions of Labor, 2020

We should, perhaps, erect new institutions to manifest and welcome our productivity and pure life: institutions of the commons. Every city in Europe and elsewhere could have its institutions of labor in the form of a classical form or a generic volume, almost the same everywhere, for celebrating "working together" and "being together" in every neighborhood, city, for everyone like us that keeps moving and changing life for life. Does a monument make our lives visible is what is yet to come.

From: Colectivo Warehouse
To: **Natalie Donat-Cattin**
Subject: What is the key aim of your architecture?

Colectivo Warehouse, Community kitchen of Terras da Costa, Almada, 2014

Community is what we are interested in. We strongly believe in architecture as a process more than a project. It is about triggering reactions in response to an urban problem, a necessity, a common will. Architecture is a city tool, it is a methodology, it is an ecological issue. Architecture is about appropriation, activation of non-space and social inclusion.

From: Collectif Etc
To: **Natalie Donat-Cattin**
Subject: What is the key aim of your architecture?

We're always learning and questioning our values, our methods, our projects. We're not working with specific mottos or manifestos: we build a practice step by step, with tangible projects more than words and discourses. We're going with a mix of adventure and reinvention of our practice: a sort of permanent "reinventure"! We are fighting for that, sometimes even working for free for situations we believe in but that don't get enough means. We don't want to get bored, and we want to stay long-lasting beginners—almost on the same level of many of the volunteers we are organizing our workshops with. The reality behind that is that it is really hard to find economical stability when you want to keep your values and keep learning! At the end, we're trying to reach what we're getting inspired by: self-government, trying to break the codes, radical ecology. And to do so in a strong cooperative and friends group.

Collectif Etc, "Ne travaillez jamais!," 2020

From: constructLab
To: Natalie Donat-Cattin
Subject: What is the key aim of your architecture?

In this network we have the common will to work with the physical material. We are not architects. There are also artists, graphics, cooks, sociologists, anthropologists, writers, and all of those people who converge in this common desire of doing. We meet and we build friendships through sharing. The way we work is a critique of architecture as we currently conceive it. We put our research at the scale of interaction, trying to achieve an output close to the concept, or at least to forge a link between these two phases, concept and realization. This is not necessarily a criticism of technology. The desire is not to go back to the past and work like in the Middle Ages but to invest in a more applied kind of research, so to bring ingredients from the past to contemporary challenges. Our attitude is to mix eras and take everything; in a naively poetical way, to look for another method of work; new approaches to building and in how to act within the built environment, the city, the public space, and study the interactions between people. All this, without necessarily having a manifesto, rather a sensitivity specific to each member.

Dylan Perrenaud, *Caillasses*, Geneva, 2020

From: false mirror office
To: Natalie Donat-Cattin
Subject: What is the key aim of your architecture?

We see architecture as an eloquent language in which forms, materials, images, and functions come together to form the backdrop of that fantastic play that is our contemporary reality. This leads us to work on a narrative level at different scales of intervention, trying to produce each time something meaningful and somehow newly familiar for the city and its community. When designing at an urban scale, we try to push the background to a new level, even unearthing forgotten elements that, through our manipulated misunderstandings, find new roles and upset the urban balance, its metabolism and collective consciousness. We never stopped believing in the symbolic value of the rites and myths, no matter whether they're old or new. This is why we like to play with the forms and fragments of the past and present, downgrading them to a sort of storybook to be reread, retold, and at best, rewritten.

Our creative process is strongly based on the concept of invention, as from its Latin root *invenio*, which refers to the act of collecting rather than creating: "the only ones able to create are God or the hairdressers," one of our many mentors used to say. This idea has nothing to do with historicism; it is a proactive process, between the serious and the facetious in which the result is never the icastic reproposition of the original, but rather a distorted reflection deformed through processes and actions, whether they are borrowed from literature, semiology, or from a certain artistic avant-garde. For us, design is a process that, if it were to be depicted, would be a kind of magic mirror whose reflection would never be an honest reproduction of a certain reality, but a misrepresentation of something that was not really, but perhaps may have been a kind of, which certainly is not and hopefully will be a sort of.

false mirror office, Mirror, 2020

Not very surprisingly, *representation* is a key word in our toolkit, intended as an integral part of the architectural project and not as a mere figurative tool. Hence the constant research toward new expressive forms, welcoming the idea that a project can be a new language born from its representation code.

From: Fosbury Architecture
To: Natalie Donat-Cattin
Subject: What is the key aim of your architecture?

If the collective serves as a platform to observe and question the status quo, a common thread in most of the projects of Fosbury Architecture is the use of the project to measure the transformations of the context in which we live and operate. Whether the condition of the young architect, the impact of social media, the relationship between physical and digital space, the global warming and so on, projects are often used as a pretext to prove an intuition. The "project to come" is necessarily structured around the investigation of the contingent, rather than an idealized view of the future.

Fosbury Architecture, Architecture, 2020

From: la–clique
To: Natalie Donat-Cattin
Subject: What is the key aim of your architecture?

la–clique, "Dîner exquis," 2020

From: La Col
To: Natalie Donat-Cattin
Subject: What is the key aim of your architecture?

Probably our main vectors are social (human life) and sustainability.

Lacol, La Comunal, 2020

From: n'UNDO
To: Natalie Donat-Cattin
Subject: What is the key aim of your architecture?

To build Future. To improve people's lives.

From: orizzontale
To: Natalie Donat-Cattin
Subject: What is the key aim of your architecture?

orizzontale give us the possibility to express somehow the subject of our architecture, which is designing bottom-up processes for the creation of common relational spaces. We try to create open transformation processes involving people from more structured institutional subjects to informal groups or individuals who care for the space in which we intervene. We think of architecture as a collective act. In orizzontale we are able to express our thinking, political ideas, and interests, which are diverse and are oriented under our sensitivity on specific topics like equity, depopulation of small villages, education, upcycle. We always try to stress the boundaries of architecture and experiment on each phase of the production cycle of a common space, from the exploration to the program of activities.

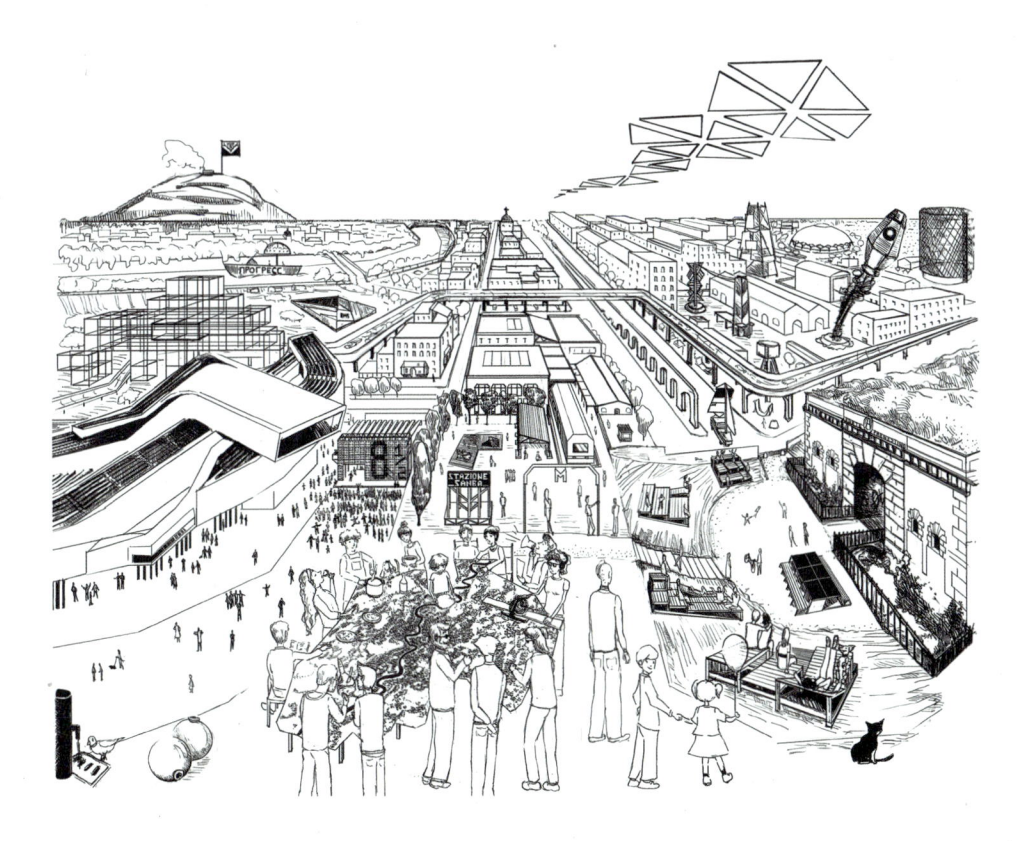

orizzontale, *Urbe*, 2015

Experimental for us means empirical, in-progress. We often try to translate in a spatial language the ideas very literally. The results of this process can be called *spatial metaphors*. Staging the ordinary and extraordinary was realized literally with a multisided stage, defined and framed by a porous screen (8½). Creating a flexible space for interaction is expressed by building a moving structure like in Gondwana, that can literally move around and "give place" to an infinite series of combinations and uses. Shifting point of view has been done by building an upper sight spot, like the terrace-observatory for Casa do Quarteirão. Unveiling hidden potentials takes the literal form of the tip of a submerged iceberg (Iceberg).

For the last couple of years, we are more focused on creating projects with an incremental process development and that we follow within a period of one to three years. Our works are primary infrastructures to build upon, like the constant flow of overbuilding the existing context. We welcome actions of rebuilding or overbuilding our intervention. What orizzontale leave behind is not necessarily a construction. Sometimes something physical remains. Some other times only knowledge and experience in the people involved remains—traces that can easily become a fertile ground for new collective visions.

From: X=(T=E=N)
To: Natalie Donat-Cattin
Subject: What is the key aim of your architecture?

We aim for an architecture that does not merely point out a reality but creates a shared experience of it. The act of architecture for us is primarily a social act; it delimits territory and lays claim to space for habitation. In this way, we measure architecture not only on its form, but by the way in which it allows the possibilities of life to happen. This can be extended to the projects we initiate and the instructions we give for building, be it questioning spatial needs, standards, or norms of construction. We need to design with the politics of space, material, labor, and economy to remain at the center of the discourse on the built environment. If we really admit it, we must confess that architecture has always been aligned to powerful interests, whether they be people, law, or money. The social political power of the architect would infer that it is valued by the former—people. At a time when architecture, or at least its promise through the image, has never been more popular, we wonder why its institutions and public figures join the professional exodus on positions of the public good. We see the potential to act.

To act is to join. Our task is to develop the sensibility to be able to recognize this and be able to respond creatively and in parity with our values.

The drawing is an overlay of 100 buildings to come. The footprints were selected from the 3500+ building sites we previously identified using Zurich open data sets and customized programming scripts. The building sites are small but buildable fragments of land in well-located urban areas. These were identified for our Distributed Cooperative project, an urban design strategy aiming to reorganize the arrangement of urban space to counteract the speculative housing market. The project responded to the 2011 referendum on affordable housing in Zurich, which legislated that by 2050, one-third of Zurich's rental housing must operate on a nonprofit basis. Although housing cooperatives account for 70 percent of the nonprofit rental sector, a lack of well-located, affordable sites combined with the rapid growth of the market housing sector, will make it increasingly unlikely that the public mandate will be reached by 2050. New models are clearly needed to address the current and future supply crisis for compact, legitimate and sustainable urban habitation.

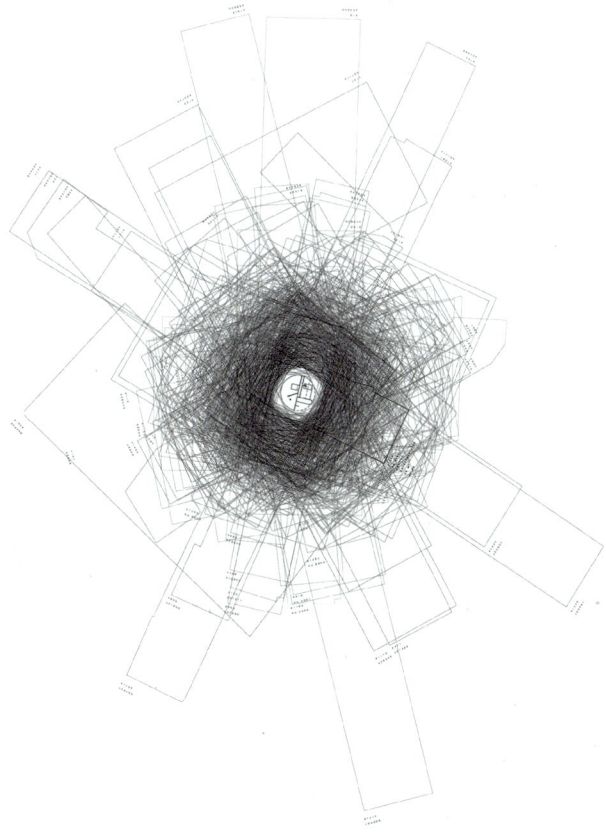

Scott Lloyd, X=(T=E=N), 1/100/3500 Odd Lots, 2020

Open Co
Rethinking

clusion/s:
rchitecture

This text aims to be a reflection on an eighteen-month experience analyzing collective processes in the European architectural scene. It is not a conclusion, rather another fragment of this analysis. It is written in collaboration with Scott Lloyd, from TEN, one of the first people I met during this experience and who, unlike me, knows what it means to be part of a collective.

The goal is to reveal the possibilities and the difficulties of working in collectives, and to suggest how these models could contribute to rethinking the architectural discipline and its institutions. It is timely to intensify such an inquiry, and to pick up on the common global movements that are currently pressuring dominant forms of social organization. These are playing out through diverse and effective mobilization against structural discrimination, and the increasing disparity in wealth, power, and resource distribution. They are aiming to undermine the power and legitimacy of traditional institutions and are prompting broader society to question the values and rules by which they operate. Among others, the common tendencies in these movements include the call for more open and representative governance and greater accountability for exploitative enterprise. The ubiquity of social media and information technologies have allowed such solidarity to be globally networked, while emerging platforms for visibility and exchange have helped to give form to previously marginalized identities and positions. While these have delivered legitimate directives for societal transformation, and indeed warrant genuine political and institutional responses, they also have appeared to reveal the dormant contradiction between the promise of modern citizenry and the dominant structures that enforce the status quo.

Until now, the power of this general shift has had little effect on the established architectural profession and is only marginally reflected in the institutions for architectural education. It could be claimed that the increasing specialization of the profession and its uncritical reliance on the property market have confirmed its retreat from visible positions on the public good. This unfortunately comes at a time of high public demand for leadership in addressing the increasingly diverse and complex conditions of building in a rapidly changing environment. Along with the interests to which established architecture answers, the centralized and hierarchical way in which it is practiced—and still being trained for—seems to render it incapable of offering alternative registers of knowledge or meaningful counterproposals. While Michel Bauwens has sketched out possible definitions of postcapitalist practice relevant to the field, Tom Holert suggests that the profession should enrich purposeful destabilization of its social and aesthetic contracts. The Architecture Lobby's recent manifesto sets out a broad call for the valorization of architectural labor, while Architects for Future demand a design-led transformation of the building industry. Meanwhile, a general reprioritization of the commons and a revival of the themes of cohabitation are being established as baselines for a new generation of architects and critical practices. These are pioneering open design processes and connecting larger narratives with architectural propositions. They reach for potentials beyond the optimization of commodity value and pursue at times radical political engagement and creative opposition to the social habits and dispositions of the everyday. Such approaches have been used through-out modern history to test the limits of the practice. Groups such as Superstudio, Archizoom, UFO, Ant Farm, and NATO, formulated through their work and actions, alternative polemics on the practice of architecture. Today, we are far away from the revolutionary positions of the '70s and '80s, which, despite their rhetoric, remained mainly suggestive in their intellectual and creative transgressions. As such, the fate of these collectives followed that of their peers, either gradual abandonment once the transformative promise of collaboration fell short, or their imagery became iconographic and superseded their message. The reactionary collective was ultimately subsumed by more immediate social and economic imperatives.

The current crop of collectives shown in this publication, however, seems to draw motivation from this genealogy but is marked by a particular nonradical—one could say humble—acceptance of an alternative yet symbiotic position within functioning systems. As opposed to building a reactionary counterpoint to society, they are postidealistic with a drive to create robust prototypical and functioning alternatives. They seem at ease with the unavoidable contradictions that shape the everyday, and seek reasonable independence from serving short-term private interests through self-initiated projects. As suggested by Bonsiepe, they act rather to cultivate a critical practice aimed less at the solution of problems and more toward the critical handling and thematization of social relations. This act of "designing in dialogue" embeds architecture into its broader contexts, whereby the constant negotiation forces it to identify and expand on its unique societal proposition. The design act becomes one of facilitation and learning from multiplicity and inclusion, an act that is commended in open, progressive societies yet marginalized in traditional institutions and private enterprise.

Given the complexity of human relations, as well as the time-consuming and often difficult decision-making processes, the question remains how can collectives remain competitive or relevant today? The publication embodies a moment of change in the profession by emphasizing the unique creative potentials of collective architecture. However, how can collective practices sustain themselves in a post-idealistic setting without the power of the myth of collaboration? Or better, how can collective practices thrive and influence the contemporary model of architectural practice?

1. By overturning the myth that individual authorship is contradictory to the collective.

2. By developing a culture of dialogue to explore the boundaries of individual knowledge and draw on collective intelligence.

3. By transforming the inefficiencies of coordination into the strengths of multiplicity.

4. By defining and publishing a set of values and codes in a statute.

5. By constantly learning from different working structures that could inform the discipline and create new business models. Each collective—architectural and not—has very different ways of working together and organizing groups.

6. By allowing for active governance not regulated government. A collective requires a lot of organization, clear mandates, and systems of participation. Like all social organization, collectives must defend against the inevitable tyranny of consolidated power and ensure that individuals are incentivized to participate. This can be achieved by building organizational structure on principles of subsidiarity, where decisions are made at the local level—a trend that is happening across all levels of governance and planning.

7. By promoting creative destruction. The collective evolves its structure in order to overcome its internal problematics. This may mean forking the organization or pivoting from original visions.

8. By allowing for freedom of thought and equal representation through fair decision-making processes. This is relevant within the collective and working with actors outside of it.

9. By broadening a preoccupation with style and aesthetics with an architecture of opportunity, finding, and rearrangement, considering relevant ecological and social imperatives.

10. By subversively adapting to the system in force, to be able to propose counterpositions.

These points were sketched out from the general analysis in this publication. Together they reveal the ambition to create architecture outside Architecture, and to develop new knowledge built from open collaboration with other disciplines and nondisciplines. This could be understood as field of exploration, moderated by the collective making of architecture. It relies on in-house processes, and direct relationships to build fairer dialogues and simplify the system by which it acts. These allow for the rediscovery of the simple joy of building yet with an understanding of the unique facets that various protagonists, specialists, and the external actors bring to the process. Indeed, for some, the collective model is the only one capable of offering opportunities for equality and agency while offering a design process aimed beyond simply consolidating the dominant legacy of architecture. In this way, it can be said that contemporary collectives still aim to rethink the most basic assumptions on the agenda of architecture. They use collaborative actions to both explore and make a type of working commons built through constant, open, and creative negotiation. This shared journey through the unknown is the transformative promise of collective architecture.

INTRODUCING THE ACTORS

INDE
PRAC

Featuring: (ab)Normal, A-A Collective, Assemble, CNCRT, Collectif Etc, Colectivo Warehouse, constructLab, false mirror office, Fosbury Architecture, la–clique, Lacol, n'UNDO, orizzontale, and X=(T=E=N)

X OF
TICES

la–clique
Zurich, Lausanne

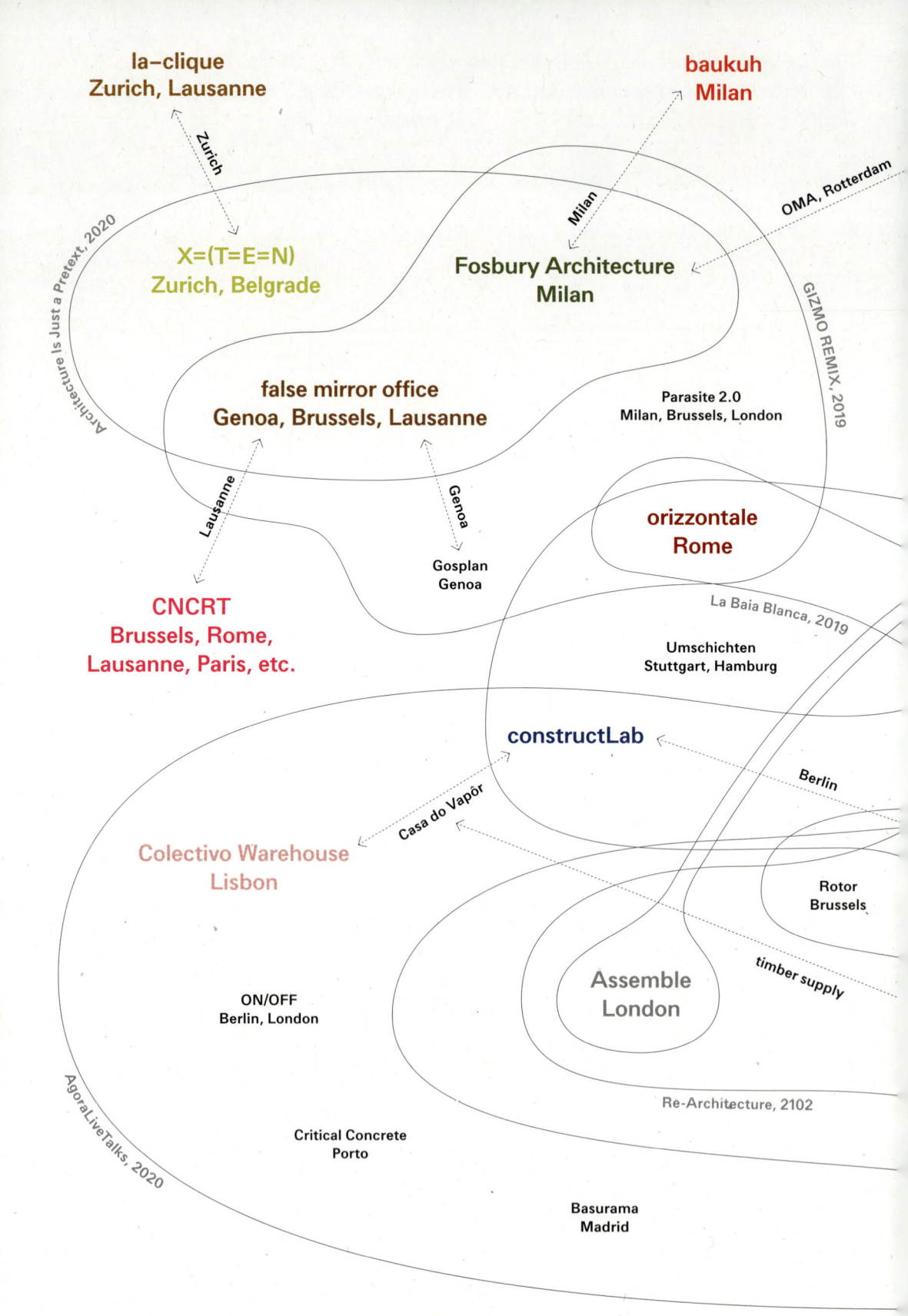

baukuh
Milan

Zurich

Milan

OMA, Rotterdam

X=(T=E=N)
Zurich, Belgrade

Fosbury Architecture
Milan

Architecture Is Just a Pretext, 2020

GIZMO REMIX, 2019

false mirror office
Genoa, Brussels, Lausanne

Parasite 2.0
Milan, Brussels, London

Lausanne

Genoa

orizzontale
Rome

Gosplan
Genoa

La Baia Blanca, 2019

CNCRT
Brussels, Rome,
Lausanne, Paris, etc.

Umschichten
Stuttgart, Hamburg

constructLab

Berlin

Casa do Vapôr

Colectivo Warehouse
Lisbon

Rotor
Brussels

timber supply

Assemble
London

ON/OFF
Berlin, London

Re-Architecture, 2102

AgoraLiveTalks, 2020

Critical Concrete
Porto

Basurama
Madrid

Natalie Donat-Cattin, mapping of some collective events of the last decade

(ab)Normal
Milan, Rotterdam

Herzog & de Meuron, Basel

n'UNDO
Madrid, Saint-Gilles,
Barranquilla

Publico Design Fest, 2015

A-A Collective
Milan, Basel,
Copenhagen, Warsaw

Zuloark
Berlin, Bologna,
La Coruña, Madrid

Torino Stratosferica, 2020

Todos por la praxis
Madrid

EME 3, 2012

Lacol
Barcelona

OSTHANG, 2014

Urbanités Inattendues, 2011

Collectif Etc
Marseille

recetas urbanas

pez estudio
Madrid

raumlabor
Berlin

Coloco
Paris

Cabanon Vertical

EXYZT

Bruit du Frigo
Bordeaux

Paris

Bellastock

Les Saprophytes
Lille

Les Arpenteurs
Fontaine

Le Détour de France, 2011–12

(ab)Normal is a graphic novel without chronology. Obsolete 3ds and rejected timelines are reconfigured in spatial narratives. (ab)Normal is firstly an experiment on architectural representation. Location: Milan, Rotterdam

(ab)Normal was founded in 2017 and comprises four members:
Marcello Carpino
Mattia Inselvini
Davide Masserini
Luigi Savio

MACHINE(S) OF LOVING GRACE
Installation, Teatro Ringhiera,
Milan, May 2019

Machine(s) of Loving Grace is an exhibition, part of a wider research developed starting from two different projects presented at Politecnico di Milano: Logistics Landscape by Captcha and Googleburg by (ab)Normal, that investigate the emerging spaces generated by computational systems that are driving our lives; in the first case with a study on logistics and its fulfillment centers; and in the second with an analysis on data centers. The title of the exhibition takes inspiration from the poem "All Watched Over by Machines of Loving Grace" by Richard Brautigan, published by the American author in 1967 in a collection of poems with the same name.

The poem describes, following those years of fascination with and faith in technological development, a technological utopia where machines help and protect men in a new relationship with the natural environment. A distinction between technology and nature doesn't exist anymore: both these elements are programmed in a mutual harmony that allows men to be free of labor and to join back to nature.

DICHTELUST
Commissioned artwork,
Swiss Architecture Museum,
Basel, November 2018

Commissioned work for the entrance portal of the exhibition *Dichtelust*. The term *density* is conspicuously negative in Switzerland. In the political discussion about the urban planning and spatial planning development of Switzerland, *density* is often used as a battle concept and conjures images of the horrors of "built-up" cities and scenarios of high-rise buildings that "overgrow" urban centers. This negative image needs to be corrected. The exhibition illustrates what *density* really means, namely a meaningful exploitation of the developable territory. How density materializes in the city is one of the key questions. Because *density* does not automatically mean "building high" but, above all, building compact. And density, used properly, is the best means of avoiding density stress.

PARAPHERNALIA
Interactive installation,
The State of the Art of Architecture,
Milan Triennale, 2020

The State of the Art of Architecture Milano is intended to be an invitation to reflect on the creation of new forms of contemporary architectural thought through the involvement of 38 innovative and emergent architecture studios and researchers. The exhibition focuses on future generations in order to understand current lines of development and new directions in design.

Portrait:
(ab)Normal, Group photo, 2020

MACHINE(S) OF LOVING GRACE, MILAN

Piercarlo Quecchia, *Machine(s) of Loving Grace*, 2018, close-up

Piercarlo Quecchia, *Machine(s) of Loving Grace*, 2018, detail

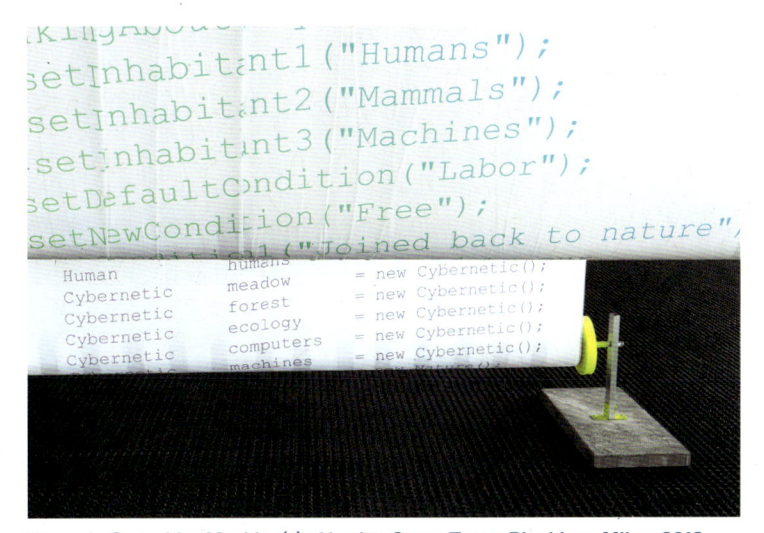

Piercarlo Quecchia, *Machine(s) of Loving Grace*, Teatro Ringhiera, Milan, 2018

DICHTELUST, BASEL

Piercarlo Quecchia, *Dichtelust*, S AM, Basel, 2018

Piercarlo Quecchia, *Dichtelust*, 2018, S AM, Basel, entrance

Piercarlo Quecchia, *Dichtelust*, 2018, S AM, Basel, detail

PARAPHERNALIA, MILAN

(ab)Normal, *Paraphernalia*, Triennale, Milan, 2019

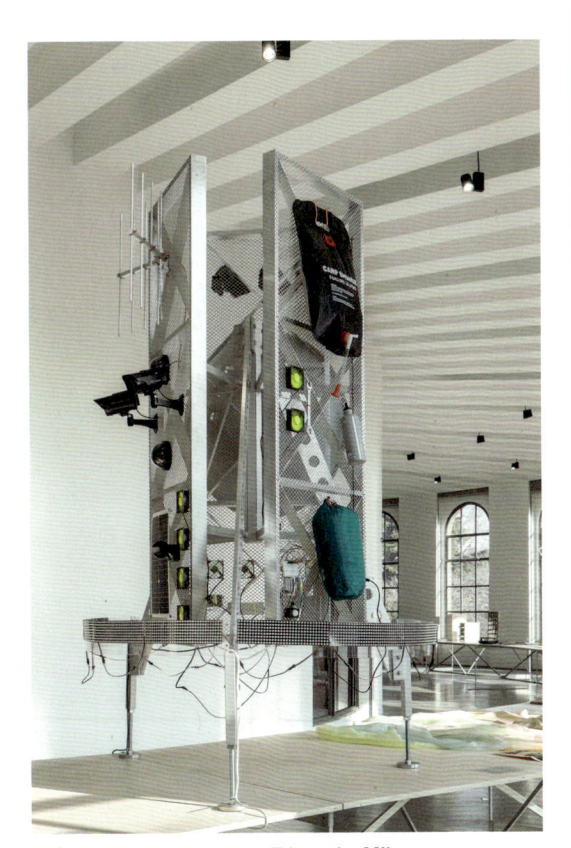

(ab)Normal, *Paraphernalia*, Triennale, Milan, CGI, 2019

(ab)Normal, *Paraphernalia*, Triennale, Milan, 2019, close-up

A-A Collective is an interdisciplinary practice focused on architecture with members in Basel, Copenhagen, and Warsaw. The collective came together in Switzerland and operates from three different countries by putting together local backgrounds and knowledge to face the contemporary global complexity. A-A Collective was founded in 2018 and comprises four members: Zygmunt Borawski, Martin Marker Larsen, Furio Montoli, Srdjan Zlokapa. Location: Basel, Copenaghen, Warsaw

WARSAW CENTRAL SQUARE
Restricted competition entry,
1st place, Warsaw, 2018

The idea for the reconstruction of the Central Square is based on a multilayered reading of the past, present, and future of Warsaw. The drawing of the paving emerges from a cartographic study that takes in consideration precise maps of prewar Warsaw as well as old maps from the archives of the city. Vegetation will be introduced as a binding material to connect the diverse layers of history and as a characteristic feature of the public space of this city: giving new character to the square while enabling new uses. To be able to show this dialogue between past and present we decided to design a new paving that mixes the existing granite cobblestones with new ones. Some of the existing elements of the Communist past will be reinterpreted. The final aim is to give the square back to the citizens of Warsaw.

AN ARCH FOR SØNDERJYLLAND
Open competition, 1st place,
Christiansfeld, Denmark, 2020

This monument will be built to celebrate the 100th anniversary of the historic reunification of the region of Southern Jutland to Denmark through a referendum vote after the First World War. The Arch is designed as a sequence of steel modules inspired by the arches that were installed in sequence to decorate the street where the king was passing to celebrate the reunification. The powerful motif of the structure is constantly changing depending on where you see the work from. The portal can appear both massive and porous. It's a physical monument, but it celebrates something fragile and precarious. An important part of the concept study was planning together with the municipality of Kolding the transportation and installation of the monument to the Reunification and Border Museum. Here, over time, the plants and nature will take over the monument until it ages into the realm of ruins.

PIVOT (with Magdalena Stadler)
Open competition, 1st place,
Steckborn, Switzerland, 2020

The existing ensemble had a strong history and a powerful character: a sixteenth-century tower house flanked by a long and low building along the lake and an ensemble of heterogeneous constructions that came later, with a pier and views to the lake. In order to keep the balance between built substance and natural elements, the decision was to keep the *qualities* and replace the *objects*. The *long building along the lake* became a *new long building along the lake* maintaining the same tension between horizontality and verticality as the old one. A shed closing the southern flank of the big courtyard was replaced by a school building that keeps the same horizontality and directness toward the outside. The same happens on the side to the park, where the new *mehrzweckhalle* is defining the new-old border. All the functions are grouped around a central schoolyard, the heart of the ensemble. The light and filigree constructions blur the lines between inside and outside. The school becomes a campus.

A-A Collective, Founding partners' collage based on original portraits by Hans Memling, 2020. Original images by Hans Memling from left to right: Hans Memling, *Portrait of a Young Man praying (recto)*, Museo Nacional Thyssen-Bornemisza, Madrid, ca. 1485; Hans Memling, *Portrait of a Young Man before a Landscape*, Gallerie dell'Accademia, Venice, ca. 1480; Hans Memling, *Portrait of Jacques of Savoy*, Kunstmuseum Basel, ca. 1470; Hans Memling, *Portrait of a Man with a Pink*, The Morgan Library & Museum, New York, ca. 1475

WARSAW CENTRAL SQUARE, WARSAW

A-A Collective, Warsaw Central Square, 2020

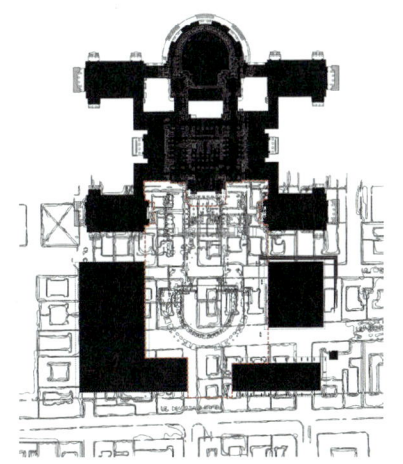

A-A Collective, Warsaw Central Square, 2018, eclectic drawing of historical layers

A-A Collective, Warsaw Central Square, 2019, visualization

AN ARCH FOR SØNDERJYLLAND, CHRISTIANSFELD

A-A Collective, An Arch for Sønderjylland: King Christian X of Denmark, 2020, concept sketch

Koliding Kommune, Frank Cilius and A-A Collective, An Arch for Sønderjylland, 2021, inauguration

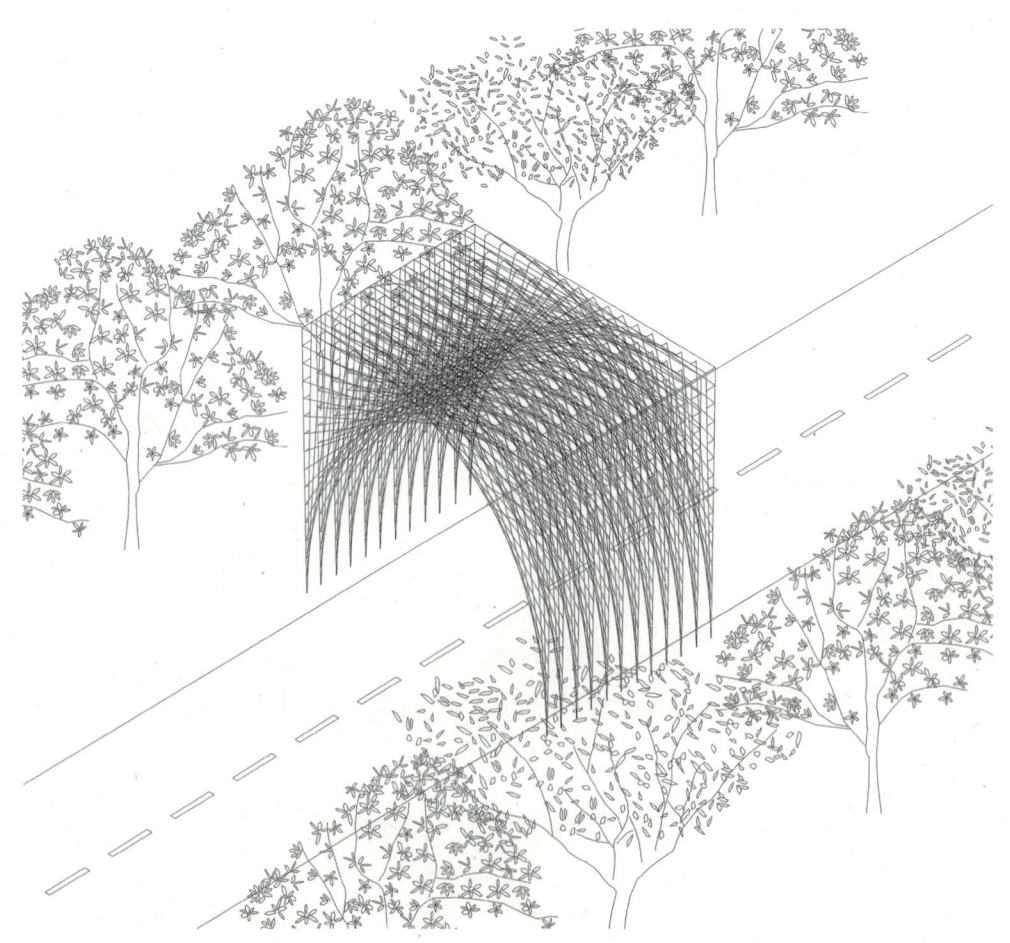

A-A Collective, An Arch for Sønderjylland, 2020, isometric drawing

198

PIVOT, STECKBORN

A-A Collective + Magdalena Stadler, PIVOT, 2020, exterior visualization

A-A Collective + Magdalena Stadler, PIVOT, 2020, interior visualization

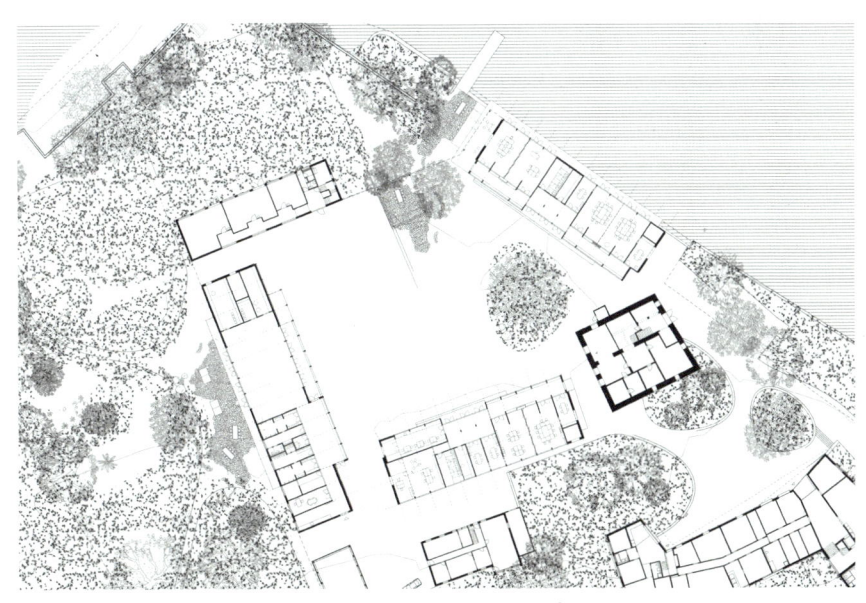

A-A Collective + Magdalena Stadler, PIVOT, 2020, situation plan

ASSEMBLE

Assemble is a multidisciplinary collective working across architecture, design, and art. Founded in 2010 to undertake a single self-built project, Assemble has since delivered a diverse and award-winning body of work while retaining a democratic and cooperative working method that enables built, social, and research-based work at a variety of scales, both making things and making things happen. Assemble was founded in 2010 and is composed of twenty members. Location: London

GRANBY FOUR STREETS
Ongoing, Liverpool, 2013

Granby Four Streets is an ongoing community-led project to rebuild Granby, a Liverpool neighborhood that was nearly made derelict by decades of poorly planned regeneration initiatives. The demolition of all but four of Granby's streets of Victorian terraces during decades of "regeneration" initiatives saw a once-thriving community scattered. Assemble worked with the Granby Four Streets CLT and Steinbeck Studios to present a sustainable and incremental vision for the area that builds on the hard work already done by local residents and translates it to the refurbishment of housing, public space, and the provision of new work and enterprise opportunities.

GRANBY WINTER GARDEN
Liverpool, 2019

Assemble and Granby Four Streets CLT have converted the derelict terraced houses at number 37 and 39 Cairns Street in Granby, Liverpool, into a new shared garden, freely accessible to local residents and the wider neighborhood. The Granby Winter Garden sits at the heart of the Granby neighborhood, housing a communal indoor garden, a meeting and events space, and accommodation for artist residencies. Assemble's design strategy for the Winter Garden sought to transform the typically private space of the terraced home into a focus for neighborhood activity, an unexpected indoor garden and unique resource for creative community action, cultural production, and exchange.

THE BRUTALIST PLAYGROUND
London, 2015

Assemble worked in collaboration with artist Simon Terrill to create the *Brutalist Playground*, an immersive installation that recreated a trio of postwar play structures out of foam. Designed for the Architecture Gallery at the RIBA, the *Brutalist Playground* consisted of full-size fragments of three distinctive London housing estates: Churchill Gardens in Pimlico, the Brownfield Estate in Poplar, and the Brunel Estate in Paddington. Assemble recast these concrete-and-steel playground structures in reconstituted foam in order to allow people to consider their formal characteristics separately from their materiality, and in doing so to allow them to be reappraised as places for play.

Portrait:
Assemble, Group portrait on the timber frame of Yardhouse, 2014

GRANBY FOUR STREETS, LIVERPOOL

Assemble, Granby Four Streets, Liverpool, 2013

Assemble, Granby Four Streets, scale model of a terraced house, Liverpool, 2013

Assemble, Granby Four Streets, exhibition display for the Turner Prize, The Tramway, Glasgow, 2015

GRANBY WINTER GARDEN, LIVERPOOL

Assemble, Granby Winter Garden, 2019, conceptual image

Assemble, Granby Winter Garden, Liverpool, 2019, model close-up

THE BRUTALIST PLAYGROUND, LONDON

Tristan Fewings and RIBA, *The Brutalist Playground*, girl running up the Brunel steps, 2015, RIBA, London

Alun Bull and RIBA, *The Brutalist Playground – The Tunnel from Park Hill*, 2016, S1 Artspace, Sheffield

Alun Bull and RIBA, *The Brutalist Playground – The Flying Saucer*, 2016, S1 Artspace, Sheffield

CNCRT is a collective of architects who challenge contemporary practice within architecture by exploring new forms of work organization based on the principle of common and temporary cooperation. CNCRT works on architecture, urbanism, and territory, trying to link research and design. Location: scattered around Europe

CNCRT was founded in 2014 and is composed of twelve present and former members:
Antonio Paolillo
Ezio Melchiorre
Giovanna Pittalis
Greta Torsello
Hubert Holewik
Jacqueline Luduvice
Luciano Aletta
Magdalena Jendras
Marson Korbi
Matteo Novarino
Ophélie Dozat
Tommaso Mola Meregalli

WE ARE BEAUTIFUL!
Proposal for the Tallinn Architecture Biennale *TAB 2019: New Habitats, New Beauties*, Competition, 2019

Writing, studying and yet our capacity to be creative has shifted from the terrain of beauty to the terrain of productivity. Working penetrates the personal intimacy of the domestic sphere, turning it into a productive space and isolating any possibility of collectivity. Not many choices are permitted within a room which seems an office rather than a place of beautiful creativity. *We Are Beautiful!* refers to us, architects, researchers, creative workers. A multitude living within a society that with the rhetoric of beauty tries to hide the political problematics of precariousness, instability, and all-day working. We propose coworking as a first step to escape from isolation in which we are constrained and to gain a new condition where beauty is accepted for its nature: a common terrain within individual labor.

DOMES (AULE) OBSERVATORIES OF COLLECTIVE WORKING

Research and project presented as part of the installation for the event *RI-RED, Ripensare il Redentore*, The Salesian Institute SS Redentore, Bari, 2020

Observing the Moon and studying space in the research of new planets represents the highest aspiration of human intellect. Marx intends this form of labor as part of the general intellect, including here all the scientific and intellectual inventions of the "social brain," a fruit of the global work made in cooperation. In a context where labor absorbs affectivities, individual care, free time, all life, we propose DOMES: Communal Aule for liberating ourselves from the discipline of the office/factory and for finding time to observe space. DOMES are communal rooms, designed as generic architectures to be collocated within the capitalistic metropolis as places to organize ourselves as workers, where to cooperate deciding together democratically when to produce, when to play sports, and when to create microcosms of nature.

URBAN CARPET
School campus with collective facilities, including a park, sport fields, and workshops (Paolo Caselli Competition), Rome, 2020

The area around Borghetto Caselli in Rome is characterized by a series of dispersed elements and objects, including the Aurelian Walls and the Non-Catholic Cemetery, where the only common part is ground. Ground could be intended as the whole soil underneath our feet, or as just a piece of land and surface able to open up new possibilities for collective use. Indeed, ground is the most tangible element that can physically represent the concept of *common*. The reading of this condition represents the starting point of our proposal for a school campus with sport facilities, parks, and workshops in the Testaccio district. We used the metaphor of the carpet as a system of strips, paths, and punctual elements, which, together with the existing buildings, create a series of programmatic landscapes that reconnect this undefined urban block to the historical city.

Portrait:
Jeff Wall, *After* Invisible Man *by Ralph Ellison*, the Prologue,1999–2000

WE ARE BEAUTIFUL!, TALLIN

CNCRT, *WE ARE BEAUTIFUL!*, Proposal for the Tallinn Architecture Biennale TAB 2019: *New Habitats, New Beauties*, Competition, 2019

CNCRT, *WE ARE BEAUTIFUL!*, 2019, collage

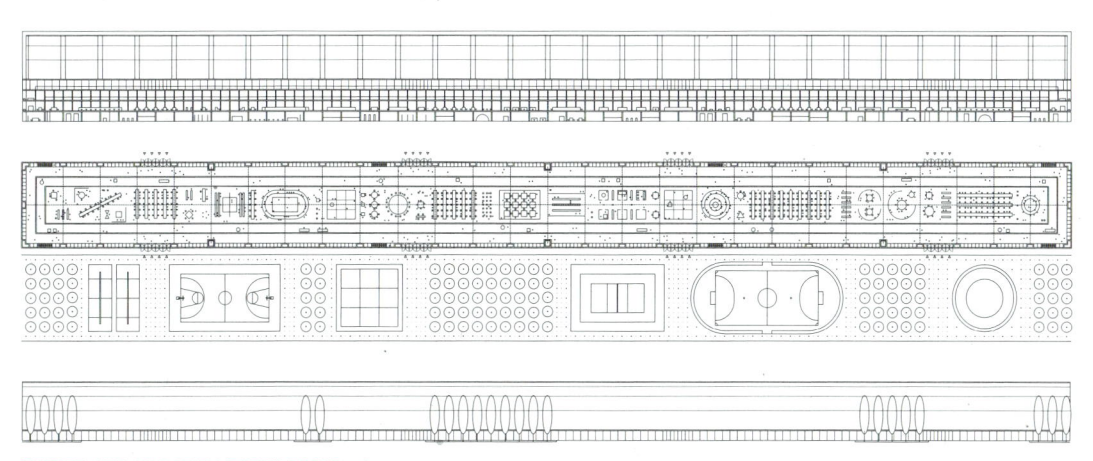

CNCRT, *WE ARE BEAUTIFUL!*, 2019, plan

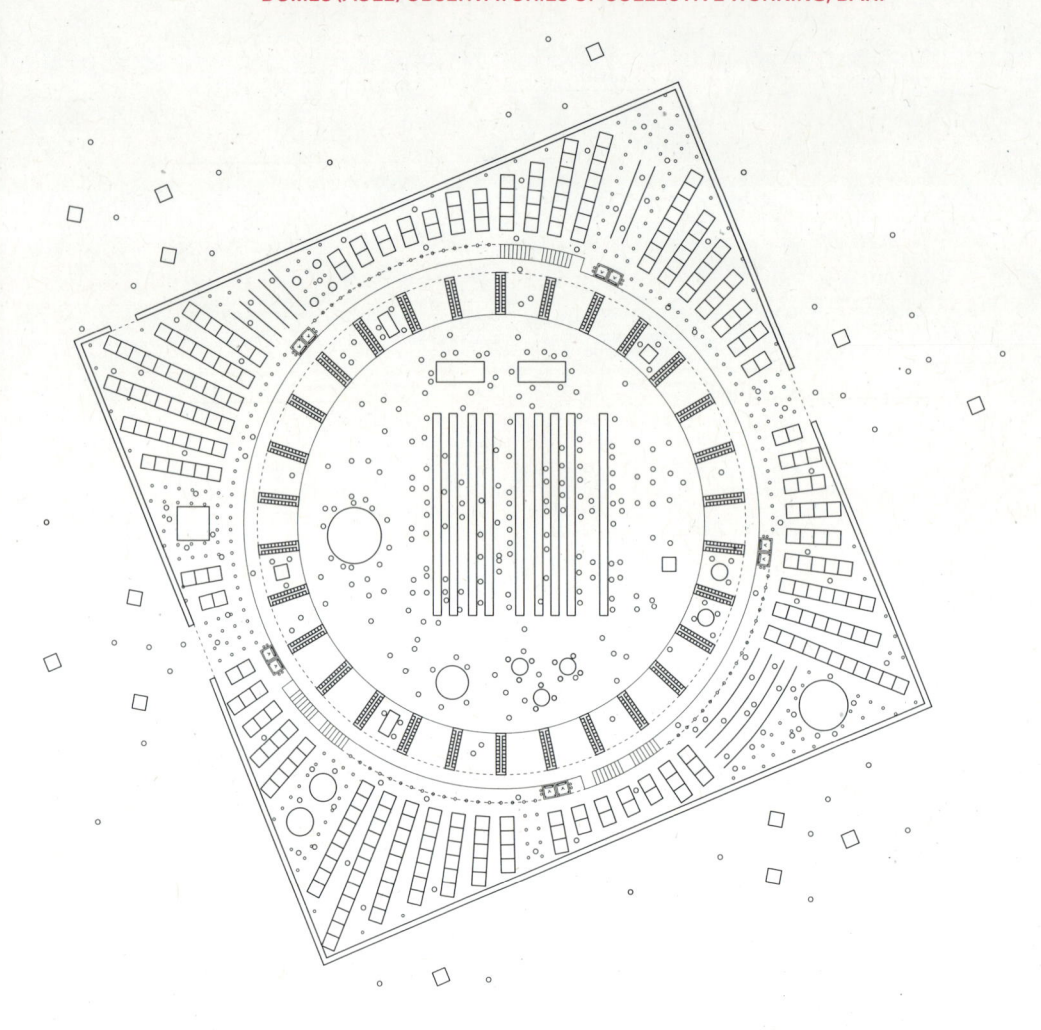

DOMES (AULE) OBSERVATORIES OF COLLECTIVE WORKING, BARI

CNCRT, *DOMES (AULE) OBSERVATORIES OF COLLECTIVE WORKING*, 2020, plan

CNCRT, DOMES (AULE) OBSERVATORIES OF COLLECTIVE WORKING, Research and project presented as part of the installation for the event *ri-Red, Ripensare il Redentore*, The Salesian Institute SS. Redentore, Bari, 2020

URBAN CARPET, ROME

CNCRT, *URBAN CARPET*, 2020, collage

CNCRT, URBAN CARPET, School campus with collective facilities, park with sport fields and workshops, Paolo Caselli Competition, Rome, 2020

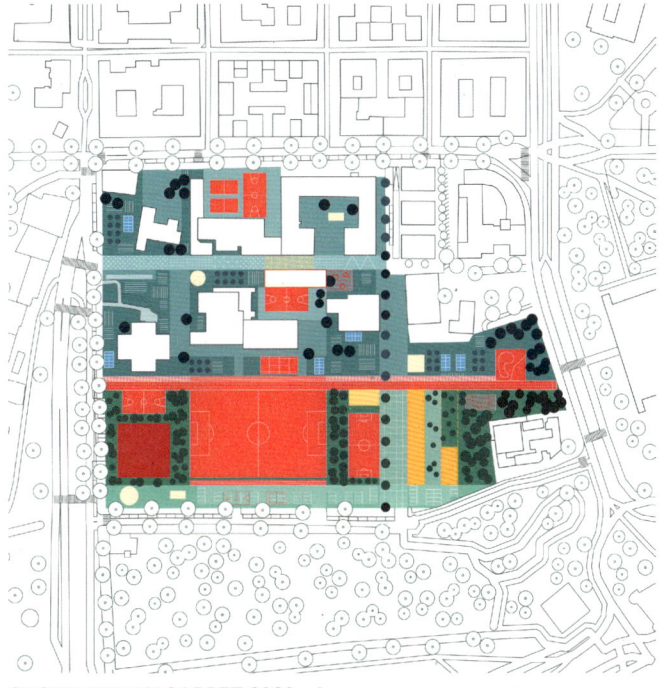

CNCRT, *URBAN CARPET*, 2020, plan

COLECTIVO WAREHOUSE

Colectivo Warehouse is an architecture and art collective, seeking to understand what architecture is nowadays and what role architects play. Warehouse funds its architectural praxis through design, experimentation, mediation, civic participation processes, collaboration, and practical intervention. Warehouse develops participatory architecture projects in the cultural and social scope. Hands-on approach is transversal in their practice. Warehouse develops collaborative projects because they believe that through multidisciplinary cocreation, it is possible to achieve better results. Location: Lisbon

Colectivo Warehouse was founded in 2013 and is composed of four members:
Sebastião de Botton
Monica Di Eugenio
Raquel Santos
Rúben Teodoro

COMMUNITY KITCHEN OF TERRAS DA COSTA
Almada, 2014

Terras da Costa is an isolated territory, where the locals feel forgotten except for frequent severe police interventions.

It is a strip of land between the town of Caparica and the cliffs, a highway and the ocean. Precarious shacks without water and sanitation are the homes and lifestyle of nearly five hundred people who live in an informal settlement. The project seeks to fight against the marginalization of Terras by strengthening its sense of identity, promoting exchanges among citizens in and out of the neighborhood and empowering them to take action, allowing for a nonconflictual dialogue with local public institutions. The project created a community center that offers a multifunctional and intergenerational public space, while bringing water to the neighborhood. This project was conceived and designed by means of an extensive participatory process. Four simple wooden modules serve as a kitchen, laundry, water point and a playground, allowing for flexibility. The structure is designed by Warehouse in collaboration with ateliermob.

BRINCADEIRA CIRCULAR
Lisbon, 2020

Brincadeira Circular is a project of educational equipment designed and built through a participatory process with the aim of evolving the entire community of Escola Fernanda de Castro, located in Tapada das Necessidades. Colectivo Warehouse was invited to coordinate this project by the Parish Council of Estrela, framed in a financing program of an environmental trust fund that encourages projects that apply principles of circular economy and sustainability. The project was born out of the recognition of the existence of underused spaces outside the school. Through the organization of collaborative sessions with parents, students, and professionals, an artistic temporary installation was built. The creation of this equipment aims to provide an educational space where the themes of circular economy, upcycling, reuse, and ecological responsibility will be addressed with activities proposed by teachers. The project was created using reused wood and milk packages collected by parents and students during the months before the building period. An art gallery was created with works made by students crafted with the leftovers from the construction itself.

HABITABIS FESTIVAL
Lisbon, 2018

Habitabis Festival is a collaboration tool based on the festival format, which addresses the themes of rehousing and social housing, promoting conferences, workshops, and debates between institutions, technicians, and communities, aiming for more inclusive processes. Its format is based on direct sharing, horizontal collaboration, and the coconstruction of diagnostics and solutions. It involves different actors: institutions (representatives); technicians; and communities (representatives or inhabitants).

Portrait:
Colectivo Warehouse,
Collective photo, Fundão, 2021

COMMUNITY KITCHEN OF TERRAS DA COSTA, ALMADA

Colectivo Warehouse, Community kitchen of Terras da Costa, Almada, 2014, daily use

Colectivo Warehouse, Community kitchen of Terras da Costa, Almada, 2014

Colectivo Warehouse, Community kitchen of Terras da Costa, Almada, 2014, structure

Colectivo Warehouse, Brincadeira Circular, Lisbon, 2020

Colectivo Warehouse, Brincadeira Circular, Lisbon, 2020, close-up

Colectivo Warehouse, Brincadeira Circular, Lisbon, 2020, structure

HABITABIS FESTIVAL, LISBON

Untold stories, lecture, *Habitabis Festival*, Lisbon, 2018

Untold stories, *Habitabis Festival*, Lisbon, 2018

Untold stories, discussion, *Habitabis Festival*, Lisbon, 2018

COLLECTIF ETC

Collectif Etc is a nonprofit organization since 2009. We support common spaces through actions that gather people around construction workshops.

political engagement · *action-based* · *social-oriented* · *external participation* · *urban practice* · *artistic practice* · *architecture* · *representation & narrative* · *research* · *ecology*

We're using various mediums like edition, screen printing, sewing, filmmaking, artistic process. We hope that architecture can be a tool to change our world toward a more social, democratic, and ecological way of life. Location: Marseille (but about to emigrate to the countryside).

Collectif Etc was founded in 2009 and is composed of six members: Cécile Kohen, Benjamin Guillouet, Maxence Bohn, Léo Hudson, Charlène Bay, Théo Mouzard

PLACE DES POSSIBLES
Saint-Laurent-en-Royans, 2019–ongoing

La Place des Possibles is a former textile factory in a rural area. Led by an association giving social support to families and young people in trouble, it gathers various associations working in the fields of ecology, crafts, reused materials, and reduction of the digital divide. Collectif Etc is creating a step-by-step rehabilitation of 2500m² with a series of open construction workshops. Instead of millions for a single architect-expert's point of view, they propose incremental and collaborative design, working with renewable resources and reusing materials of the site. Can architecture, as an act of building more than an artist's vision, be a way to bring together the community around its space? Giving care to a former building becomes a way for emancipation and solidarity between various publics in an underresourced territory.

GRAND HALLE DE CAEN
Caen, 2019

One building remains of the former industrial complex of Caen, in the north of France. Collectif Etc first built a settlement for the association in charge of turning this former building into a living and shared multifunction space. All made of reused materials, this small house allowed the association to exist and prefigure various uses during the rehab construction process. Architecture is not the image of a final built space but rather a process: Collectif Etc came before the rehabilitation was achieved, then came again during the construction to build small *dragsters*, mobile elements that allow the space of the big, empty hall to be configured for various uses. Finally, they came again after the rehab was finished to set up a series of collective workshops around reused materials for outdoors, creating a storytelling about both the heritage of this industrial place and a sci-fi-like possible sustainable future.

PAPOMO
Parlement Populaire Mobile, 2015–ongoing

This Mobile People's Parliament, or PaPoMo, is intended to be a tool at the service of these groups who meet, who debate, and who are driven by the desire to take their living conditions back in hand. For all those who have a pacifist, inclusive, generous, and optimistic approach. For all those who wish to do so in the public space: get out of confidential circles of reflection, go beyond a sometimes reassuring, often worrying, self-esteem. So that words, ideas, and experiences circulate publicly and freely. All the collaborative construction process has been done with people from the deprived neighborhood of Belle-de-Mai, Marseille, where we had our office and project Ambassade du Turfu for 4 years. PaPoMo can be use in various configurations and can be used in movement. It takes fifteen minutes to set up.

Collectif Etc, Our collectif and friends in Venice during our project for the 16th Biennale of Architecture, 2018

PLACE DES POSSIBLES, SAINT-LAURENT-EN-ROYANS

Collectif Etc reusing old ventilation system's galvanized steel for furniture, Saint-Laurent-en-Royans, 2020

Collectif Etc, A party in front of the building, with collaborative screen-printing flags, Saint-Laurent-en-Royans, 2020

Collectif Etc, Open and collaboration construction workshop in former factory, Saint-Laurent-en-Royans, 2020

GRAND HALLE DE CAEN, CAEN

Collectif Etc, Working outdoors with reused materials, creating a narrative about possible low-tech science fiction futures, Caen, 2020

Collectif Etc, First intervention all made of reused materials from a house just nearby during the rehabilitation construction process, Caen, 2016

Collectif Etc, Dragster-like mobile elements to allow various types of uses inside the big empty hall, Caen, 2019

PAPOMO, MARSEILLE

Collectif Etc, Collaborative construction process with inhabitants of the neighborhood and young migrants, connected to our Ambassade du Turfu project, Marseille, 2020

Collectif Etc, Latest prototype, 2020

Collectif Etc, First prototype, later destroyed by the police when used during a protest against a municipality project, Marseille, 2015

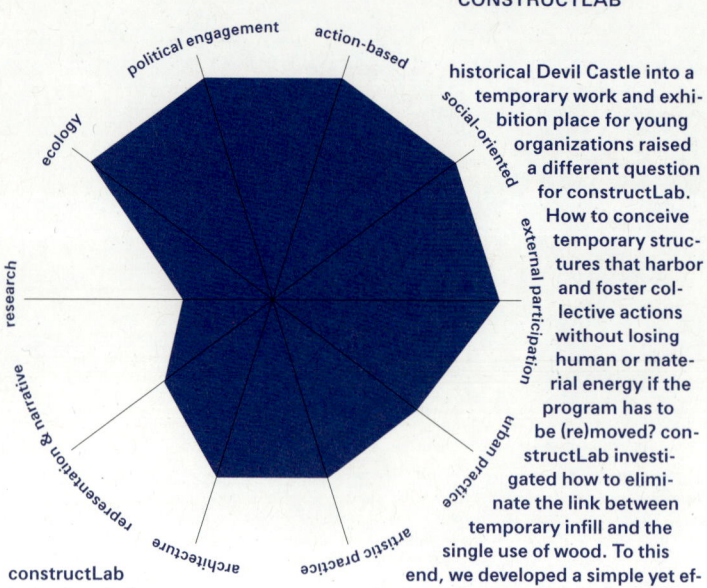

CONSTRUCTLAB

constructLab is the description of a collaborative spatial practice, working on both ephemeral and permanent projects. Breaking with traditional divisions of labor, the network includes multitalented practitioners—designer-builders as well as sociologists, urban planners, graphic designers, curators, educators, and web developers—who carry the creative process from the drafting table into the field, enabling design to mindfully respond to the possibilities and constraints posed by materials, sites, and ecosystems. At the heart of constructLab's work, which includes projects commissioned throughout Europe, is the desire to explore practices that transform territories through commoning and conviviality. Location: scattered around the world, postbox in Berlin.

constructLab was founded in the 2010s and is composed of a large network of people, involved on different levels.

THE DEVIL CASTLE
Geraard de Duivelstraat,
Ghent, Belgium, 2020

constructLab entered the medieval castle of Geeraard the Devil as a strange area to be discovered whose potential we collectively explored. constructLab initiated modular pioneering structures that make it possible for youth organizations to develop themselves in this formerly cold, inhospitable medieval environment. The issue of transforming the historical Devil Castle into a temporary work and exhibition place for young organizations raised a different question for constructLab. How to conceive temporary structures that harbor and foster collective actions without losing human or material energy if the program has to be (re)moved? constructLab investigated how to eliminate the link between temporary infill and the single use of wood. To this end, we developed a simple yet effective connector piece that combines the versatility of scaffolding connections with affordable wood sections.

CAILLASSES—EXPLORATIONS OF A TERRITORY IN TRANSITION

constructLab was invited to reflect on the transformation of a large part of the city of Geneva: the PAV, a perimeter historically dedicated to craft and industrial production. The issues of the PAV project could not be approached only from the point of view of the planners, politicians, architects, citizens, elected representatives, companies, investors, trade unions, and inhabitants' associations. Therefore constructLab started by questioning the quietest but most present actor in the PAV project: the stone. Passive, inert, cold: the mineral is among the elements that humanity has most easily domesticated. Working beyond disciplines has enabled them to listen to the stone, to open a dialogue with animals, water, plants, backhoe loaders, but also with people, their hopes and fears. *Caillasses* is a learning experience, a contribution to the collective intelligence of the territory, in order to reach a common objective: to work toward an alliance between minerals and the living species that design and inhabit this milieu, to face together the climate challenges of the coming decades.

CASA DO VAPÔR
Cova do Vapôr, Almada,
Portugal, 2013

Cova do Vapôr is a small fishing settlement opposite Lisbon, at the bank of the river Tejo. Inspired by the creativity of the locals, the genuine DIY ethic and to have discovered a community that still lives up to its name, constructLab decided to self-initiate Casa do Vapôr, a support structure to the local association in order to serve local initiatives. Its various structures have accommodated an open-air classroom, a public library, a kitchen, a bike workshop, a skate ramp, a playground, and a pizza oven. Casa do Vapôr was built out of reused wood from the construir juntos project in Guimarães ECC 2012. Due to building restrictions, the installations can only be temporary. However, Casa do Vapôr has become a common that survives. The same material is used over and over, disguising Casa do Vapôr in temporary forms from time to time, like a new community kitchen—cozinha das terras—and a public library—biblioteca do vapôr and biblioteca do mare—which are ongoing.

Portrait:
constructLab, Osthang Project, Darmstadt, 2014

THE DEVIL CASTLE, GHENT

Michiel De Cleene, *The Devil Castle*, Geraard de Duivelstraat, Ghent, Belgium, 2020

Michiel De Cleene, *The Devil Castle*, Geraard de Duivelstraat, Ghent, Belgium, 2020, toilet detail

Michiel De Cleene, *The Devil Castle*, Geraard de Duivelstraat, Ghent, Belgium, 2020, new intervention

CAILLASSES—EXPLORATIONS OF A TERRITORY IN TRANSITION, GENEVA

Dylan Perrenaud, *Caillasses*, mission 1, 2020, Geneva

Dylan Perrenaud, *Caillasses*, 2020, Geneva

Dylan Perrenaud, *Caillasses*, mission 1, 2020, Geneva

CASA DO VAPÔR, ALMADA

constructLab, Casa do Vapôr, painting the kitchen facade, Cova do Vapôr, Almada, Portugal, 2013

constructLab, Casa do Vapôr, inauguration day, Cova do Vapôr, Almada, Portugal

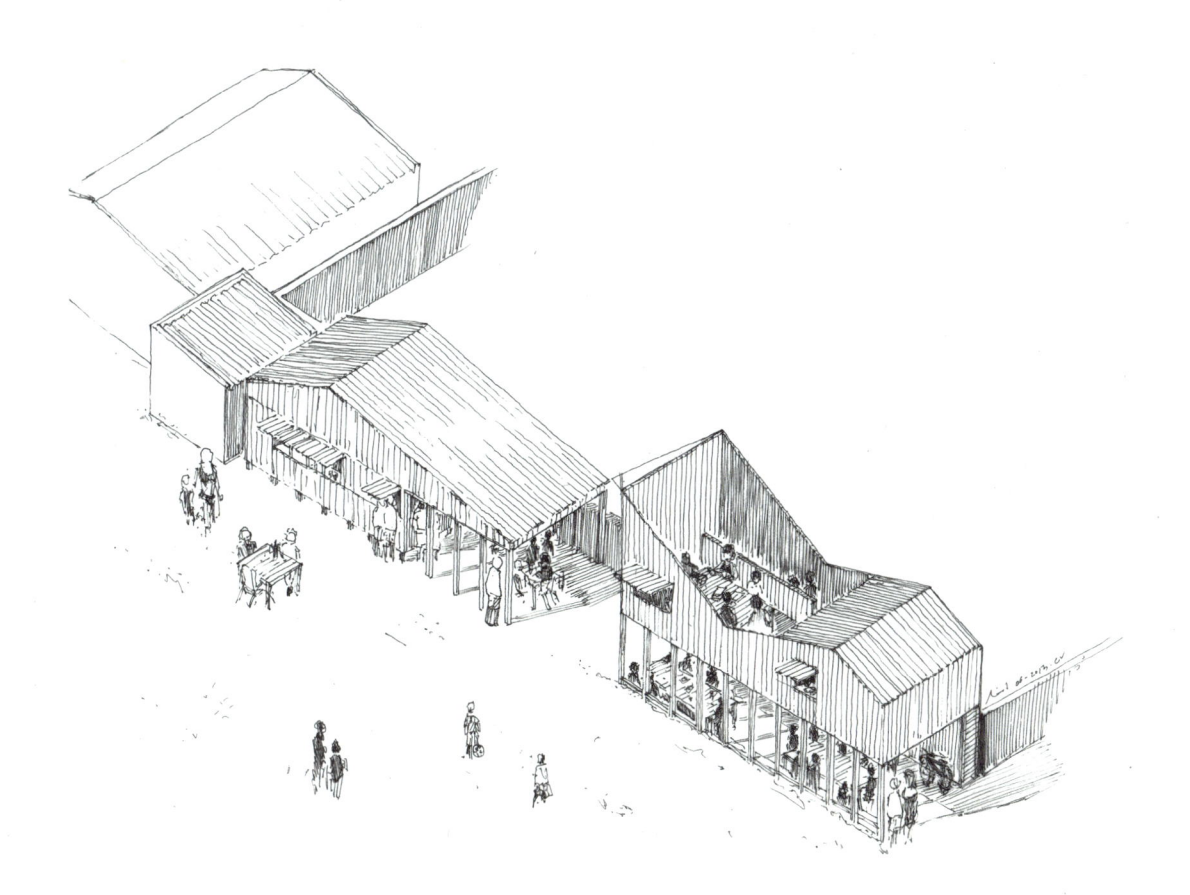

Miguel Magalhães, Casa do Vapôr, 2013, illustration

FALSE MIRROR OFFICE

false mirror office gathers five architects who share the Polytechnic School of Genoa as a common background. While collaborating with leading European firms, its members share an interest in selected themes of major relevance, spanning from disciplinary topics to unrelated matters. If architecture design combines them in the form of a conclusive reasoning, theoretical research and debate set them up for requestioning. Believing that new only originates as a reaction to the existing, false mirror office rediscovers the past as the present, resignifies high as mass culture, revalues forms and functions. As a matter of fact, false mirror office misrepresents architecture. Location: scattered around Europe

false mirror office was founded in 2015 by six members:
Andrea Anselmo
Gloria Castellini
Filippo Fanciotti
Giovanni Glorialanza
Boris Hamzeian
Guya Di Bella (former member)

FALSE MIRROR PROJECT
Europan 13, 1st prize,
Trondheim, 2015

False Mirror Project is the winning project for the competition held by Europan 13 Norway to redevelop a suburban harbor district in the city of Trondheim as part of a reflection on adaptability, temporality, and sustainability. Our response is based on the development of an abacus of devices of different scale, nature, and use. Against the idea of yet another playground of standardized and generic toys, these devices are local and specific because they arise from the recovery of archetypes belonging to Trondheim's harbor, its canals, its barges, its historic warehouses and its blue line. Contextually adapted rather than generically adaptable is the formula for those in search of a slogan.

ZUPPA ROMANA
Research Project, 2016

This project originated with an invitation to participate in the exhibition *Re-Constructivist Architecture* curated by Jacopo Costanzo and Giovanni Cozzani at the Iermonti Gallery in New York with the aim of bringing together two generations of architects on the theme of the Roman villa in the countryside. Our proposal was born from the discovery of a rich and complex universe made of architectures, paintings, posters, movies but also of the most kitsch characters, recipes, and songs. In Zuppa Romana all this took the form of a villa homage, where a nymphaeum of Villa Adriana the animated surfaces of Paolo Portoghesi Casa Baldi, and the unauthored barracks of the suburbs are juxtaposed in a fresco of the collective imagination of the Roman countryside where this villa is no longer even a foreground figure but becomes the background of a bulimic iconography where high and low culture joyfully coexist.

TOWARD A NEW DOMESTIC HABITAT
Research project, GUD, 2020

This project is part of a search for new forms of domesticity that merge living and production spaces. This research began as an experiment five years ago in the framework of the fourteenth edition of the Europan competition and has been transformed by the confinement due to the Covid-19 pandemic into a response to a real and urgent problem. In order to react to the forced coexistence of living and production spaces in our homes, it is necessary to think of an environment in which intimate spaces for private life, flexible spaces for collective life, technological devices, and symbolic objects find a synthesis. From traditional models of dwelling, therefore, it is necessary to recover some of the founding elements such as the wall, the room, the hearth, and the piece of furniture, and transform them to give life to a device in which they interact actively with the body and the psyche of the individuals who live there. Through the conception of this ecosystem a domestic model that is no longer a traditional dwelling but a habitat is born. From existenz-minimum to existenz-maximum.

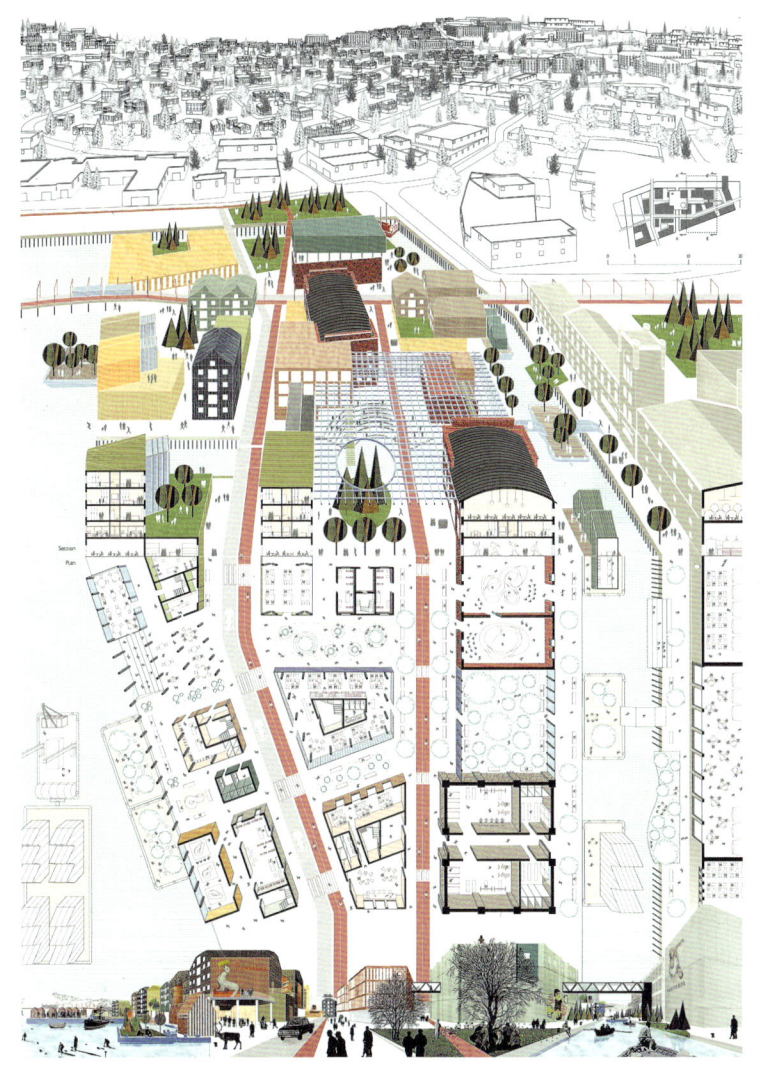

FALSE MIRROR PROJECT, TRONDHEIM

false mirror office, False Mirror Project, Europan 13, first prize, Trondheim, 2015, planche total

false mirror office, False Mirror Project, Europan 13, first prize, Trondheim, 2015

ZUPPA ROMANA, ROME

false mirror office, Zuppa Romana, research project, 2020

TOWARD A NEW DOMESTIC HABITAT, GUD

false mirror office, Toward a new Domestic Habitat, research project, GUD, 2020

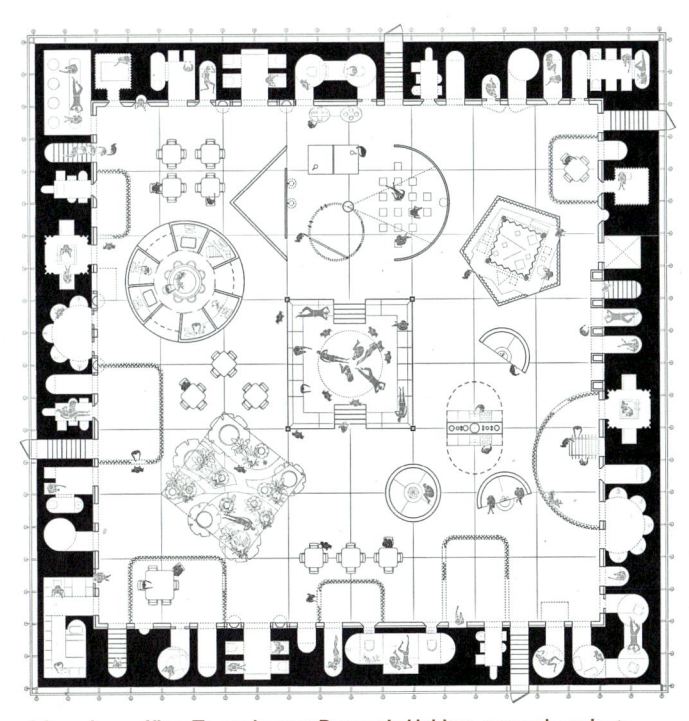

false mirror office, Toward a new Domestic Habitat, research project, GUD, 2020, plan

FOSBURY ARCHITECTURE

Fosbury Architecture is a collective of design and research. Location: currently based in Milan.

Fosbury Architecture was founded in 2013 and is composed of five members:
Alessandro Bonizzoni
Claudia Mainardi
Giacomo Ardesio
Nicola Campri
Veronica Caprino

GANZFELD
Research, 2016, with Marco Gambarè and Stefano Gariglio

The environments on display try to activate a relationship between life and form that is not fulfilled in mere functional terms, but that challenges life to survive under abnormal conditions; without any ambition to change the habits of anyone other than perhaps those who designed them.

J'AI PRIS AMOUR
Chicago Architecture Biennale, *Make New History*, 2017, with Matteo Bassi and Matteo Frangi

The installation investigates the disrupting effects of productive leisure on the space of the home. While domesticity permeates every human activity, work invades all aspects of everyday life, blurring the boundaries between private and public.

The figure of the video blogger is Gianluca di Ioia, probably the one that best embodies this brand-new condition: the YouTubers are immaterial workers making profits by broadcasting their personal life from the intimate space of the home. They represent the tangible transfiguration of the general intellect in the late capitalism of the twenty-first century.

THE LABYRINTH
Private commission, 2017–ongoing

In the larger frame of an operation of recovery and redevelopment of the Villa Arconati's garden in Bollate, it was decided to restore a labyrinth, following the traces of an ancient plan of the villa produced by Marc'Antonio Dal Re. For economic, logistical, and ecological necessities, the labyrinth has been built in phases in three subsequent years.

The three stages of development have been translated into a design that envisage every year an autonomous and finite architectural effect: the *hortus conclusus* (or enclosed garden), the enfilade, the labyrinth.

Fosbury Architecture group photo, La Triennale di Milano, 2019

GANZFELD, 2016

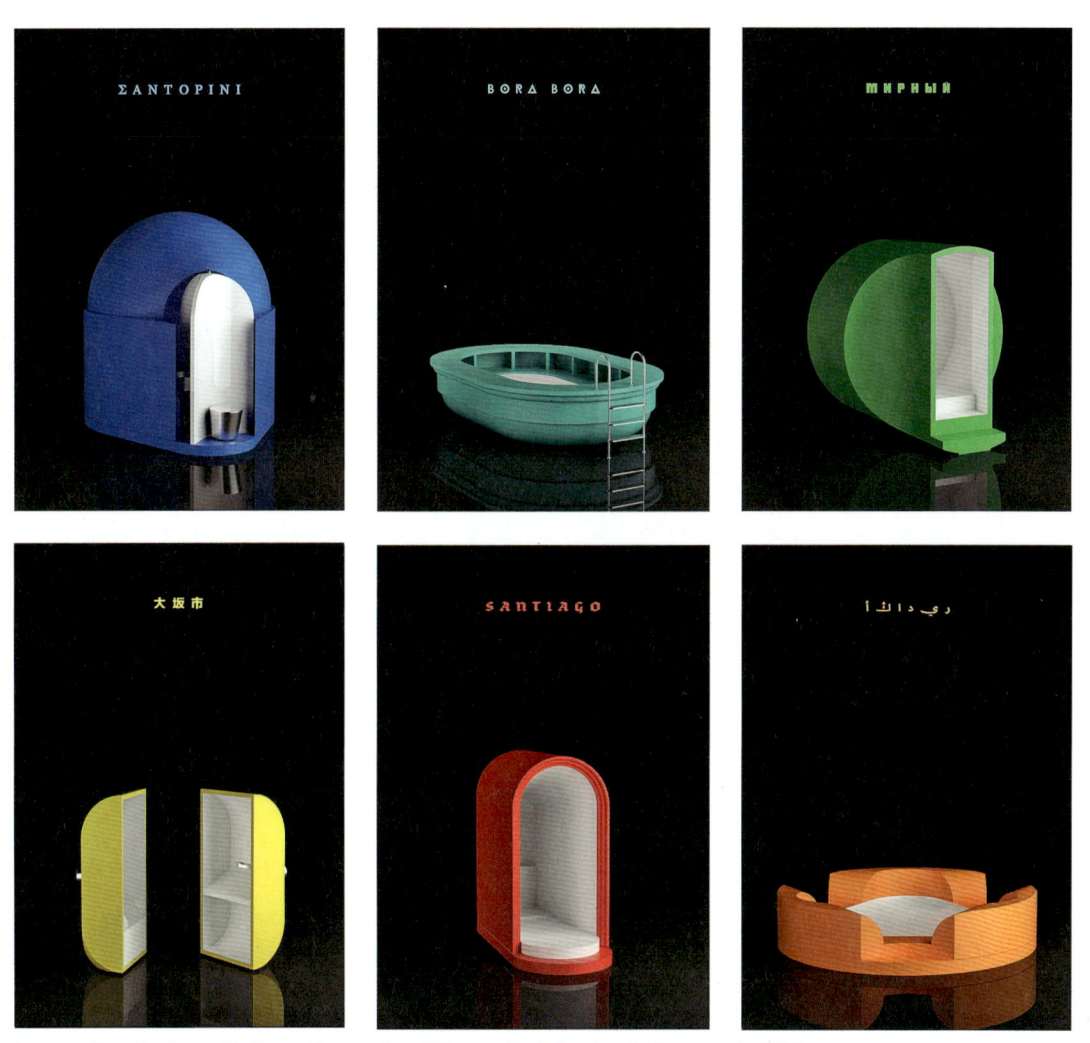

Fosbury Architecture with Marco Gambarè and Stefano Gariglio, Ganzfeld, research, 2016

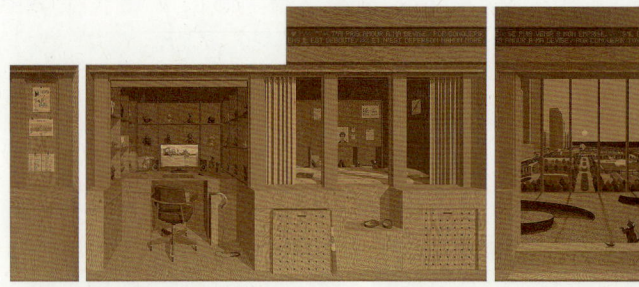

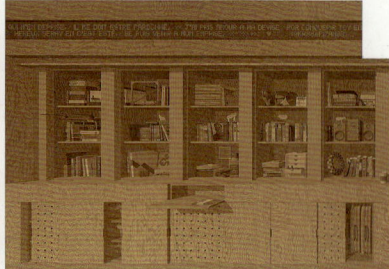

J'AI PRIS AMOUR, CHICAGO

Fosbury Architecture with Matteo Bassi and Matteo Frangi, *J'ai pris amour*, Chicago Architecture Biennale, *Make New History*, 2017

Fosbury Architecture with Matteo Bassi and Matteo Frangi, *J'ai pris amour*, Chicago Architecture Biennale, *Make New History*, 2017, detail

Fosbury Architecture with Matteo Bassi and Matteo Frangi, *J'ai pris amour*, Chicago Architecture Biennale, *Make New History*, 2017, detail

THE LABYRINTH, MILAN

Fosbury Architecture, The Labyrinth,
private commission, Bollate, 2017–ongoing, plan

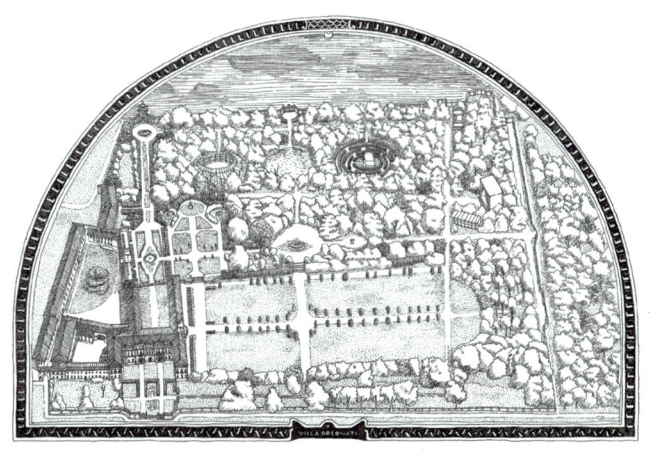

Fosbury Architecture, The Labyrinth, private commission,
Bollate, 2017–ongoing

LA–CLIQUE

la–clique is a Swiss collective of architects, urban planners, landscape architects, researchers, artists, craftsmen, musicians, and photographers. Interested in interdisciplinary and collective forms of work, its members form an independent platform for exchange and experimentation around architecture. As a collective, la–clique develops projects in the field of tension between politics, sociology, and ecology, on different scales and taking into account different practices, from craftsmanship to urban planning. Location: scattered around Switzerland

la–clique was founded in 2019 and is composed of twenty-two members:
Adrien Grometto
Alexandre Figueiredo
Amalia Bonsack
Anna Maciver-Ek
Axel Chevroulet
Charline Dayer
Claartje Vuurmans
Donia Jornod
Gabrielle Rossier
Jeremy Ratib
Jonas Meylan
Luca Rösch
Marie Page
Mathilde Berner
Maximilian Fritz
Nicolas Marx
Pierre Marmy
Pierre Métrailler
Sarem Sunderland
Sven Högger
Thibaud Sulliger
Zoé Laubeuf

BOCTO
Versegères, Valais, 2019

For this third edition, the infrastructures provided for artists' comfort and public reception have been built by la–clique based on the remnants of previous editions. Logs planted into the ground during the first edition of Bocto were used as masts on which large reclaimed boat sails were stretched. The workshop, used as a collective workspace and as a canteen, was enlarged and improved since the previous edition, and completed by a series of wooden benches. Steel sheets for roofing and white sheets serving as a curtain-facade constituted a space encouraging work and discussion. The only construction existing on-site was a garden shed, and so setting up these temporary structures was essential for the duration of the residency. These spaces favored artistic and social cohesions, and allowed to organize meetings, discussions, and work groups.

SPEAKERS' CORNER
Manifesta, Marseille, 2020

The project seeks to shed light on the role of urban space in the problems of social integration of stigmatized people—those affected by mental disorders, homelessness, or belonging to ethnic minorities. A collaboration with actors of the local associative scene offers the opportunity for an in-depth reflection on the role that architecture can play in supporting social integration in the urban environment. The project is based on the implementation of a place of expression and speech in the public space of Marseille: the Speakers' Corner. By offering a space for different forms of expression, by promoting exchanges and self-telling, the intervention aims at a reappropriation of the urban space by often marginalized citizens.

MEP—MÉTRO M3
Lausanne, in collaboration with Johanne Roten and Julien Mercier, 2019–20

In order to carry out the parallel study mandate M3 Line Identity, we partnered with Julien Mercier—multimedia designer—and Johanne Roten—freelance graphic designer: together we formed the team Les Carreleurs. Tile is a material often used in the underground world of underpasses. It is the basic unit of a whole that leads to an entire grid. We propose to further explore this material to develop the identity of the M3 subway line, the different stages it connects, and the other materials with which it will be inserted. While each station is designed individually, this materiality becomes the binding thread between them. As the subway line progresses through the city, the production of visual and sound atmospheres is inspired by local data such as the density of buildings in the neighborhoods or the altitude.

la–clique, Speakers' Corner, Manifesta, Marseille, 2020

BOCTO, VALAIS

la–clique, Bocto, Versegères, Valais, 2019, close-up

la–clique, Bocto, Versegères, Valais, 2019, detail

la–clique, Bocto, Versegères, Valais, 2019

SPEAKERS' CORNER, MARSEILLE

la–clique, Speakers' Corner, Manifesta, Marseille, 2020

la–clique, Speakers' Corner, Manifesta, Marseille, 2020, detail

la-clique with Johanne Roten and Julien Mercier, MEP – Métro M3, Lausanne, 2019–20

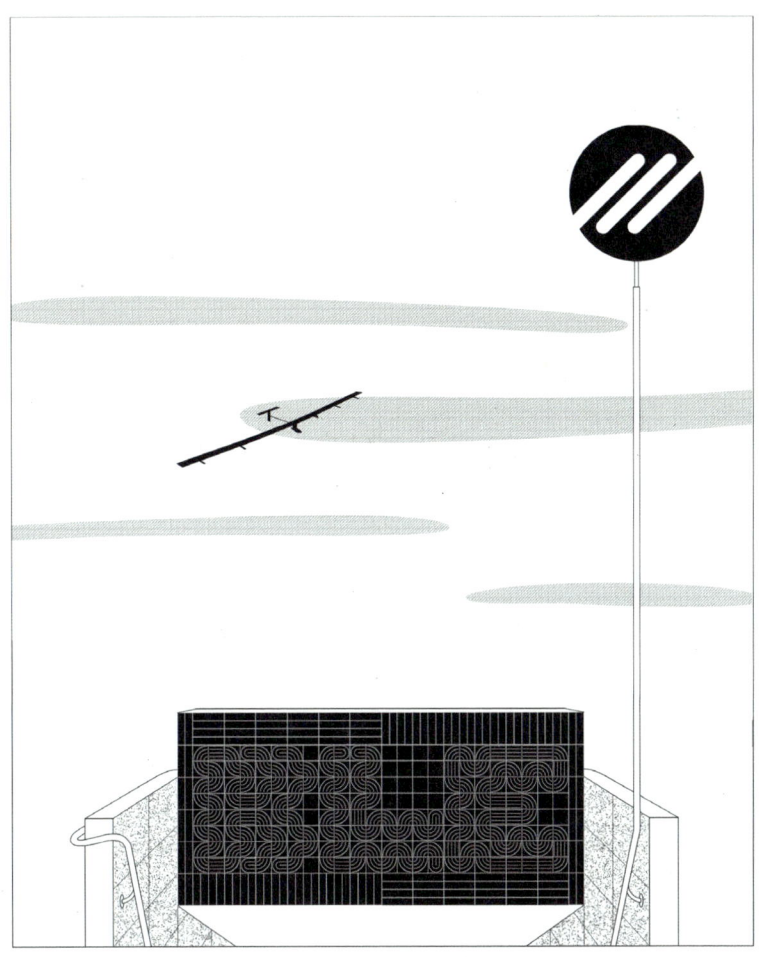

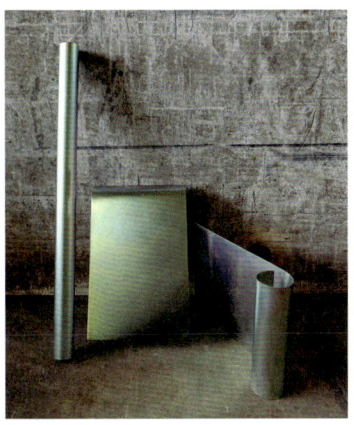

la-clique with Johanne Roten and Julien Mercier, MEP – Métro M3, Lausanne, 2019–20, materials

la-clique with Johanne Roten and Julien Mercier, MEP – Métro M3, Lausanne, 2019–20, detail

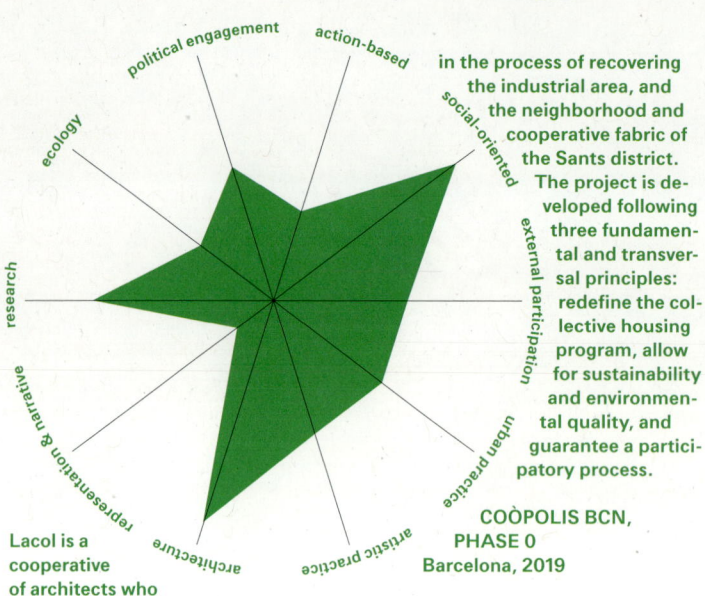

LACOL

Radar chart axes: political engagement, action-based, social-oriented, external participation, urban practice, artistic practice, architecture, representation & narrative, research, ecology

Lacol is a cooperative of architects who work in the neighborhood of Sants, in Barcelona. They work toward social transformation using architecture as a tool to intervene critically in the environments that are the closest to them. They root their activity in a horizontal system of labor, acting alongside society with justice and solidarity in mind. Location: Barcelona

Lacol was founded in 2009, became a cooperative in 2014 and is composed of fourteen members:
Arnau Andrés
Eliseu Arrufat
Ari Artigas
Carles Baiges
Anna Clemente
Lali Daví
Cristina Gamboa
Ernest Garriga
Mirko Gegundez
Laura Lluch
Lluc Hernàndez
Pol Massoni
Jordi Miró
Núria Vila

COOPERATIVA D'HABITATGE LA BORDA
Barcelona, 2014

The La Borda housing cooperative is a self-organized promotion for its users to access decent, nonspeculative housing that puts its use value at the center through a collective structure. The idea of cooperative housing was born in 2012 as another Can Batlló project promoted by the community in the process of recovering the industrial area, and the neighborhood and cooperative fabric of the Sants district. The project is developed following three fundamental and transversal principles: redefine the collective housing program, allow for sustainability and environmental quality, and guarantee a participatory process.

COÒPOLIS BCN, PHASE 0
Barcelona, 2019

Coòpolis BCN wants to become a comprehensive facility for the promotion and encouragement of the social and cooperative economy in Barcelona located in Can Batlló, with plans to be located in Block 4 of the site. It wants to be a space of reference for all those initiatives of the social, cooperative, and community economy that require training, support, advice, or support, establishing a new pole of economic promotion in the city.

TRANSFORMATION OF THE OLD PRISON LA MODEL
Barcelona, 2018

Project awarded in the AJAC XII Awards, in the field of participatory processes

The recovery of this unique space for the city represents a unique opportunity of urban regeneration in Barcelona. The aim of the participatory process was to discuss and jointly determine the future of this space, taking into account the degree of heritage protection, the uses it should accommodate, and the urban configuration it should have.

During the process, different activities, thematic workshops, and actions with groups were carried out in order to reach a great diversity of people and gather the plurality of existing opinions. As a result, twenty-three criteria have been drafted that include the different voices of the process and that constitute the guidelines to be followed for a future transformation project.

Lacol, group photo, Barcelona, 2015

COOPERATIVA D'HABITATGE LA BORDA, BARCELONA

Lluc Miralles, Covered courtyard in La Borda, 2014

Lacol, South facade of La Borda, Barcelona, 2014

Lluc Miralles, Ground floor in La Borda, Barcelona, 2014

Álvaro Valsecantos, Incubator spaces for new social economy initiatives in Coòpolis, Barcelona, 2021

TRANSFORMATION OF THE OLD PRISON LA MODEL, BARCELONA

Lacol and Equalsaree, Participatory process for the transformation of the old prison La Model, 2018

Lacol and Equalsaree, Participatory process for the transformation of the old prison La Model, discussion, 2018

n'UNDO was founded in 2011. More than 120 people have collaborated and been part of the office in these years. Location: Madrid, Saint-Gilles, Barranquilla

KALMAR MASTER PLAN
Europan 12, first prize,
Sweden, 2013–14

In Kalmar, an intervention is proposed based on economic, social, environmental, and cultural sustainability, through urban development based on density and complexity, prioritizing the conservation of the environment and the territory. The project follows a series of principles: no construction, consolidating and protecting existing landscapes and voids; minimization, with criteria of minimum impact; reuse of existing spaces and infrastructures; and densification of the existing plot without moving away from the human scale.

ATOCHA TRAIN STATION INTERVENTION PLAN
Madrid, 2018

In 2018 ADIF contracted the services of the technical office of n'UNDO (n'OT) to carry out an intervention plan in the historic Madrid Puerta de Atocha Station. Since 2012, n'UNDO has worked in the Atocha environment, carrying out workshops and urban actions, to show that improvement from subtraction is not only possible but also necessary. This proposal has been made following the n'UNDO criteria and methodology, with subtraction as a mode of action, for the recovery and enhancement of the heritage building. The project does not intend to provide a single or closed solution but rather to provide a tool for decision-making without losing the reference of the general strategy.

URBAN VOIDS PLAN: RENATURALIZATION AND DECARBONIZATION
Malaga, 2019

The document is an approach to the problem of urban dispersion in Malaga through the study of its gaps, based on its strategic importance for the development of different lines of intervention that promote sustainable urban development. The existing problems in the periphery of the city of Malaga define the general objectives of the plan: decarbonization and renaturalization of the studied areas as ways for a sustainable urban and territorial development, pertinent in the case of study of Malaga, and always under the framework of the New Spanish Urban Agenda.

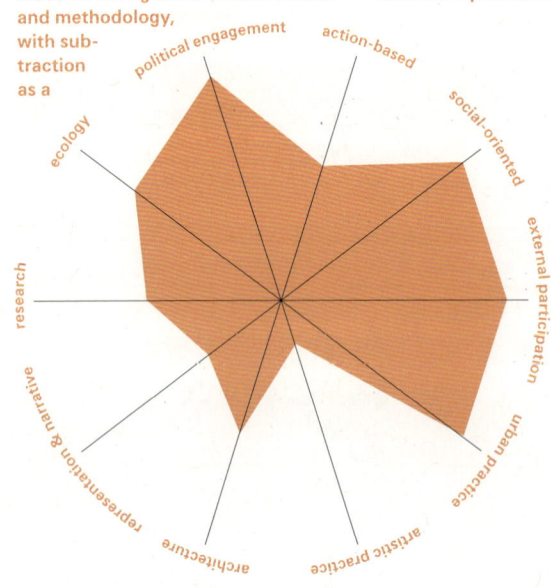

Portrait:
n'UNDO, Collective photo, undated

KALMAR MASTER PLAN, SWEDEN

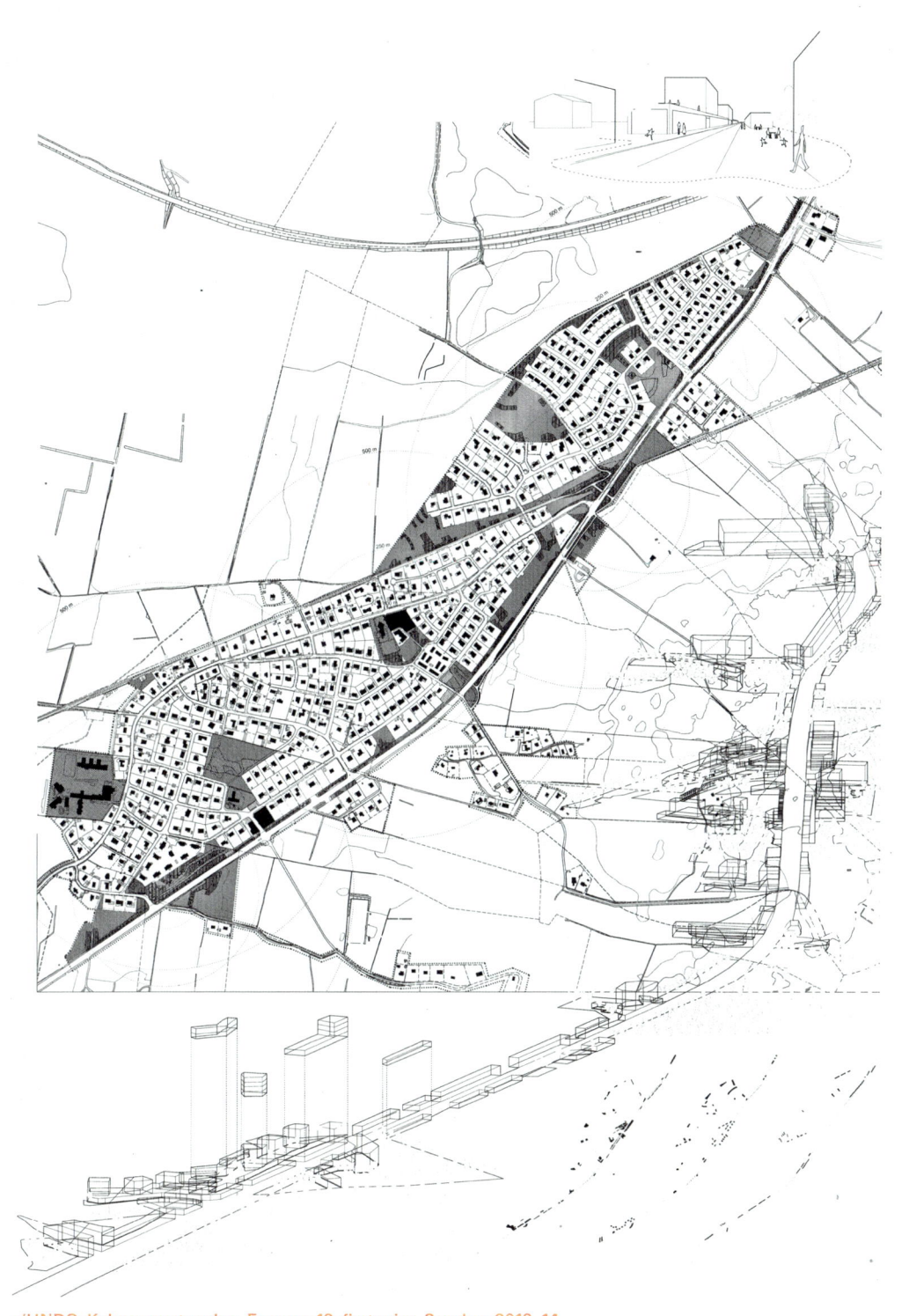

n'UNDO, Kalmar master plan, Europan 12, first prize, Sweden, 2013–14

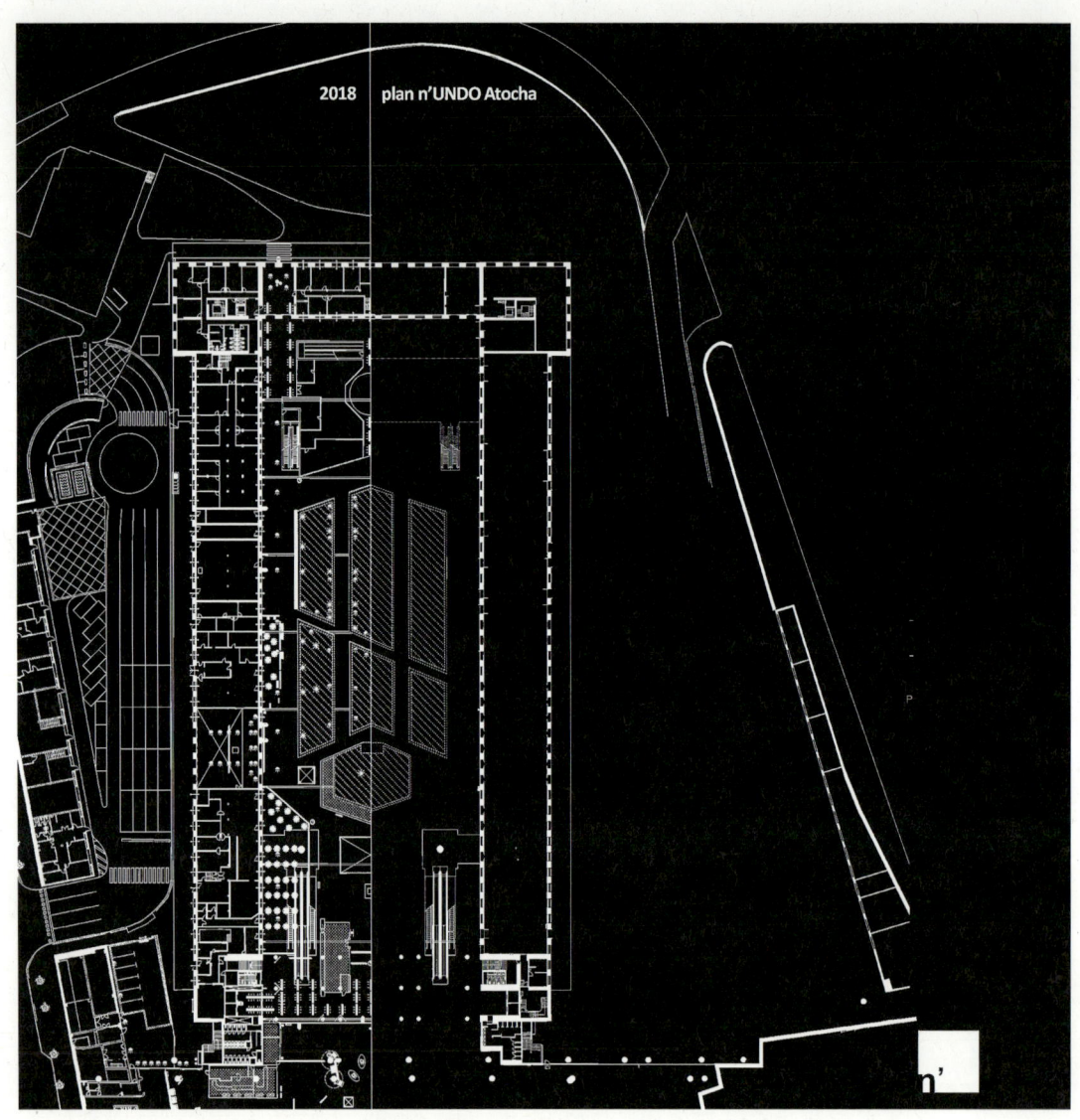

ATOCHA TRAIN STATION INTERVENTION PLAN, MADRID

n'UNDO, Atocha Train Station intervention plan, Madrid, 2018

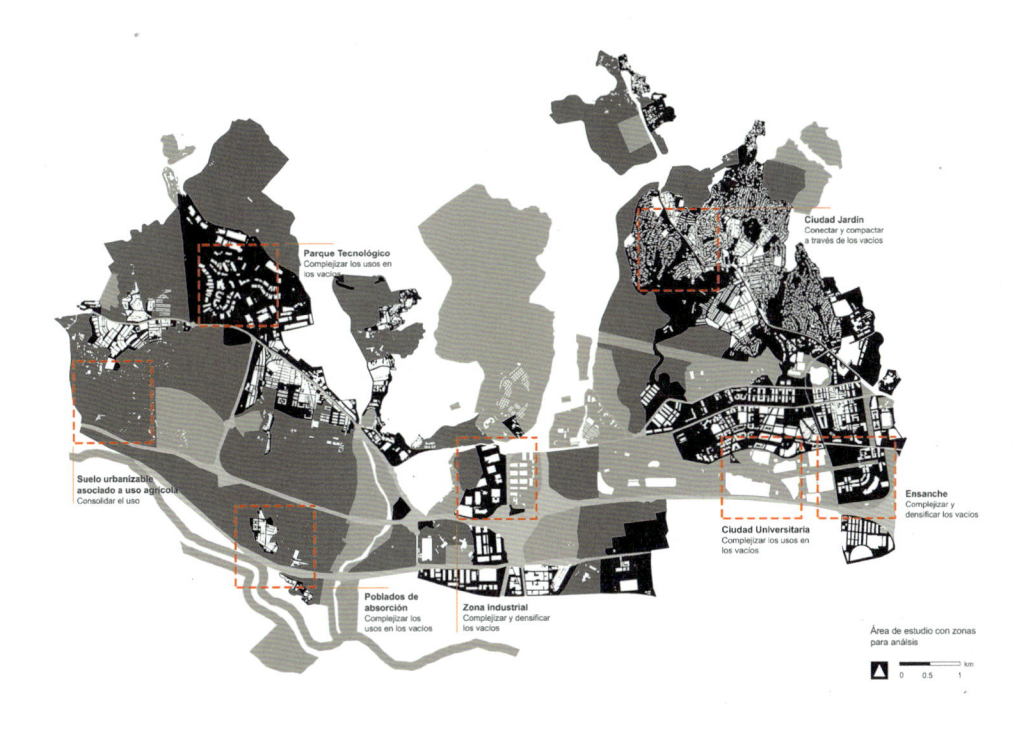

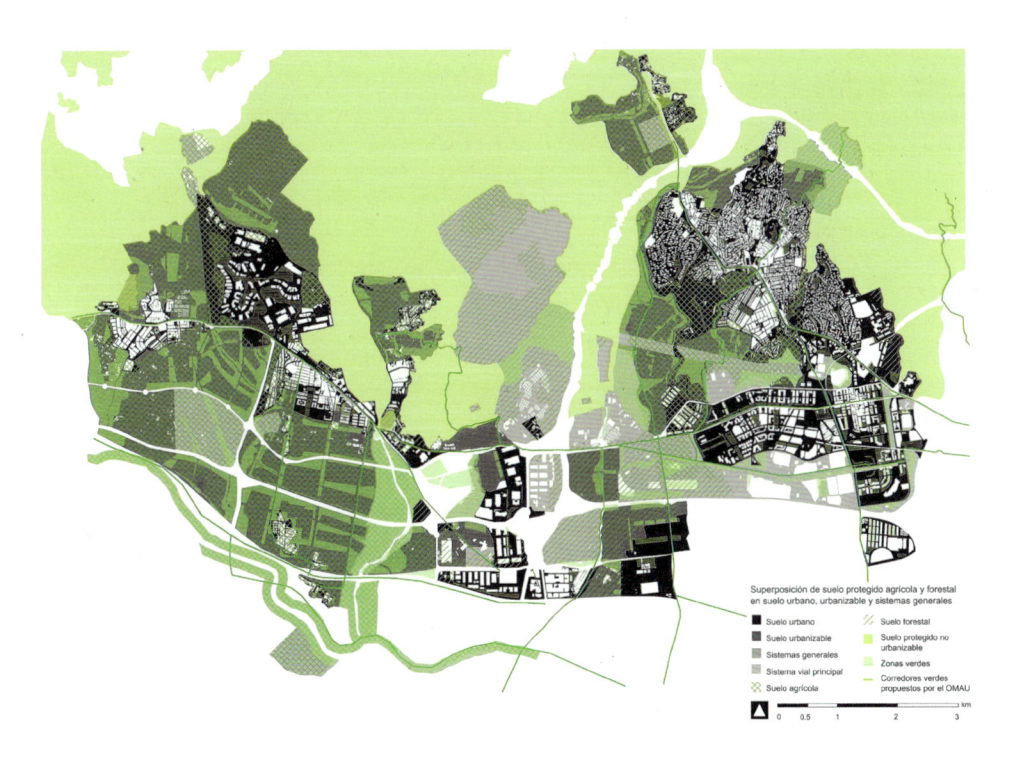

URBAN VOIDS PLAN: RENATURALIZATION AND DECARBONIZATION, MALAGA

n'UNDO, Urban Voids Plan: Renaturalization and Decarbonization, Malaga, 2019 orizzontale is an architects' collective based in Rome whose work crosses the fields of architecture, urbanism, public art, and DIY practice. orizzontale since 2010 has been promoting projects of common relational spaces, giving form to both dismissed and unseen images of the city. These projects have represented the ground for experimenting with new kinds of collaborative interactions between city dwellers and urban commons as well as occasions to test the boundaries of the architectural creation process. Location: Rome

orizzontale was founded in 2010 and is composed of seven members:
Jacopo Ammendola
Juan Lopez Cano
Giuseppe Grant
Margherita Manfra
Nasrin Mohiti Asli
Roberto Pantaleoni
Stefano Ragazzo

CASA DO QUARTEIRÃO
Walk&Talk, Ponta Delgada,
São Miguel Island, Portugal, 2016

Casa do Quarteirão is a project developed within Walk&Talk 2016 and it was born out of the community that lives and works in the neighborhood, reclaiming a physical space for convivial and collaborative use. We were invited to realize an installation in the core of the neighborhood and to collaborate with NO-ROCKET (Francesco Zorzi, an Italian visual designer and illustrator based in Amsterdam). The project feature is metaphorically a *Viveiro*, a collective greenhouse to make "O Quarteirão" flourish and develop spontaneously. The idea was also to recreate the intimacy of a traditional Azorian house. Thus we worked on two elements, creating new inviting entrances to the space: a pavilion to provide a place for people to gather and organize events (Rua Pedro Homem) and a small structure with a tiny terrace (Rua d'Acoa), to give a cozy and unusual view of the area. Between these structures a new square took shape.

8½
YAP MAXXI 2014, Rome, 2014

8½ is a mobile theater, a machine to experience public space. It investigates the dual nature of public space as the place of intimacy and elective relationships and in the meantime the preferential territory of event and spectacle. The installation intends to be a reflection about the transition that changes public space from being the background of private encounters and individual moments to being the scene of public events and collective representations. 8½ was built in four weeks; the construction site became for two weeks a workshop open to students from all over Italy. 8½ consists of two complementary elements: the wall and the arena. The participants worked on the wooden structures of the arena and on the upcycle process of turning plastic beer kegs into lampshades for the wall.

CIVICO CIVICO
Lurt 2020,
Riesi, 2020

Human laboratory of territorial regeneration (LURT) was opened in its first edition to twenty-one participants (nineteen students and two professionals) under the age of forty. The working group, composed of Flora La Sita and orizzontale, intervened in the phase of the self-construction laboratory. Civico Civico is the name of the renovated space. According to the principle of self-construction, the elements that distinguish the project (flexible and modular furnishings, the wooden floor of the old garage, the portal) were designed and built on-site, transforming the street into an outdoor joinery. The splash of color represents the reappropriation of a space that becomes collective, crowded, pushing the inhabitants to mix with different voices and ideas, as in the festive moment of the inauguration.

Portrait:
Giacomo Costa,
orizzontale team, Largo Milano,
Cinisello Balsamo, 2014

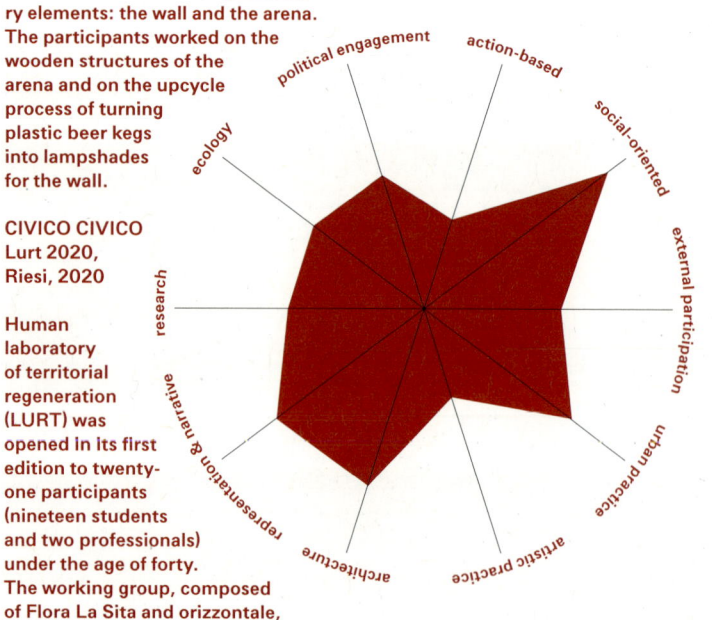

CASA DO QUARTEIRÃO, SÃO MIGUEL ISLAND

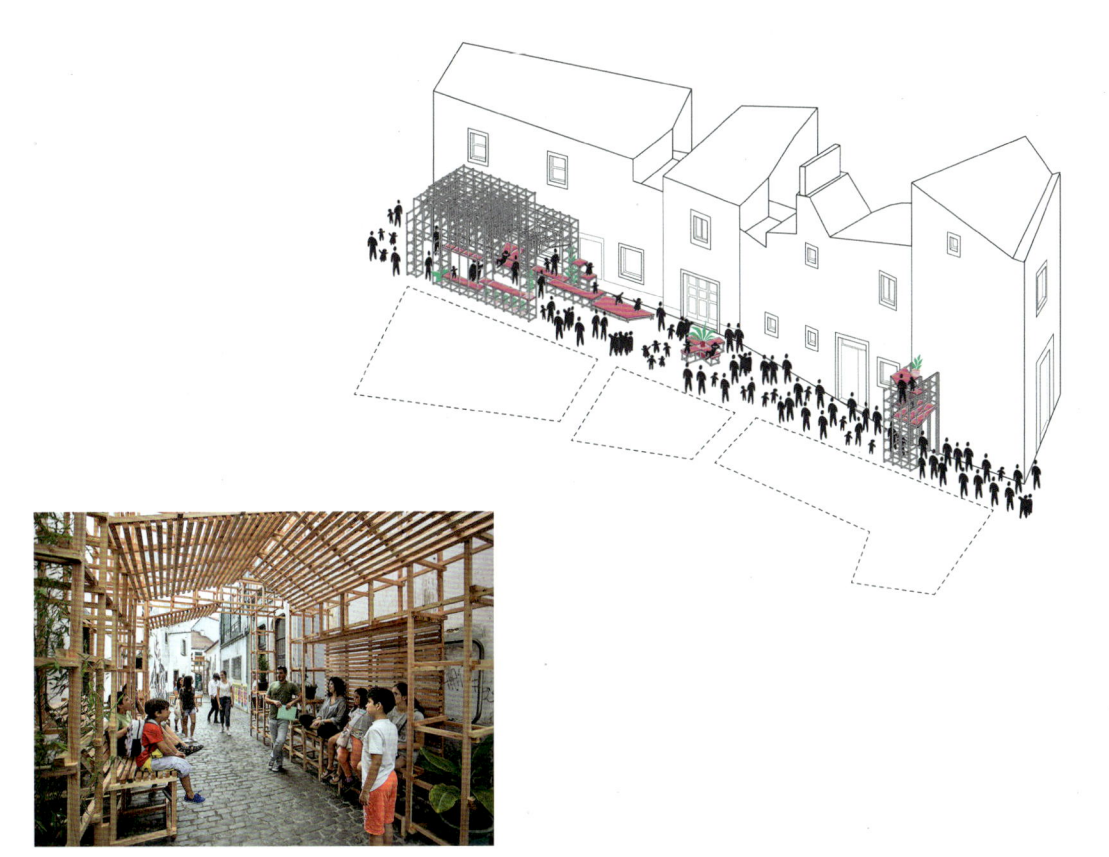

Sara Pinheiro, Casa do Quarteirão, São Miguel Island, Azores (PT), 2016, close-up

Sara Pinheiro, Casa do Quarteirão, São Miguel Island, Azores (PT), 2016

8½, ROME

Alessandro Imbriaco, 8½, Yap MAXXI, Rome, 2014

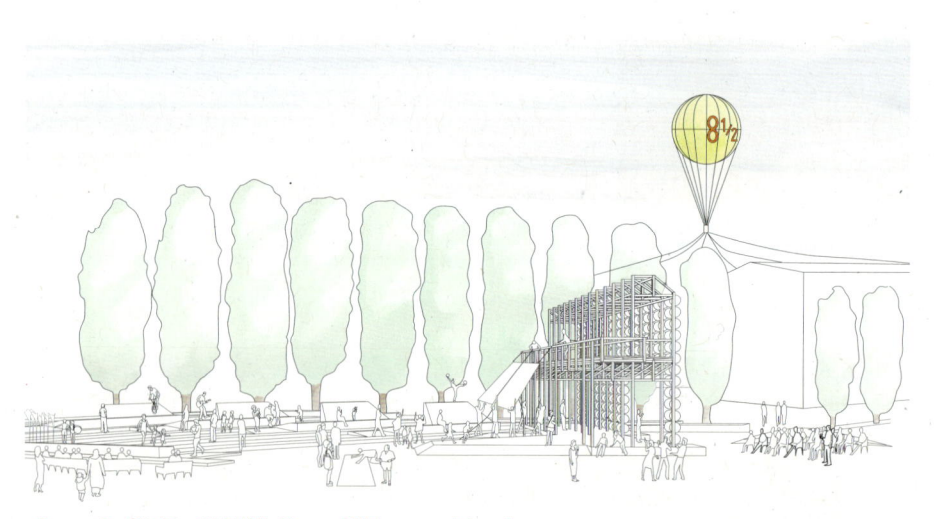

orizzontale, 8½, Yap MAXXI, Rome, 2014, general drawing

Ianniello Musacchio, 8½, Yap MAXXI, Rome, 2014

CIVICO CIVICO, RIESI

Gianluca Fiusco, Civico Civico, Riesi, 2020

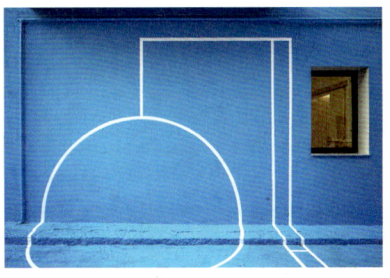

Giulio Marzullo, Civico Civico, Riesi, 2020

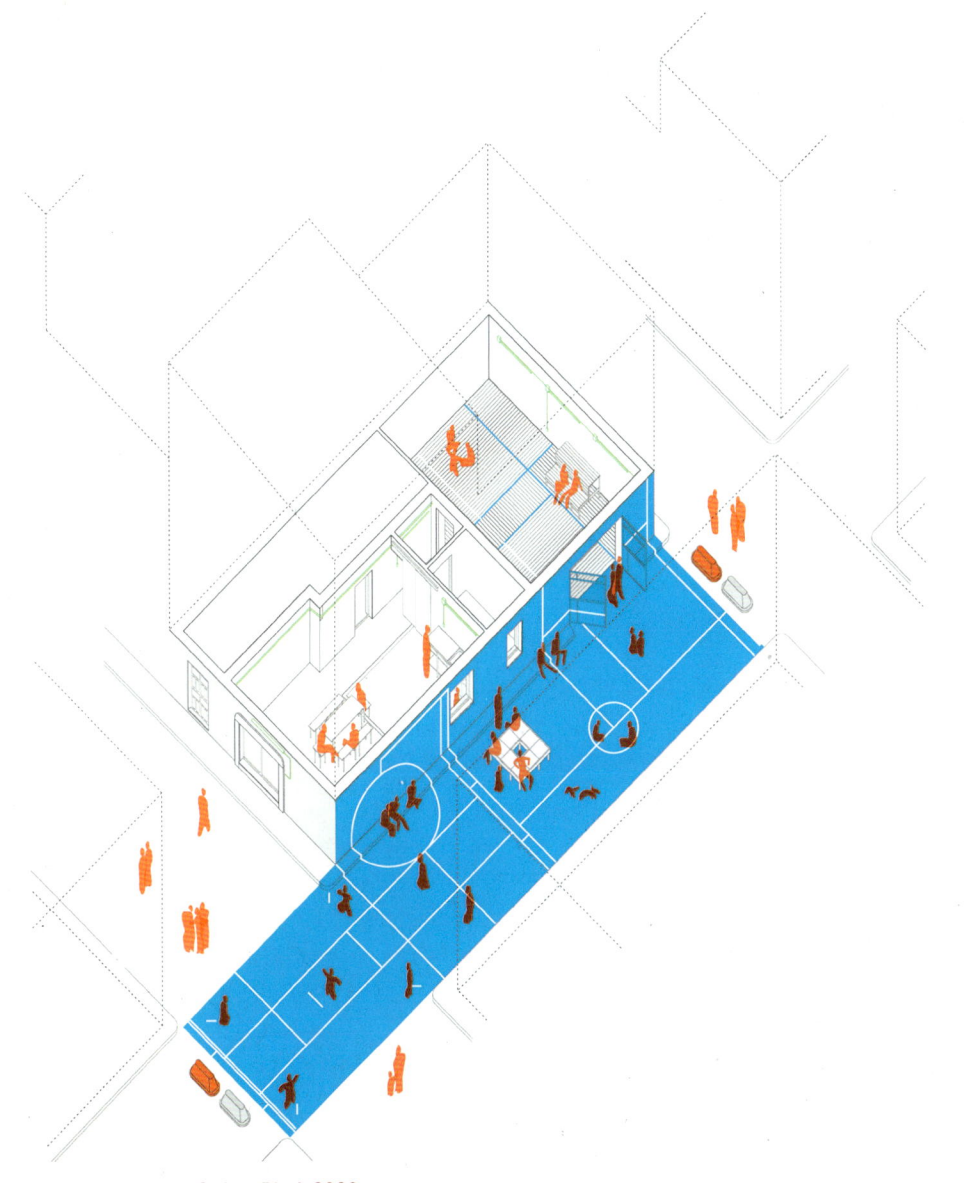

orizzontale, Civico Civico, Riesi, 2020, axonometry

X=(T=E=N)

X=(T=E=N), 2021, collective photo

X=(T=E=N) is both a studio and an institute based in Zurich and Belgrade. X=(T=E=N) is composed as a record label, providing possibilities for forming independent work constellations for each project. X=(T=E=N) was founded in 2015 and is composed of a series of fixed members and of a network of people around it.
Current members:
Scott Lloyd, Nemanja Zimonji, Ognjen Krašna, Jana Kuli, Nicolas Rothenbühler, Luka Piškorec, Lukas Burkhart. Former members: Emma Letizia Jones, Guillaume Othenin-Girard, Karl Rühle, Alexa den Hartog, Marija Blagojevic, Josip Jerkovic, David Stöger

THE DISTRIBUTED COOPERATIVE
Zurich, Switzerland, 2019

The project investigates the architectural and urban potentials of underutilized, well-located sites within the city of Zurich in order to offer a replicable and scalable method for inner-city densification. The research responds to the 2011 affordable housing referendum that resulted in legislation to ensure by 2050, one-third of Zurich's rental housing must operate on a nonprofit basis. Working with the City of Zurich open data and the Bauhaus University in Weimar, we developed specialized computational scripts to automatically identify more than three thousand potential sites in Zurich. For these we are developing architectural prototypes that offer high-quality living spaces within the constraints of the sites for the affordable housing segment. Sites within a five-minute walking radius are clustered into "distributed cooperatives" with shared spatial assets located one per site. This offers an innovative and contemporary strategy for cooperative urban living.

STUDIOLO
Swiss Art Award 2018 (winner), Zurich / Basel / St. Gallen, Switzerland

Studiolo was an applied research project undertaken by every member of X=(T=E=N) within an experimental decentralized project organization. The project reinterprets the space and form of the private study by referencing the Studiolo, an architectural archetype established during the Renaissance. The project was shaped through the act of writing, drawing, and making. Furan sand—a material generally reserved only for casting molds—became both our object and our means of study to explore the limits of its properties. Outside its usual application, it is possible to crease, shave, smear, tear, chip, split, cut, drop, remove, curve, inlay, impress, heap, scatter, arrange, bond, and mark the material into new forms. These experiments were conducted by X=(T=E=N) at the art foundry in St. Gallen. The final pieces were transported across Switzerland and installed at Art Basel for the 2018 Swiss Art Awards.

HOLLIGER SUPERSTRUCTURE
Bern, Switzerland, 2020

The Holliger tower follows a staked three-floor approach to spatial, structural, and building systems design to offer unique social, economical, and ecological possibilities. The scheme combines a highly efficient primary structure of precast concrete cores and in situ concrete slabs set at every third-floor level with an infill prefabricated timber element system. Both concrete (compression, robustness, longevity) and timber (precision, adaptability, ecology) are applied to where their properties are best suited and most complementary. Vertical atrium spaces connecting the three floors between the slabs offer secondary circulation, shared services (laundry, drying room) and flexible use to suit the evolving requirements of the residents (library, café corner, winter garden for houseplants, exercise rooms, home offices, adult and children's playrooms). This spatial offer encourages engagement, increases chance encounters, and offers a shared departure from the private isolation of high-rise living.

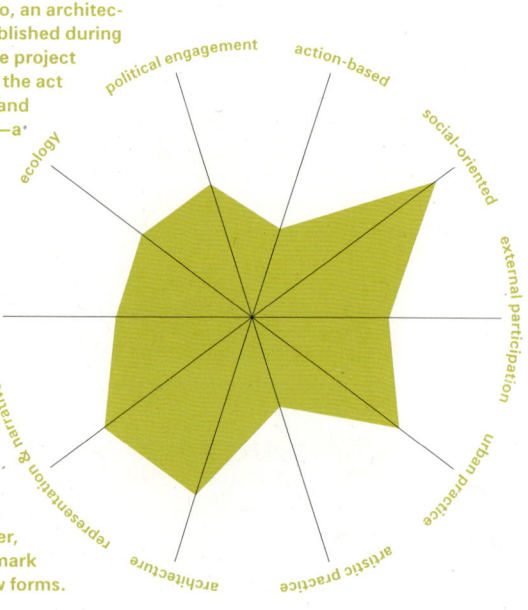

244

THE DISTRIBUTED COOPERATIVE, ZURICH

X=(T=E=N), The distributed cooperative, Zurich, Switzerland, 2019, axonometry

X=(T=E=N), The distributed cooperative, Zurich, Switzerland, 2019, model

X=(T=E=N), The distributed cooperative, Zurich, Switzerland, 2019

STUDIOLO, ZURICH

X=(T=E=N), Studiolo,
Swiss Art Award 2018 (winner),
Zurich / Basel / St. Gallen,
Switzerland, 2018

X=(T=E=N), Studiolo, Swiss Art Award 2018
(winner), Zurich / Basel / St. Gallen, Switzerland,
2018, detail

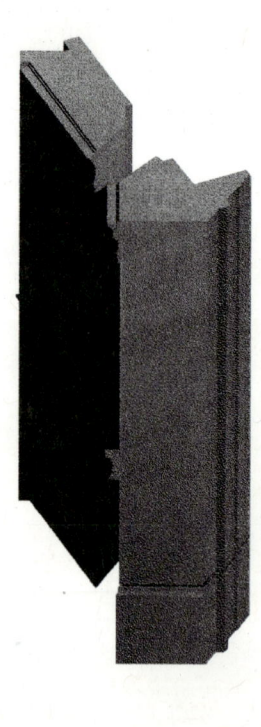

X=(T=E=N), Studiolo, Swiss Art Award 2018 (winner),
Zurich / Basel / St. Gallen, Switzerland, 2018, axonometric view

246

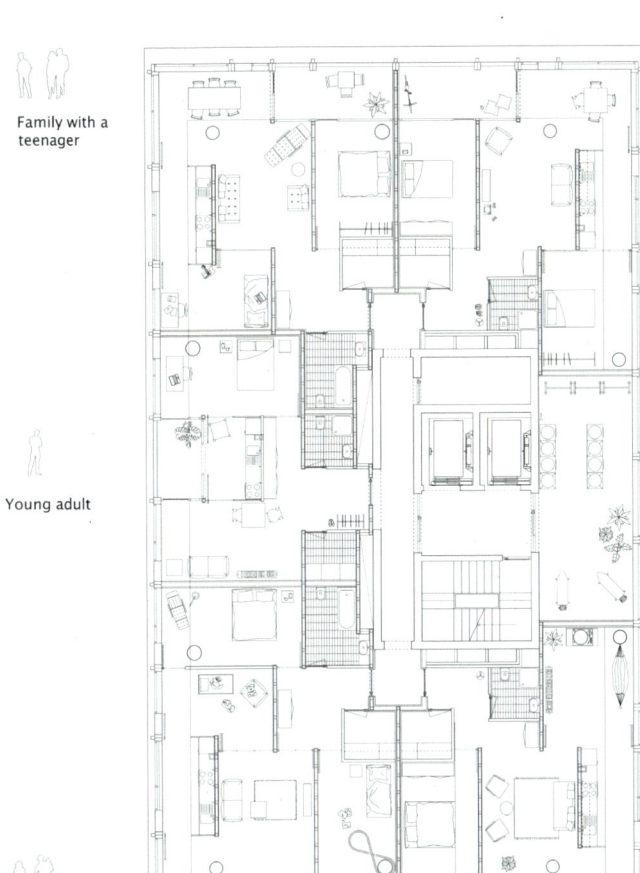

HOLLIGER SUPERSTRUCTURE, BERN

Family with a teenager

Roomies

Young adult

Family with two kids

Young couple

X=(T=E=N), Holliger Superstructure, Bern, Switzerland, 2021

X=(T=E=N), Holliger Superstructure, Bern, Switzerland, 2021, model

X=(T=E=N) with ArtefactoryLab, Holliger Superstructure, Bern, Switzerland, 2021

A special thanks to: Professor Roberto Gargiani for giving me the opportunity to undertake this research and showing me "the premises for the genesis of an ideal tension towards a possible future, a collectivity to come"; all the members of the collectives with whom I have worked closely during this experience for their openness, availability and engagement; Barbara, Irini and Tobias for their constant support; Antoine, Martin and Matthew for their constructive criticism; the Laboratoire de Théorie et d'Histoire de l'Architecture LTH3, directed by Professor Roberto Gargiani at the École Polytechnique Fédéral de Lausanne, for its financial support towards the publication and the research behind it; Fiona Pia Architectes for the additional sponsoring; Alain Brülisauer for the contribution; Baharak Tajbakhsh for her trust in the project and extreme dedication; Lorenzo Mason and Simone Spinazzè for their hard work on the book design; Regina Herr, Amelie Solbrig and Keonaona Peterson for their constant availability, time and involvement in the making of the publication.

Supported by

pro helvetia

EPFL

Sponsored by

fiona pia architectes

Concept:
Natalie Donat-Cattin

Texts:
Natalie Donat-Cattin, Scott Lloyd

Copy editing:
Keonaona Peterson

Project management:
Baharak Tajbakhsh, Regina Herr

Production:
Amelie Solbrig

Design:
Lorenzo Mason Studio,
Lorenzo Mason, Dafne Pagura,
Simone Spinazzè

Paper:
Diva Art 1S
Recytal Matt

Printing:
Gutenberg Beuys Feindruckerei GmbH, Langenhagen

Image Editing:
prints professional, Jan Scheffler & Kerstin Wenzel GbR, Berlin

Library of Congress
Control Number:
2021945356

Bibliographic information published by the German National Library
The German National Library lists this publication in the Deutsche Nationalbibliografie; detailed bibliographic data are available on the Internet at http://dnb.dnb.de.

This work is subject to copyright. All rights are reserved, whether the whole or part of the material is concerned, specifically the rights of translation, reprinting, reuse of illustrations, recitation, broadcasting, reproduction on microfilms or in other ways, and storage in databases. For any kind of use, permission of the copyright owner must be obtained.

ISBN
978-3-0356-2470-0

e-ISBN (PDF)
978-3-0356-2471-7

© 2022
Birkhäuser Verlag GmbH,
Basel P.O. Box 44, 4009
Basel, Switzerland
Part of Walter de Gruyter GmbH, Berlin/Boston

9 8 7 6 5 4 3 2 1
www.birkhauser.com